2nd edition

Sociology
of
childhood

MARVIN R. KOLLER

Kent State University

OSCAR W. RITCHIE

Prentice-Hall, Inc., Englewood Cliffs, New Jersey 07632

Library of Congress Cataloging in Publication Data

KOLLER, MARVIN R
  Sociology of childhood.

  (Prentice-Hall sociology series)
  Authors' names appeared in reverse order on 1st ed.
  Bibliography.
  Includes index.
  1. Child development.   2. Socialization.
I. Ritchie, Oscar W., joint author.   II. Title.
HQ781.R54 1978   301.15'72   77-13314
ISBN 0-13-821074-8

© 1964, 1978 by Prentice-Hall, Inc., Englewood Cliffs, New Jersey 07632

Printed in the United States of America

10   9   8   7   6   5   4   3   2   1

PRENTICE-HALL INTERNATIONAL, INC., *London*
PRENTICE-HALL OF AUSTRALIA PTY. LIMITED, *Sydney*
PRENTICE-HALL OF CANADA, LTD., *Toronto*
PRENTICE-HALL OF INDIA PRIVATE LIMITED, *New Delhi*
PRENTICE-HALL OF JAPAN, INC., *Tokyo*
PRENTICE-HALL OF SOUTHEAST ASIA PTE. LTD., *Singapore*
WHITEHALL BOOKS LIMITED, *Wellington, New Zealand*

Dedicated

to the memory of

OSCAR W. RITCHIE

There is an old legend that says that ten righteous persons appear every century to remind humanity of the directions it should take. Surely, those of us who were privileged to know him best would nominate Oscar W. Ritchie to this select circle. His untimely passing makes only more poignant his memory. It is altogether fitting that Oscar was sensitive to the beginnings of life and so invested his energies in the interests of the very young.

His compassion for children carried over into his teaching, study, work, and efforts on behalf of the powerless, subjugated, deprived, and rejected. Oscar transformed difficulties into challenges and opportunities to grow. To be numbered among his students, colleagues, friends, or family was and is honor, indeed. If this volume, originally conceived, initiated, and coauthored with him captures a fragment of his sweet nature and purpose in life, it merits attention.

Contents

Preface

Some fourteen years have elapsed since the publication of the first edition of *Sociology of Childhood.* In that time, the nature of the world and American society, in particular, has changed drastically. The postwar years of World War II with the remarkable promise of the Kennedy Administration were ending tragically with the loss of a charismatic leader and with losses of other inspirational leaders such as the revered Dr. Martin Luther King, Jr. and Robert Kennedy. Three short years later, Oscar W. Ritchie passed away and left the sadness felt for a warmhearted brother and colleague. The Vietnam conflict escalated and brought student confrontations to a climax in deaths and woundings on our home campus of Kent State University on May 4, 1970. The nation witnessed the withdrawal from Vietnam only to be further tested in the Watergate conspiracies and the resignation of its President. A healing process seems to have been operating throughout the land as Americans continue to confront the pressing domestic issues of achieving a healthier economy, environment, energy system, and rekindling of ethical efforts in behalf of human rights.

Sociological studies have continued unabated, and new data and theories have been accumulating during these years. A second edition of *Sociology of Childhood* is, thus, long overdue and needed. Completely rewritten, this edition updates the work of both research and theory specialists in sociology and related fields. Its substantive focus is upon the first twelve years of the human life cycle, the status of childhood with its multidimensional qualities, in the midst of contemporary American society struggling to find its way through the final decades of a twentieth century and into the beckoning twenty-first century.

The civil rights struggles begun in the late 1950s and continued into the 1960s, which concentrated on the rights of blacks, have broadened to include all persons regardless of race, religion, ethnicity, class, region, sex, or age. The second edition reflects the human rights movement in its conscious efforts to apply these rights to the children of America and the world. In the hands of the students and teachers, this new edition of *Sociology of Childhood* can be a useful tool to direct attention and efforts in behalf of the newest arrivals in our midst.

Appreciation unbounded is due to Oscar Ritchie, who requested that, as a "marriage and family" specialist, I should give more attention to childhood than I had ever done before. Appreciation unbounded goes to Edith Ritchie and her family who gave me full rein to revitalize the text over which Oscar and I labored so many years ago. Respect and gratitude goes to Edward H. Stanford, Sociology Editor of Prentice-Hall, Inc., and his entire staff and associates for urging me on. And finally, to my wife, Pauline, and son, Bob, Dad can come out of his "kiva" for a few hours more each day until "the next one." Maybe, if we all keep trying long enough, we can "get things right" for the whole human family.

M.R.K.

ONE

Introduction to childhood

1

Childhood:
a multidimensional
status

The first twelve years of life for an individual are filled with significance whether judged from the perspective of that individual, the groups, organizations, or associations with whom that individual is related, or from the collective viewpoint of the society in which the individual spends his or her lifetime. In these early years, it is quite clear that the foundations of unique personalities are laid down, that the general directions that lives will take are given orientation, and that the social futures of generations are begun. To treat these momentous years of any given life in terms of their personal-social dimensions in some sensible, systematic, and sufficiently satisfying manner is a task of enormous proportions. Nevertheless, it is one to which we dedicate ourselves because it is an effort that should give us "understanding." With understanding can come thoughtful actions, which prevent the pitfalls that shatter lives and lead to those alternatives that enhance lives.

A distinction should be made from the beginning between *childhood* and *children*. Childhood is held to be a status, a position in a society relative to other age groups older than twelve years of age. Essentially, childhood is a universal phenomenon involving ascription or an assumption on the part of others that children are to behave in some "approved," acceptable manner. Children, however, are young individuals just acquiring the ways of the persons who are older than themselves. How readily or reluctantly children acquiesce to their ascribed behavior, the expectations of others, becomes a complex question with which our study deals.

In a sense, we should be free to examine childhood and children everywhere and throughout history. Further, it would be profitable to draw upon every discipline that bears upon childhood and children. But there are practical limits to what can be accomplished within the confines of a single text, a single course of study, and a single quarter or semester of an academic year.

We limit our concerns with childhood and children, therefore, to America and to the years ending the twentieth century and beginning the twenty-first. Where childhood and children in other parts of the world or in other historical times can be instructive, however, we do not hesitate to draw upon such useful and illuminating information. Finally, the key discipline from which we draw our analyses and syntheses of childhood and children is sociology.

In our stress upon the sociological, however, there must be recognition of the values insights of other fields of study. Because childhood and children are multifaceted and not the exclusive topics of interest in any one discipline, we need to consider the multiple approaches available to students.

APPROACHES TO THE STUDY OF CHILDHOOD

General Background

Each approach to the study of childhood has its advocates as well as its skeptics. Further, within any single approach, there are "schools of thought," factions that maintain that certain aspects should be emphasized or made paramount.

Within sociology, for instance, there has been prolonged debate about being neutral, detached, or uncommitted to any single value-stance. Students being trained in sociology have long been cautioned to be objective, to stand "outside" the subject matter and diligently consider all possible data before arriving at "tentative" conclusions. The one allowable value was to use the scientific method as rigorously as possible before deciding what the facts really are.

Such a stance, however, is most difficult to maintain in the face of a value-laden, value-generating world. Consequently, it is not heretical to identify, acknowledge, or be aware of one's own set of values. Sociologists and students of sociology have begun to state their values and so let others know why they believe something is "good" or " bad." We, obviously, believe that children are precious beings in their own right or we would not devote so much time and energy to pulling together sociological data or thinking about children.

Historical Approach

An approach that should yield great insight is one that makes use of historical materials. There is sound logic to the premise that in order to understand the present, there is need to understand the past. Treatment of children and childhood has varied in time, and a tracing of the earliest interest in youngsters from prehistory through the recorded history of ancient, medieval, European, African, Asian, and American periods would be a rewarding venture. Of particular value to students of childhood would be the historical changes and consequences of transforming contemporary societies into urbanized, industrialized, high energy consumption enclaves that rapidly dissipate limited resources.

An historical approach, at best, should prove to be an effective antidote to the all-too-common bias of *temporocentrism*.[1] This bias stresses the present as the most important of all times, a perspective that does not square with the reality of the infinite time-slices that came before the present and will occur into the distant future.

One fascinating finding in historical study is that behavior considered quite modern and unique is really quite ancient or long-established. The ancient laments of children in their reluctance to devote long hours to their academic studies have, for example, a familiar and modern ring. One ancient Egyptian pupil wrote to his former tutor, "I was with thee since I was brought up as a child. Thou didst beat my back and thy instructions went into my ear."[2] This was in keeping with the ancient Egyptian maxim that "a boy's ears are on his back and he harkens when he is beaten."[3] Such a maxim came from one of numer-

[1]Robert Bierstedt, *The Social Order*, 3rd ed. (New York: McGraw-Hill Book Company, 1970), pp. 177–179.
[2]Adolf Erman, trans. by Helen M. Tirard, *Life in Ancient Egypt* (New York: The Macmillan Company, 1894), p. 329.
[3]James H. Breasted, *A History of Egypt* (New York: Charles Scribner's Sons, 1924), p. 99.

ous "morality" books written by childhood "experts" of antiquity.[4] Undoubtedly, such advice reflected the needs of adults to bring children under control, but it did not consider the needs of the children themselves. Positive or negative sanctions, rewards or punishments, the familiar "carrot-or-stick principle" continue to be debated among those who seek conformity to norms whether it be in the context of family, school, church, prison, or employment.

There have been changes, of course, and these have evolved slowly, laboriously, almost imperceptibly throughout human history. One such change would be *the increasing value placed upon children.* Far back in the past, children were not particularly esteemed or accorded special attention; little was required of them other than general service and obedience to their elders. Children were to be subdued, subordinate, and servile. The dominant themes expressed by the "speak-when-spoken-to" and the "be-seen-but-not-heard" precepts for yesterday's children come to mind, as well as the exploitation of children in mines or factories.

Otto Bettmann has written a most revealing history of America's disregard for children in times well within the memories of living elders.[5] Bettmann reminds us that in this "land of the free," children were put into hazardous mills, mines, and factories to earn twenty-five cents for a twelve to fourteen hour day. Parents would be paid one dollar to release a company of all claims when a child was injured or handicapped for life. "Charitable" employers volunteered a single payment of five dollars for an injured child.[6]

It would take many years before a turnabout could occur, but eventually child-labor laws were made part of the legal codes. Children were to attend schools to prepare themselves for adult roles. The *extrinsic* value of children for what they could *produce* was gradually abandoned in favor of the *intrinsic* value of children for what they *are.* Childhood viewed as preparation rather than an opportunity for exploitation was a profound shift for adult Americans to make.

Some would take the position that the swing of the historical pendulum went too far. American society has been held to be a "youth-oriented" or "youth-centered" society. It is the adults, rather than the young, who have to be defensive, and a countervailing movement has begun. This is the central concern of the gerontologists who seek ways

[4]Margaret Murray, *The Splendour That Was Egypt* (New York: Philosophical Library, Inc., 1949), p. 107.
[5]Otto L. Bettmann, *The Good Old Days—They Were Terrible!* (New York: Random House, 1974).
[6]Ibid, pp. 77–78.

and means to integrate or incorporate older persons into ongoing society rather than dismissing them as inconsequential and expendable, a status once accorded children.[7]

A third result of historical study of childhood is to discover neither stability of patterns nor complete reversals of established treatment of the very young. Instead, children have experienced uncertain, cyclical strategies of "bringing children up." Children, we have noted, have been treated as slothful, as subhumans who are sorely in need of discipline. If this discipline grows too harsh, the unconscionable conditions found among children lead to remorse and dissatisfaction. Modifications are begun to help children enjoy their childhood and so grow in whatever directions they see fit. When and if this "self-actualization" culminates in discord and disregard for the needs of others, new adult controls are instituted and the cycle begins again. In brief, the *run of attention* in child rearing seems to be more in terms of *fads and fashions.* One bit of evidence supporting this emphasis-deemphasis-reemphasis thesis is found in *Infant Care,* a booklet issued by the Children's Bureau of the Federal Government for many years.[8]

In sum, the historical approach to the study of childhood does yield valuable insights in terms of the evolution of conditions that affect children. Further, those patterns that are unaffected by the passage of time or those subjected to rapid changes are brought under observation. Some relationships concerning children will be linear or accumulative while others will display the characteristics of cyclical growth-decline-return to growth.

In the course of this book, we need not apologize for drawing upon social historians when they furnish us with illuminating examples of childhood. But the more comprehensive analysis and synthesis of historical data as it relates to childhood will not occupy a central place in this discussion. It will remain in the well-qualified hands of our fellow social scientists, the historians.[9]

----

[7]There are numerous publications in the burgeoning field of Social Gerontology, but a few sources that would help ground a person in this field would be: Matilda White Riley, Director, *Aging and Society,* Vol. One; *An Inventory of Research Findings,* Vol. Two; *Aging and the Professions,* Vol. Three; *A Sociology of Age Stratification* (New York: Russell Sage Foundation, 1968, 1969, 1970); Robert C. Atchley, *The Social Forces in Later Life, An Introduction to Social Gerontology* (Belmont, California: Wadsworth Publishing Company, 1972); and Douglas C. Kimmel, *Adulthood and Aging* (New York: John Wiley & Sons, Inc., 1974).

[8]*Infant Care,* Washington, D.C.: Children's Bureau, Health, Education, and Welfare Department.

[9]A useful source that gives a useful perspective on the historical treatment of children is Stuart A. Queen and Robert W. Habenstein, *The Family in Various Cultures,* 4th ed. (Philadelphia: J. B. Lippincott Company, 1974).

Developmental Approach

One of the most appealing frames of reference concerning child-hood has been that which emphasizes the various phases of developing children, their stages of growth and, at times, their regressions or failures to move beyond certain levels of growth or abilities. The miraculous creation of life in the fertilized ovum, literally a microscopic speck, to its gradual transformation into mature adulthood has fascinated observers for years, particularly those who identify closely with this growing organism from the stages of foetus, infant, child, and adolescent to that of mature adult. As both the *object* and the *subject* of attention, each individual has a deep investment in his or her own growth-stages and, generally speaking, looks forward to "growing up some day."

The developmental approach to the study of childhood, then, could be said to rest upon biological, physical, and physiological processes that occur involuntarily in response to inherent genetic codes. The increasing refinements of musculature, neural, glandular, and other body systems form the foundation for what is known as "age-grading" of children in numerous cultures.[10]

Little is expected of such a helpless, vulnerable, dependent creature as the infant. Indeed, the general treatment most accorded babies is *acceptance* of their lack of control over body functions. Some would express this as a state of voluntary *resignation* to the need of infants for attention almost every hour of the day or night.

Newly arrived babies in their very state of utter dependency are, figuratively speaking, "kings or queens" of households. Note the numerous preparations anticipating the arrival of these "royal" creatures, the careful, meticulous marking and celebration of birthdays and the seemingly endless years of nurturance, support, protection, and encouragement given "little ones." All unknowingly, unconsciously, babies must be taken into account by the more mature, independent adults and so, in a real sense, control situations.

Of course, there are notable exceptions to what we would expect as a normal response to infants or very little children. One such exception that has aroused public furor is apparent in cases of abused or battered children.[11] We will have occasion to return to this venting of aggression against defenseless infants or young children. For the present, suffice it to note that child-abuse is an extreme form of reject-

[10]See for example, Monica Wilson, *Good Company, A Study of Nyakyusa Age-Villages* (Boston: Beacon Press, 1967).
[11]See Jerome E. Leavitt, ed., *The Battered Child, Selected Readings* (Morristown, New Jersey: General Learning Corporation, 1974).

ing, resenting, repudiating the presence of lives in development. Milder, subtler, but nevertheless highly meaningful reactions of gradually withdrawing support so that children may stand, walk, talk, eat, sleep, play, dress, and control elimination with increasing facility still seems threatening from the perspective of little children.

The relationship between parents and children is inverse. As children develop and gain, thereby increasing abilities to attend to their own needs, adults gradually pull away, diminish, their attentive, hovering, ever-present supports and place children "on their own." This is the *weaning process* that occurs among other species, but is socially significant for children and for those who are closest to them. Parents, siblings, relatives, friends, or their surrogates comment on how well children are progressing in terms of this displacement of physical dependency by physical autonomy

Something else, however, is also going on as this type of shifting occurs. This is the *nonacceptance* of childish behavior because children have supposedly acquired or developed enough personal control of their minds and bodies "to do better" than they have in the past and so release others from certain responsibilities. Pressures mount upon children in these stages of development. Persons attending children ask more and more of them. Baby-talk or other childish behavior must give way to adult behavior. If, for instance, something happens that seems to suggest that children are arrested, retarded, or handicapped in their normal growth and development, then parents may be sorely tested to continue to sustain their offspring. Such "special children" are discussed in a later chapter.

The internal changes, the changes in organs, systems, and coordinating mechanisms, of the human body are the special province of pediatricians and other medical specialists. These are accompanied by the external, easily seen changes that occur with developing children. These latter changes seem to excite the greatest comment from observers. Children's increasing heights, weights, skills in manual dexterity, and communicating their needs are a constant source of amazement to proud parents and relatives. Most of us can recall numerous instances in our childhood when relatives or friends exclaimed, "My, how you have grown!" Under our collective breaths, we might have said to ourselves, "What did you expect?," but if we were cautioned to deal with such moments, we politely thanked them for their interest in our normal development.

These developments are greeted with approval and acclaim because they have social significance in terms of the child soon to be a participant in the social order. Reaching one level, stage, or plateau in development means that the next "higher" levels of accomplishment are within the individual's grasp. The work of Gesell and associates laid the foundation for this type of thinking.[12] Children under observation simply were expected to demonstrate increasing control of their bodies in some progressive fashion.

The error in this developmental theory is that children are expected to perform in some lockstep manner as they reach a particular age. Failures to perform at progressive levels as anticipated alarm some parents. If, on the other hand, children perform far better than anticipated, parents bask in the reflected glory of their "precocious" children. It is the assumption of a fixed series of developmental stages that brings on undue fears or overbearing pride on the part of parents. Such reactions are magnified still further when they are communicated to growing children who may also doubt their abilities or acquire a scornful conceit of others. *Invidious comparisons* have left scars of envy, hatred, and resentment that mar the personalities of children for the remainder of their lives.

One last observation should be made concerning the developmental perspective. It is that untold numbers of children in the world do not have "an equal chance" to develop physically and physiologically. Rather, there are wide differences in children's development because of social circumstances and these social limitations (nutrition, sanitation, and physical care) prevent optimal growth. Because these social circumstances are not immutable, there is reason to believe that they will yield to persistent efforts to exchange vital medical or health knowledge and skills.

Outstanding medical professionals such as Albert Schweitzer, Tom Dooley, and Gordon Seagraves have taken their expertise to remote regions of the world and so earned worldwide acclaim for their humanitarian efforts. Not many years ago, the *U.S.S. Hope*, a floating hospital, cruised world ports providing a teaching function for medical practitioners. Project Hope continues in a wide variety of land-based operations to diffuse the necessary knowledge to give children a healthy start in life. Arthur Goodfriend's *The Only War We Seek* dramatized the need in a photographic essay that urged "a war" against the ancient enemies that attack all humanity, namely, poverty, disease, hunger, and illiteracy.[13] The work goes forward on multiple fronts to this day to

---

[12]See Arnold L. Gesell, *Infancy and Human Growth* (New York: The Macmillan Company, 1928); Arnold L. Gesell, *Atlas of Infant Behavior* (New Haven: Yale University Press, 1934); Arnold L. Gesell, *How a Baby Grows* (New York: Harper & Row, Publishers, Inc., 1945); Arnold L. Gesell and Frances L. Ilg, *The Child From Five to Ten* (New York: Harper & Row, Publishers, Inc., 1946); Arnold L. Gesell and Frances L. Ilg, *Child Development* (New York: Harper & Row, Publishers, Inc., 1949).

[13]Arthur Goodfriend, *The Only War We Seek* (New York: Farrar, Straus and Young, 1951).

reduce wherever possible the unnecessary suffering of innocent children. Whether close to home or abroad, children's rights to healthy survival and development merit continued vigilance.

Psychological Approach

Under the aegis of psychology, a close "sister" science to sociology, there are subsumed such specializations as psychiatry, psychoanalysis, and social psychology. All of these and many current manifestations such as transactional analysis, transcendental meditation, and encounter groups share the common denominator of an abiding *concern for and with individuals.* Whenever generalizations are made about categories or groups of people, as sociologists are committed to do, the inevitable counterobservation is that these generalizations do not apply to *all* individuals. The central theme that unites the various advocates of a psychological approach to childhood may be summarized by simply saying, "individuals differ." In short, each child is not exactly the same as any other child.

As those using a sociological approach to childhood, we have no quarrel with those who persist in an abiding concern for unique individuals. Indeed, as we shall stress throughout our discussions, students of sociology need to be sensitized to individual needs and not necessarily devote their allegiance to some abstract " society." The perception we would favor would be that there needs to be a division of labor among those who seek to understand childhood. To investigate childhood with rigor calls for specialized tools and specialized concerns. In the end, the interests of each child and, subsequently, of all children should be served.

In this brief space, we can only highlight some of the major concerns of those identified with the psychological approach to childhood.[14] Conditioning and learning certainly have psychological dimensions and are paramount when children are involved. Rewards and punishments, popularized as "the carrot and the stick" principle, loom large as processes in connection with acquiring new behaviors. Intelligence, habits, and genetics are involved in the educational experiences of children and we are indebted to the work of educational psychologists in regard to these major factors in the "inner environment" of children. We would be foolish to rule out these matters in our commitment to "outer" environments.

[14]See Benjamin Wolman and Rudolf Dreikors, eds., *Handbook of Child Psychoanalysis; Research, Theory, and Practice* (New York: Van Nostrand Reinhold Company, 1972); M. Fordham, *Children as Individuals* (New York: Putnam, 1970); and James O. Palmer, *The Psychological Assessment of Children* (New York: John Wiley and Sons, Inc., 1970). See also, E. Mavis Hetherington and Ross D. Parke, *Child Psychology* (New York: McGraw-Hill, 1975).

Educational Approach

Following closely on the heels of the psychological approach is the educational approach to childhood. The key concept in the educational approach is that children are to be "school-processed." This is to view children as entities who enter at one end of a formal educational process lacking in human knowledge to be finally released at the other end of the process saturated with as much of the accumulated learning of humankind as possible. This has been dubbed "the vessels-to-be-filled" conceptualization of formal schooling.

There are other perspectives among educators, which in all fairness should be noted. For example, the *formal* curricula to which children are exposed, the content or substance that they are asked to study, constitute only one part of their school experiences. Equally important to many educators are the *informal* educational experiences that occur in and around schools, outside formal classrooms, in such settings as playgrounds, corridors, lunchrooms, dispensaries, restrooms, auditoriums, libraries, offices, and gymnasiums. Indeed, extracurricular activities are planned and carried out as integral parts of the educational growth of youngsters. Drama, music, sports, field trips, entertainment, and interest groups are considered valued adjuncts to children's learning experiences. In a real sense, children in the primary-elementary grades from kindergarten to sixth grade are school-involved, taken up with a multitude of school-oriented, school-associated activities. The process continues well into adolescence as children move on to enter junior and senior high schools that complicate and consume the time and energies of the young.

Aside from the what, how, when, and where questions in education, the why questions are probably the most salient. By contemporary standards, it is not sufficient to pour educational experiences into empty vessels. There has been rising concern for and by the children themselves. Their rights, needs, readiness, feeling-states, and perspectives need to be considered if formal and informal education are to be effective. Through mass media, television in particular, children of the seventies and eighties are far more exposed to contemporary scenes than many educators have given them credit. The already enriched experiences of children require abilities to order, to build, to further enlarge upon the store of knowledge and ability children bring to their schools.

Children may have been passive participants in formal schools of the past and they may continue to be agreeable to whatever is being done in their behalf in schools. But there is evidence that children and their advocates are now far more vocal. One instance has been the furor created by the discovery that some school records contained cruel and unfair comments about children that followed them throughout their formal schooling. The right to examine school records was sustained by the passage of laws that gave access to these heretofore damaging documents.

It is interesting to note that the word long associated with education is *pedagogy,* the study of children. What has been assumed is that education is something that belongs in childhood and not particularly in other and later stages of life. Educators have long held that they are preparing children *for life.* A newer and more inclusive view is that education occurs throughout life, and consequently education is *for a lifetime. Andragogy,* the education of adults, is an emerging arena of educational activity, and this calls for even greater respect for learners than ever before.[15]

With education associated with every age, there are inevitable criticisms that the educational processes are not as effective as they once were believed to be. The abysmal lack of ability of high school graduates, for example, to write clear sentences and paragraphs, to read an income tax report, to write a check, or to do simple mathematics has brought charges of the miseducation of the young. While educators are willing to take responsibility for whatever shortcomings might be exposed, the responsibilities must be shared by other constituencies in the educational process. Learners, themselves, may adopt resistance to learning for a variety of reasons. Parents of children may or may not provide receptive and positive attitudes toward education or educators. A whole community of adults may nullify or undermine the educational groundwork of educators for children. In brief, we are stressing the *social* context in which education occurs.

Therapeutic Approach

For children in need of help, a therapeutic approach is in order. Knowledge that has been thoroughly tested is applied in some pragmatic fashion. Therapists, however, differ as to procedures and objectives. Some would modify; others would radically change the conditions under which certain children live. Some would build protective systems around children while others would help children cope with the existing circumstances.

Therapy is necessary because children are vulnerable to assaults from hostile, thoughtless, aggressive, and violent adults. Their fundamental state is that of helplessness or dependency, and this prompts

[15] *Never Too Old To Learn* (New York: Academy for Educational Development, 1974), p. 47; *A Trainer's Guide to Andragogy: Its Concepts, Experience and Application* (Washington, D.C.: U.S. Government Printing Office, 1973).

sympathetic and empathic persons to become child-advocates. Certainly those children who are the innocent victims of neglect, unconcern, or abuse need immediate attention. Other children warrant prolonged protection and guidance in terms of placement or care. Human rights have a long history in our freedom-conscious society and have notably included the rights of women; racial, religious, and ethnic minorities; and the elderly. Children's rights are an integral part of the whole human rights movement.[16]

The therapeutic approaches to children are characterized by warm, humane, gentle treatment of children. Homage is due those talented and perceptive men and women who daily render inestimable comfort to children in need. The practical, everyday care and treatment of children, however, is not the chief characteristic of the sociological approach.

Sociological Approach

What, then, is the sociological approach to childhood? It may draw upon the historical, developmental, psychological, educational, or therapeutic approaches, but it has its own uniqueness. The sociological approach studies children in terms of their *introduction to and interaction with social systems.* Holding childhood as the dependent variable, the phenomenon being studied, we seek to investigate the impacts of independent variables, the factors or circumstances that affect childhood. Or, at times, we may reverse the procedure and seek to understand in what ways childhood affects societal conditions or nonchildren, the adults.

Sociology emerged in the late nineteenth century in response to the needs of an increasingly complicated industrial-urbanized life style. What the application of scientific principles to physical materials and forces had accomplished could hopefully be emulated if applied to personal-social phenomena. The application, development, adaptation, and refinement of the physical science model to relationships and processes within person-to-person, person-to-group, or group-to-group situations has continued for almost a century and culminates, at present, in a kaleidoscope of perspectives among contemporary sociologists. Expressed differently, it would be both audacious and fallacious to claim that all the extant sociological analyses and syntheses are comprehensively treated in this text.

Instead, to operate in manageable units, we opt to select certain sociological theories or conceptualizations that we believe seem to offer

[16]See Paul Adams, et al., *Children's Rights, Toward the Liberation of the Child* (New York: Praeger Publishers, 1971).

the most effective and insightful information concerning children and their childhood.

First and foremost, we will utilize the dominant theory in sociology, *structural-functionalism.* In a nutshell, this theory concentrates upon social order, social forms, or social frameworks and the manner in which they operate. Applied specifically to childhood, this theory suggests that children are brought into contact with preexisting ways of doing things; are constantly taught to conform, to adapt, to adopt, or to internalize the ways of adults; or are trained, schooled, and raised "to get along with all others" as they grow up.

The central process within this structural-functional thesis, for children, is *socialization.* Children are viewed as individuals ill-equipped to participate in a complex, adult world. Rather, they are held to have the potentials of being brought slowly and carefully into contact with human ways. The procedure is alleged to be smooth, deliberate, calculated, gradual, and fairly one-sided because it places responsibility, importance, and authority in the hands of adults. In a sense, socialization can be viewed as an endless, self-perpetuating plan of action in which older persons, already socialized, seek to mold the next generation in their own images.

From this perspective, social structures and functions remain awesome, unchallenged, immutable, and relatively fixed preconditions with which children must deal. There is a reverse side to the coin, however.

One of the early challenges to this unquestioning allegiance to the existing social order came from Dennis Wrong. Wrong cautioned structural-functionalists that they should guard against being overzealous in their dedication to socialization. While disclaiming a deliberate attempt to play on words, we cannot resist agreeing that *Wrong was right!* It was his observation that *persons are social creatures without being entirely socialized:*

> Socialization may mean two quite distinct things; when they are confused an over-socialized view of man is the result. On the one hand socialization means the transmission of the culture, the particular culture of the society an individual enters at birth; on the other hand the term is used to mean "the process of becoming human," of acquiring uniquely human attributes from interaction with others. All men are socialized in the latter sense; but this does not mean that they have been completely molded by the particular norms and values of their culture.[17]

[17]Dennis H. Wrong, "The Oversocialized Conception of Man," *American Sociological Review*, 26, No. 2 (April 1961), 183–193.

Over the past ten or fifteen years, other theories have been advanced that help temper the dominance of structural-functionalism. These include *symbolic-interaction, exchange,* and *conflict* theories.

In brief, symbolic-interaction is concerned with *bonding,* decisions to join and to identify with others, through common *symbols,* meanings attached to items. Perhaps the best example, particularly as it applies to childhood, is the acquisition and use of language, the means of communication among those speaking the same "tongue."[18] Children spend a great deal of their time learning the vocabulary, grammar, and meaning of verbal interaction. Symbolic-interaction, of course, goes beyond the verbal into nonverbal symbolisms. Certain body postures, facial expressions, or gestures convey meanings to those initiated into their significance. Further, certain signs such as a cross or a Star of David, certain places such as a church or temple, or certain acts such as praying or fasting are cues to behavior that take time to learn.

Exchange theory focuses upon reciprocity, checks and balances, rewards and punishments, gains and losses, moves and countermoves among participants in social settings.[19] Rearing children demands strategies, thoughtful planning to achieve desired ends. Anticipating a series of actions and reactions, both children and adults engage in endless interchange that we may profitably explore.

Finally, there is conflict theory which deals with nonalignment, nonacceptance, nonagreement with other persons or systems. Conflict may or may not take violent form such as highly aggressive, hostile behavior. It may easily involve the nonviolent forms of rejection, deviance, or nonadaptation of ways being promoted by others.

Most important of all, growing out of conflict theory is *control* theory.[20] Control theory provides an effective way to examine and test older assumptions that children simply are compliant, cooperative, docile creatures who are willingly obedient to the demands of their elders or peers. Control theory is a useful way to de-emphasize the static interpretations of the past that children accept a priori societal conditions and so provide a new set of agents to perpetuate a given social order. Instead, control theory places greater emphasis upon children, consciously or unconsciously, controlling their own lives by determin-

[18]See Jay D. Schvaneveldt, "The Interactional Framework in the Study of the Family," in *Emerging Conceptual Frameworks in Family Analysis,* eds. F. Ivan Nye and Felix M. Berardo (New York: The Macmillan Company, 1966) and Ralph H. Turner, *Family Interaction* (New York: John Wiley & Sons, Inc., 1970).
[19]See Peter Blau, *Exchange and Power in Social Life* (New York: John Wiley & Sons, Inc., 1964); George C. Homans, *Social Behavior: Its Elementary Forms* (New York: Harcourt, Brace, and World, 1961).
[20]See James T. Duke, *Conflict and Power in Social Life* (Provo, Utah: Brigham Young University Press, 1976); Paul Sites, *Control, The Basis of Social Order* (New York: Dunellen Publishing Company, 1973).

ing the extent to which they conform to social pressures. The interplay of control, power in action, between and among those being socialized and those doing the socialization determines, in large measure, how persons of all ages eventually act toward each other.

CHILD-CENTERED, CHILD-ORIENTED, AND CHILD-DOMINATED SYSTEMS

Three different systems are interlocked in the socialization of children and in the assignment of the status of childhood. These are designated as child-centered, child-oriented, and child-dominated.

Child-Centered Systems

Child-centered systems are those that involve the total personality, the whole child, and, allegedly at least, place the individual child as the focus of attention and concern. The key example is family life in which, supposedly, children take center-stage. Husbands and wives speak of "having a family someday" by which they mean to bring children into the world and to mold them into future citizens of their society.

Child-Oriented Systems

Child-oriented systems do not deal with the total personalities of children. Rather, they deal with facets of children's lives.

Further, they are designed, created, and sponsored by adults. A prime example is the school. In this setting, children are expected to acquire the conventional customs of their society and so prepare themselves for a place among adults as those who have gone before them have done.

Another way to understand child-oriented systems is to think of them as "prepackages" developed by adults that are said to be "for the good of the child." A tremendous variety of programs have been so developed and we will devote a portion of our studies to them. The programs of the Scouts, 4-H, Indian Guides, Bible School, and summer camps are examples of child-oriented systems that will come under consideration.

Child-Dominated Systems

Despite all the allegations and good intentions of adults, child-centered and child-oriented systems carry with them an aura of adult-control; a "father or mother-knows-best" attitude prevails.

Child-dominated systems help children escape the manipulations of adults and provide, in their place, opportunities for children to take control. Children themselves become the authorities, sponsors, and makers of regulations. Supervision and control are derived from age-peers. Adults are persona-non-grata, because they are, by definition, members of the out-group. This does not mean that adults are simply forgotten because, symbolically, there is widespread imitation, rehearsing, and reacting to the life styles of older persons.

Play groups, gangs, cliques, and friendships are examples of child-dominated systems and play a major role in personality formation. What occurs within these systems may or may not have the approval of adults, but at least the young have taken some control over their destinies. There is a school of thought that would stoutly maintain that these child-dominated systems are far more significant than families in the socialization of children. The influences of peers certainly will occupy our attention as we move ahead in our study of childhood and children.

SUMMARY

Defining childhood as the status accorded persons twelve years of age or younger and concerning children as unique individuals who are beginning to acquire the ways of persons older than themselves, we have begun the process of understanding childhood and children from a sociological perspective.

The multiple approaches to the study of childhood beyond that of the sociological include the historical, the developmental, the psychological, the educational, and the therapeutic. Each has its merits, and each is subject to outside criticisms. The same applies to the sociological approach utilized in this text.

No single discipline or approach holds childhood or children as its exclusive province because these areas of interest concern multiple disciplines. While drawing upon other disciplines or approaches, the major emphasis of this text will be sociological. By this we mean the introduction of children to, and their interaction with, social systems. The social structures and their functions are of prime importance in this approach together with stress upon the process of socialization.

There are cautions, however, that we do not error in terms of oversocialization. Accordingly, other considerations from symbolic-interaction, exchange, and conflict theories should help temper our use of data and their interpretations. Further, control theory will guide us when we discuss such aspects of childhood as power, authority, and internalization of social dicta. In the end, we may be able to determine for ourselves if children are docile, receptive youngsters or more dynamic, active participants in the processes that initiate them into relationships with all others.

2

Childhood
in sociocultural
settings

If the status of childhood is to be understood, it is essential that an overall, comprehensive view be gained at the outset. Thereafter, such a view can be filled in and tempered with a closer, more detailed examination of the subvariations, subdivisions, or component portions of childhood status in comparison with other age-statuses.

To present the broadest possible view of childhood, then, is the prime objective of this chapter. The next chapter will provide the more restricted, segmented perspective.

For sociologists, perhaps the largest units of study are *societies* and their *cultures*. The former, societies, refers to the variety of ways people organize themselves to live together in groups or collectivities with a sense of common identity. The latter, cultures, refers to those processes and products the various societies evolve or redefine over time. In brief, the term society refers to people living together, and the term culture refers to their way of life.

CHILDHOOD: AS AN AGE-GRADE, GENERATION, OR PART OF THE LIFE CYCLE

Thousands of known societies provide some form of recognition that their people may be differentiated on the bases of their age-grades, generational cohorts, or locations within the life cycle. The key term here, *differentiate* or make distinctions, provides the rationale for *differential treatment*, dealing with sets of people in unique ways that are bound to manifest themselves in unique results.

Childhood, adolescence, adulthood, and old age are the most common age-grades. For more specific reasons, childhood is often broken down into infancy, the first year or so of life; early childhood, sometimes called "preschool childhood"; and later childhood, school children from the ages of about five to twelve.

Adolescence, for our purposes, covers the "teen-age years," from about thirteen to nineteen. Sometimes referred to as "the difficult years" because the persons seem to be caught somewhere between their childhood and their adulthood, adolescents are confronted with the judgment that they are half-children and half-adults. The lowering of the legal age from twenty-one to eighteen calls into question the rather arbitrary designation of "teen-agers" as adolescents, but we are more concerned here with the age-grades themselves than we are with the accuracy of the demarcation points.

Adulthood is that period of life in which individuals are said to be able to take on the full responsibilities of societal participation. In terms of freedom, adulthood means emancipation from the restrictions of childhood or adolescence. However, because this is also a period of full responsibilities, there are new social restrictions, controls, or duties imposed. In adulthood, individuals have shed one set of social bonds for another, a lesson in life that takes on significance as one grows older. It is also a lesson that has not yet been learned by children who believe adulthood is a period of doing whatever one pleases.

Adulthood may also be subdivided into young adulthood, middle age, and old age or later maturity. It would be fairly safe to assume that those utilizing this text are young adults, those in their twenties and thirties who are in the decision-making years in terms of their future careers. Middle age is a fairly vague term to cover persons who are in mid-career, those about forty or fifty years of age. The final age-grade is old age, often said to begin in the mid-sixties, but said to be beginning earlier and earlier as retirement from lifetime careers is initiated earlier in industrialized societies.

People may also be differentiated on the basis of their generational cohorts, those thousands who share a common set of experiences that mark or characterize their entire life spans.[1] From a generational point of view, children are launched into the rivers of time when their societies and their cultures are characterized by certain circumstances. That the children so "launched" take on something of this sociocultural coloration should come as no surprise to anyone.

Finally, childhood needs to be understood as the beginning of the life cycle, the life-curve that starts with growth, levels off in young adulthood, and begins a slow decline to old age, later-maturity, and inevitable death. It is a cycle because, from ongoing society's perspective, there is a perpetual regeneration of new age-grades, new generations already underway long before older generations decline and pass away. Replacements or "new recruits" enter the life cycle at fairly steady intervals unless the pattern is altered for various reasons. For example, concern for population control or freedom from unwanted pregnancies can affect the pattern. Inadvertent interruptions can also occur due to such massive upheavals as famine, war, widespread disease, or other disasters. For children, the life cycle that ends for everyone in death or "dismissal from life" seems to be a rather remote possiblity or conceptualization of life. To children, who are generations removed from death, life seems infinite. It has been said that those children who confront the death of others or who come close to death in their own experiences lose some precious part of their childhood and become "sober adults" too early in life.[2]

While we have noted the apparent separation of childhood from adulthood, the separation may not be real, depending upon how societies and their cultures treat the situation. Pre-literate hunters and gatherers as well as agriculturally-based societies have been known to dichotomize age-grades into either childhood or adulthood. On a single day, a child may enter adulthood if he or she has gone through a socially approved rite of passage or appropriate ritual. One of the interesting survivals found in contemporary society is the bar mitzvah ceremonies for thirteen-year-old boys or the bas mitzvah ceremonies for thirteen-year-old girls of the Jewish faith.[3] Through these ceremonials, a child takes on the special status of full *religious adulthood*. The years of formal training and preparation for the rituals are alleged to be worthwhile because they yield adults capable of fulfilling their religious obli-

---

[1]For a fuller explanation of generations, see Marvin R. Koller, *Families, A Multigenerational Approach* (New York: McGraw-Hill Book Company, 1974).
[2]A useful source in this matter is the compendium, Earl A. Grollman, ed., *Explaining Death to Children* (Boston: Beacon Press, 1967).
[3]See R. Brasch, *The Judaic Heritage, Its Teachings, Philosophy, and Symbols* (New York: David McKay Company, Inc., 1969), "Bar Mitzvah," pp. 283–86.

gations. In our complicated, industrial society, there are other aspects of adulthood that remain untouched by the bar or bas mitzvahs, but for children in other types of societies, such rites of passage qualify them for *full adulthood* in terms of making a living, marrying, or defending their societies against aggressors.

In sum, childhood is the first age-grade, the founding of a new generation, and the beginning of the life cycle. The context within which this initial stage of life takes place is the particular society and culture into which children have been born. What occurs is a melange of sociocultural inputs into childhood that helps shape the lives of children and, subsequently, their lives as mature adults. It is in this arena that known and unknown variables of sociological concern operate.

CHILDHOOD:
AS DEPENDENT OR INDEPENDENT VARIABLE

Sociologists have usually treated childhood as a status that is "acted upon" by external, sociocultural factors, forces, or variables. This is to say that childhood is dependent upon variants in societies and their cultures.

But there is another way of looking at childhood, in fact, the converse of the dependency thesis of childhood. This less traditional way holds that childhood should be regarded as an independent variable, a variable in its own right that can and does affect societies and their cultures.

Two different but similar images might help in visualizing the status of childhood as both a dependent and an independent variable.

In the first image, the status of childhood is seen as a point fixed in the center of a group of concentric circles. In the second image, childhood would be similar to the proverbial pebble dropped into the center of a sociocultural pool or milieu which generates larger and larger circles. The first image conceptualizes childhood as immersed in host societies and cultures. In the second image, childhood is an activator of consequences of larger and larger sociocultural import.

If we visualize childhood along the lines of the static receptor of external social forces, we fix a picture of children being controlled through adult prescriptions and proscriptions. Childhood, in this sense, is a conferred or ascribed status within the larger society. There is little that children can do in such a situation other than to react, adjust, or learn as quickly as possible what is expected of them.

There is something to be said in support of this portrayal of childhood as being "acted upon" because the arrival of children into their respective societies is anticipated by persons somewhat schooled to deal with them in socially and culturally approved ways. Children, then, do not confront a world that is baffled by their appearance, but rather one that is well stocked with ready-made responses to their presence and their demands.

It is the second image of children actively shaping their lives that seems more threatening to those concerned with established order and system. Children not only are active agents in their personal lives but are also *social agents of changes* yet to come. Expectations of conformity to sociocultural norms are no longer guaranteed, and it is the unknown social ramifications that seem to distress those assigned as children's caretakers.

The studies of Vern L. Bengtson and Joseph A. Kuypers and their underlying theory help suggest a compromise between parent's and children's generations.[4] Their theory centers around the idea of "a developmental stake," an investment on the part of parents or parental surrogates that should "pay off" in anticipated social directions. In Bengtson and Kuypers' studies, both parents and children agree that there is friction and dissension as the older generation tries to impose its views on the younger generation.

The friction and dissension, however, stem from the different positions of parents and children. Parents see their children as their heirs, as carriers of social values, as guardians of generational continuity. Children, on the other hand, see their socialization as something with which they must personally deal. It remains their decision as to what they choose to perpetuate and what they determine to shed or modify. Parents seek to *validate* themselves while children seek to *establish* themselves.

The deficiency in the thinking of those given responsibility to prepare children to enter their society and culture is in failing to learn how and when "to let go." Certainly those who rear children seek to smooth their way, to ready them for the roads ahead, to affirm their values. But adults cannot hold their children in social bondage forever. Other generations must be free to test their own judgments and to match changing circumstances with changing needs. Parents who have dominated children cannot expect that children will be carbon copies of their elders. In due time, parents grow older and complete their life

[4]Vern L. Bengtson and Joseph A. Kuypers, "Generational Difference and the Developmental Stake," *Aging and Human Development*, 2 (Farmingdale, N.Y.: Baywood Pub. Co., 1971), 249–60.

cycles. Their children, in due time, have the option of deciding what they will do with social heritages.

The Self-Fulfilling Prophecy

The self-fulfilling prophecy suggests that a preconception that individuals or groups of individuals will act in certain ways sets up the very conditions that lead to the anticipated results. Examples abound as in the cases of children labelled "difficult" or "inept" who become hard to handle or inadequate by virtue of such labels. The labelling may have been inaccurate and unsupported by the evidence, but the steady treatment of children as "problem children" ultimately leads them to accept and define themselves as rebellious.

More to the point, whole societies have prejudged children as being submissive, malleable, defenseless creatures whom they must dominate, instruct, order, sustain, and lead. It follows that children are then exposed to whatever acceptable routines exist in such matters as eating, sleeping, dressing, playing, eliminating, washing, or communicating. On the positive side, children are rewarded, reinforced, and encouraged to be like those about them and, on the negative side, are restricted, inhibited, denied, or punished if they seem to be deviating from expected behaviors. Small wonder that they turn out as they do, small replicas of the models placed before them, little children who have accepted their status in society.

One of the most dramatic examples of the self-fulfilling prophecy in action was the case brought to the attention of the general public in a televised drama of General Electric Theatre over CBS on April 23, 1974 entitled "Larry."[5] It referred to the case of a child left on his own in a facility for the mentally or emotionally disturbed. Somehow the child remained in the care of the personnel of the facility when his mother died and was treated as if he too were mentally, emotionally, and socially unable to cope with the world outside. A perceptive social worker is credited with noting that while "Larry" seemed to be like all the other patients, he was able to read, handle problems, and learn new skills. What "Larry" had done was to accept the judgments of others that he was incompetent and dependent and, in order to survive, had taken on the behaviors of those he saw about him. Based upon a true case, "Larry" was resocialized to perform acceptably in the outside world and ultimately entered it as a mature man. His potential to be a participant in his society had been sharply curtailed by the self-fulfilling

[5]Verified by the City Editor, *Akron Beacon Journal* (Akron, Ohio).

prophecy of others. It was rectified and allowed to manifest itself only after considerable effort and redefinition.

The case of "Larry" can be multiplied a thousandfold in the numerous instances of the self-fulfilling prophecy at work among children. It does suggest that it is entirely possible to alter preconceptions about childhood and to adopt a new stance that children are quite capable, sturdy youngsters who can and do make fundamental decisions about the directions their lives should take. Like the thoughtful, observant social worker who was willing to go out of her way to bring forward whatever abilities "Larry" had buried or camouflaged, so those who affect children stand in need of cautioning themselves to avoid hasty judgments and to move toward positive encouragement of children's capacities for growth and development.

The Barbarian Thesis

Another sociocultural stance concerning childhood is the deliberately overdramatized conceptualization of children as "barbarians," little "savages" who invade societies each generation and need to be contained or subdued. To do otherwise would be tantamount to standing by while revered traditions were torn down by the "uncivilized."

The Barbarian Thesis thus gives priority, preference, and privilege to societies and their cultures. It sees societies and cultures as predating and postdating children, and it is the survival and maintenance of societies and cultures that takes precedence over newly arrived children. Children and all other individuals are mortal whereas social systems are held to be ongoing, self-generating, or immortal. While not often labelled "barbarians," nevertheless children are seen as unknowing hordes by many, quite capable of demolishing all that adults have carefully built up over many generations.

If the Barbarian Thesis is accepted, it calls for strategies to convert children into standard-bearers rather than destroyers of standards of conduct. Accordingly, societies marshal their forces to assimilate the newcomers so that timetested formulas remain relatively undisturbed. Under this rubric, children become the *means* by which societies and their cultures achieve desired ends. It is only when the idea of freedom is introduced that the Barbarian Thesis becomes unacceptable.

Ethos, The Underlying
Sentiments of a Society and Its Culture

One of the most difficult tasks is to define the essential set of values that seem to guide given societies and cultures. Values are the relative worth of things and can be material or nonmaterial objects. They provide the standards of judgment that some idea or thing is "good" or "bad." Values underlie attitudes favoring or disfavoring human behavior and, of course, are social products acquired through training. Taken together, a particular set of values is known as the *ethos* of a particular society and culture.

Values or ethoes are not easily isolated by students of societies, but by treating them as social data, sociologists have found them to be useful as characterizations, explanations, or distillations that help explain why groups of people behave as they do.

As suggested in our discussion of the Barbarian Thesis, freedom is one of the values or part of the ethos of a society that makes such a judgment intolerable. Freedom means the power to determine one's own actions, to be at liberty to decide how to conduct one's self and one's affairs. To treat children as "barbarians," adults would have to plot and carry out plans to contain them. If freedom is not an important element in an ethos, then there is no hesitation about how to deal with those who seem to threaten a given social order. Control, restraint, or limits are called for in the name of a higher value, the society itself.

American society has, ideally at least, loudly and steadfastly proclaimed its dedication to *freedom for all.* While in reality Americans may fall far short of achieving freedom for all persons, they are committed to this value and so must continue their quest. One age-grade or another, one generation or another, occupants of one stage or another of the life cycle are all persons who have been given the promise of self-fulfillment, and children and childhood cannot be treated as inferior for too long without some hue and cry being raised.

Values, however, can also be in conflict. That is to say that seeking one value may thwart or deny another value. Caught between the dignity and worth of individuals and the importance of maintaining a society that controls its participants when they interfere, disrupt, or harm other individuals, a society dedicated to personal freedom has serious decisions to make.

In the face of this dilemma, it is so much simpler to stress control and domination rather than thoughtful consideration of the rights of others. Or, moving to the opposite pole, it is simplistic to take the stance that individuals can do as they please. In American society, the problem is at what juncture of events controls should be established or cast away. In childhood, the issues revolve around encouragement and permissiveness or restraint and denial.

Groups and Categories, Their Relationship to Childhood

Sociology has sometimes been summed up as the science that studies human groups, the interactional patterns and interconnections that hold persons together. Thus, *the sociology of childhood consists of examining what happens to children as they move from group to group.*

The *primary groups*, of course, are those that are characterized by prolonged, intimate associations that literally provide individual participants with personality traits or attributes. This is not to say that group participants automatically, unquestioningly accept whatever a given group promotes. Rather, individuals in primary groups select, modify, and adapt qualities that are presented to them as values. Personality can be said to be the subjective reflection of objective data. One of the most important primary groups is the family, and we will closely examine its impacts upon children and childhood in ensuing chapters. An additional primary group is the peer group, another issue in the sociology of childhood which demands attention. The issue rests upon which group, family or peer can, should, or does take precedence in the lives of children.

The *secondary groups* will also be salient concerns of the sociology of childhood. These groups may be of limited duration and involve only portions of the participants' lives. They may well be, in our language, child-centered or child-oriented, but they may or may not produce their intended effect. Schools, religious instruction, and an array of child-oriented programs calculated to serve the "best interests" of children are examples of secondary groups with which we need to be concerned.

Categories, however, differ markedly from groups and also have a serious impact upon children and their childhood. The distinction between categories and groups is that categories are classifications of types of persons alleged to have common qualities. They emerge out of the fabric of societies and their cultures and amount to identifying persons in some systematic way so that there may be short-cut ways of dealing with them. The labelling of children thus crystallizes, fixes, or freezes them into some definite status in society and legitimatizes their treatment for prolonged periods of time.

There is no quarrel with the existence of categories as sociocultural products, but there is objection to categorical thinking that prevents changes in typologies which may be in need of reformulation and rethinking. In our analysis of the place of childhood in our society, there must be extreme caution in predetermining just how and where children fit into their societies. The caution is essential because there are tremendous differences among children that call out for recognition if our abilities to distinguish them are keen and sensitive enough. Children are not simply "little people" who are brought into "a land of giants" as in fairy tales and folklore. In terms of values, they are the very young who have *pluripotentials* that need encouragement and growth.

The Tabula Rasa Thesis

The *tabula rasa* thesis holds that children are like a clean slate, an unsullied area that invites usage. Nothing has been written on this clean slate and so it arrives in a societal and cultural context in pristine condition. More contemporary equivalents of this ancient idea might be the blank typing paper that awaits the impressions of the typewriter keys or the cassettes of magnetic recording tape that have yet to be used. The point, of course, is that once used, the tabula rasa are never the same again. There can be no turning back to their original state of clear receptibility.

This conceptualization of children stresses that the experiences children have, experiences consciously or unconsciously provided through group contacts, cannot be easily erased, forgotten, or nullified. Impressionable children grow up to be adults whose recording chambers play back early experiences for the remainder of their lives. In a very meaningful way, there is a little boy speaking to the grown man or a little girl talking to the grown woman despite the passage of decades. The impressions are indelible, vivid, and instructive guides to conduct. The psycho-sexual-social history taking reported by Masters and Johnson, for example, documents how childhood experiences intimately affect the lives of adults.[6]

A further clue to the significance of the tabula rasa concept is the frequency with which adults dredge up incidents from their childhood. The untold experiences that they have had as adults would seem to have buried, blurred, or blunted the effects of childhood experiences. But such is not the case. Events that passed as trivial, meaningless, or inconsequential when a person was a child have been etched irrevocably into their memories and can be brought to consciousness through adult associations. Long-term memories provide the fundamental databanks upon which psychiatric treatment draws in searching for appropriate therapies for troubled adults. Most adults have certain areas of sensitivity in the course of their lives which are frequently traceable to some dramatic moment or some brief exchange of words or deeds that has remained figuratively branded into their personality makeup.

If there is some merit to the tabula rasa thesis for our purposes, it is that persons need to exercise considerable caution about what they say or do in the presence of children. The thoughtless words, the frightening act, or the casual remark are stamped on their memories, and children, grown to adulthood, carry these marks for their entire lives. The insignificant moment to others becomes the significant moment for

---

[6]William H. Masters and Virginia E. Johnson, *Human Sexual Inadequacy* (Boston: Little, Brown and Company, 1970).

the individual. While there is a tendency to stress the negative reper-
cussions of childhood incidents, certainly we need to acknowledge the
positive results of specific childhood experiences as well.

Childhood's Privilege of Backwardness

The relative status of societies and their respective cultural levels
have caught the attention of many observers. By comparing and contrasting the variety of ways in which people have organized themselves
to carry out their lives, some societies and cultures are thought of as
"advanced" while others are said to be "backward." These relative
positions, of course, are dependent upon a priori sets of values.

Assuming that "advanced" sociocultural contexts are at a distinct
advantage over those of "backward" societies and cultures, there would
seem to be no particular *privilege* to backwardness. But there is one
privilege that "backward" societies and cultures have—the option of
learning from the experience of those who have tried some particular
scheme or actualized their plans and ideas.

The privilege of "backwardness" applies to childhood as well as to
societies and their cultures. It is the opportunities children have to
observe what committed adults have accomplished. If grown men and
women have been successful in the implementation of their ideas, then
children may learn to emulate them. However, the persistence of adults
in carrying out their notions of what is appropriate can and does result
in failures and unresolved problems. The young have the advantage or
"privilege of backwardness" over their predecessors because they still
have options that can be exercised.

The close, participant observation of the ways in which adults
conduct themselves in sex, marriage, and family systems is one of the
most salient training grounds of children. Undoubtedly, much of childhood is spent in this sociocultural context. We need to take a closer look
at family life from the perspective of childhood, but when we do, we
can certainly remind ourselves of this "privilege of backwardness" that
the young may utilize. Although it is hoped that children enjoy their
early years in the midst of their families, evidence is also piling up that
traditional family life is being sorely tested and found wanting. Experimentation with alternative forms and procedures is increasing, according to the mass media.[7] Both young and mature adults have begun to
apply their "privilege of backwardness" which we strongly suspect is
rooted in their childhood.

[7]See for instance, Mary Walton, Knight News Service, "On the Rocks . . . Some
Fear for the American Family," *Akron Beacon Journal* (Akron, Ohio), February 15,
1976, p. H-1, 10.

SUMMARY

An overview of societies and their cultures provides the perspective that can help us see childhood as a unique age-grade in its sociocultural settings.[8] Being the first age-grade, the members of a new generation, and at the beginning of their life cycles, children are acted upon by their respective societies and cultures, or act in their own right in their respective sociocultural contexts. In sociological terms, childhood may be a dependent or independent variable. On the one hand, children are shaped and molded by their sociocultural environments, and on the other hand, they are the shapers and molders of their own lives and the lives of those they meet. Children are both the carriers of their cultures and the agents of social change.

A variety of sociological conceptualizations help expand upon this macroview of childhood in sociocultural settings. The self-fulfilling prophecy, the Barbarian Thesis, the ethos of a society, groups and categories, the tabula rasa thesis, and the privilege of backwardness were examined in terms of what these ideas mean to childhood and children. In sum, they suggest that the linkages between childhood and other age-grades are strong and binding.

[8]Prentice-Hall has developed a series concerning ethnic groups in American society; the following materials provide substance to the different sociocultural settings for childhood: Harry H. L. Kitano, *Japanese Americans*, 2nd ed., 1976; Joan Moore, Harry Pachon, *Mexican Americans*, 2nd ed., 1976; Helena Znaniecki Lopata, *Polish Americans*, 1976.

3

Childhood
and
social stratification

The previous chapter examined childhood in the broad perspective of sociocultural settings. This chapter provides a closer view by looking at childhood within social class systems.

The study of social classes or social stratification within societies has remained one of the major contributions of the field of sociology.[1] Despite all the claims to the contrary, the evidence overwhelmingly

[1]See Joseph Alan Kahl, *The American Class Structure* (New York: Rinehart, 1957); Gerhard E. Lenski, *Power and Privilege, A Theory of Social Stratification* (New York: McGraw-Hill, 1966); Melvin L. Kohn, *Class and Conformity, A Study in Values* (Homewood, Illinois: Dorsey Press, 1969); Charles H. Page, *Class and American Sociology, From Ward to Ross* (New York: Schocken Books, 1969); Celia S. Heller, *Structured Social Inequality, A Reader in Comparative Social Stratification* (New York: Macmillan, 1968, 1969); Norval D. Glenn, *Social Stratification, A Research Bibliography* (Berkeley, California: The Glendessary Press, 1970); Joseph Lopreto, and Lawrence E. Hazelrigg, *Class, Conflict, and Mobility, Theories and Studies of Class Structure* (San Francisco: Chandler Publishing Company, 1972); and Richard F. Hamilton *Restraining Myths, Critical Studies of U.S. Social Structure and Politics* (New York: Halsted Press, 1975).

documents the *differential opportunities* of children based upon their families of origin. Their fortuitous arrival within "privileged" families increases their chances to maximize their potentials within their societies. If, however, children are born to "disprivileged" families, their chances to develop their capabilities are considerably diminished. A child born to a royal family will be welcomed as a prince or princess, and most doors will be opened for him or her. A child born in poverty will struggle against great odds to find doors closed to him or her. Both children will have been given the gift of life, but the accident of birth to families of high or low socioeconomic status will be a determining factor in their success within the identical society.

Further, there are different *types* of social class systems, and these types differ in the degree to which they provide for mobility within a given social system. The *open-class* system provides for the most opportunities for children to improve their status above that of their parental families. The *estate* system provides some chances for upward social mobility, while *castelike* systems provide the least opportunities to move beyond the conditions imposed upon children by their families of origin.

OPEN-CLASS SYSTEMS

Opportunities for Children in Open-Class Systems

Open-class systems operate on the principle that merit is recognized. Channels or ladders are provided that enable a child to move to a higher position in society than that of his or her parents. These "channels" or "ladders" may be such advantages as effective schools, extensive travel to enlarge one's perspective of the world, contacts with influential persons, or access to and usage of skills and knowledge. Under an open-class system, if an individual can demonstrate ability to occupy a higher position than the one he or she currently occupies, then such a position is allegedly made available to that person. That is the way the social class system is "supposed" to work, at least in the model that is held up to view for most children in American society.

What is easily overlooked in this optimistic picture is that social mobility in open-class systems may be "down" the social ladder as well as "up." In this event, children may fail to preserve the social levels achieved by their parental families and so fall well below their original social class positions. It is a grim perspective that tends to be de-emphasized in the greater efforts to encourage children to strive for greater social rewards.

Childhood, then, is a starting point, and one's ultimate destination within a social system is problematic. Some children will opt to improve their chances in life while other children will reject their opportunities to rise above their original socioeconomic levels. But, again, the choices alone are not sufficient to assure future social class positions. There may well be extenuating circumstances that nullify the efforts of the most ambitious of children. While many persons may, indeed, have the ability to adequately fill certain high positions in society and so reap the social rewards, the positions may become nonexistent or very limited if the ability of the society to accommodate its ambitious members changes substantially. Saturation points can be reached in terms of utilizing the existing engineers, teachers, technicians, civil servants, entertainers, or attorneys-at-law. Developing nation-states in Africa and Asia, for instance, while improving education for their children, find that they cannot place as many educated persons in various positions in society as they may like to do. In American society, displacement of industries and businesses can occur rather quickly and leave many persons socially stranded.

Those Americans who postulate that their society is characterized by growing and expanding frontiers can readily understand that children should be encouraged to grasp opportunities provided for them by their families of origin. These same Americans, however, have difficulty comprehending why some children summarily reject their opportunities and enter into conflict with the social systems they encounter. Instead of being controlled by the social class system, these particular children begin to take control of their destinies and move, in their case, in unanticipated directions. While not being an adequate answer as to why some children choose the downward path, we can only suggest at this point that the values of the "underprivileged" are more important to them than the values of the "privileged" or "overprivileged." What may be lacking in material comforts is more than made up for in honesty, strength, and relaxation from tensions as far as they can learn about less privileged life styles.[2]

Open-class systems not only provide freedom to move up or down vertically, but share with all other social class systems the quality of *horizontal mobility.* By this, we mean the likelihood that children will identify closely with the social stratum of their parents and so remain

[2]See for example, Robert B. Hill, *The Strengths of Black Families* (New York: Emerson Hall Publishers, Inc., 1971, 1972).

well within the socioeconomic level with which they are most familiar. Relatives, friends, and associates, all of the same social class as the children's parents, will reinforce parental class loyalties and forge bonds that are not easily broken.[3]

Estate Systems

Estate systems are those social class systems that allow some vertical mobility upward *provided those in higher positions approve.* This is to say that while persons may have merit, they must be *recognized* for that merit by those in positions to bring them into higher ranks in a given society.

The feudal systems of medieval Europe, for example, developed a landed aristocracy with the nobility at the highest levels of prestige and power and the serfs at the lowest disprivileged levels. Only if those in the highest ranks were pleased with the behavior or achievements of those in the lower ranks could these individuals hope to improve their station in life.

However, we do not have to point to the feudal systems of Europe for examples of the estate system. We can turn to the promotions in rank that occur in our own times in schools, businesses, industries, or professions. For those who move up the ranks, the estate system is quite acceptable. Those persons, however, who fail to move up or who see others get promotions rather than themselves are understandably critical or bitter.

While the demonstration of merit is alleged to be the basis of promotions in rank, there is also the unspoken feeling that sheer merit cannot guarantee desired results. There is the intangible matter of promotional decisions by influential persons which are made rather subjectively. This so-called "pull" or "inside track" determines who shall be chosen for high office and who will be bypassed.

It follows, then, that many children are carefully taught to "get along" with as many different types of persons as possible. Friendships, common courtesies, or sensitivities to the needs of others are assets in their own right, but they are also invaluable in securing desired positions or stations in a lifetime. This is a matter that does not escape the attention of those who socialize the young and so becomes a part of the litany of training for the adult years that lie ahead.

[3]Miles E. Simpson, "Social Mobility, Normlessness and Powerlessness in Two Cultural Contexts," *American Sociological Review,* 35, No. 6 (December 1970), 1002–13.

Castelike Systems

The most rigid social class system is caste. It freezes persons in the same social strata as their parents because birth alone is held to be the most significant event in any person's life. One simply inherits the mantle worn by one's family of origin and submits to whatever ensues. Vertical mobility upward is nonexistent, and no amount of talent or influence can change one's station in life.

Most scholars point to ancient India as the locale of a prime example of a caste system. More likely, the extremes were never reached, and a "close-to-caste" or "castelike" set of conditions existed in antiquity. In modern times, however, the State of India has legally outlawed castelike conditions. The remnants of these conditions have, nevertheless, continued well into the present.[4]

As students of childhood, we would be remiss if we did not seek to determine the extent of castelike conditions in contemporary American society. It would seem to be wholly out of place to find castelike conditions in a society that prides itself on freedom and individual opportunities. But study does reveal that being born to certain families does mean minimized chances of upward mobility for numerous children in America.[5] Equal opportunity is one of the social fictions promoted by those who prefer to deal with their own successes rather than with the failures of others to enjoy whatever benefits American society can provide. We shall return to this theme when we treat other elements of the picture such as race, religion, ethnicity, physical conditions, and education.

ADVANTAGES AND DISADVANTAGES OF SOCIAL CLASS FOR CHILDREN

The American social class system, with which we are most concerned, is not a pure open-class, estate, or castelike system. Rather, it is a mixture of elements from each of the three systems we have discussed. On the one hand, there are opportunities for some children to move far beyond the socioeconomic levels of their original families. On the other hand, there are few or no opportunities to change substantially the circumstances surrounding the childhood of numerous individuals.

[4]See Robert S. Newman, "Caste and the Indian Jews," *The Indian Journal of Sociology*, 3, Nos. 1, 2 (March, September 1972), 35–54.
[5]Shirley Jenkins, "Child Welfare as a Class System," *Children and Decent People*, ed. Alvin L. Schorr (New York: Basic Books, 1974), pp. 3–23.

When Americans speak of "freedom," they mean that opportunities exist within the limitations of social classes. Some children have "more" and some children have "less" freedom depending upon their origins. It is not freedom in the sense of "doing whatever one pleases."

It would seem that the higher one moved in the social class system, the freer one would be to act in those ways that are self-satisfying. Such is not the case. Leaders are accountable to their followers. Royalty cannot walk roughshod over subjects. Even dictators must carefully guard themselves against the disapproval of the masses they command. Military leaders are responsible for the orders they issue. Professors must be conscious of how they treat their students, and so on. The Watergate years, as they have been called, have taught sobering lessons to those in high offices and, even perhaps more importantly, have left their mark on the lives of small children. One study dramatically pointed out the cynicism and distrust concerning political figures that has become a part of the makeup of elementary school children.[6] Accountability for one's actions is thus both a privilege and a constraint. Those in advantaged positions have also acquired a whole new set of social responsibilities.

There is another consideration for those in lower levels which concerns survival itself. In addition to the feeble, the injured, and the very elderly, children particularly suffer from lower class status because they are the most vulnerable to harm. One of the most sensitive barometers of the level of living is the infant mortality rate, the number of infants under one year of age dying per thousand of live births.[7] Almost without exception, unless counter measures are taken, lower-class children die in great numbers before the first year of life is over. Disease, nutritional neglect, accidents, and insufficient health care take a tremendous toll in the lower levels of a society.

It is gratifying to find that the infant mortality rate has fallen in the United States. These figures, however, take all socioeconomic levels into consideration and thus mask the profound suffering that occurs mainly to children in the lower classes.

If disprivileged children can survive the rigors of infancy, there remain many more needs that must be satisfied before these children can reach the state of being "self-actualized" or truly expressive of their personal qualities. Food, shelter, and clothing are basic needs that must

[6]F. Christopher Arterton, "The Impact of Watergate on Children's Attitudes toward Political Authority," *Political Science Quarterly*, 89, No. 2 (June 1974), 269–288.

[7]See *Historical Statistics of the U.S., Colonial Times to 1957* (Washington, D.C.: Bureau of Census), p. 25, and *Statistical Abstract of the United States, 1975* (Washington, D.C.: Bureau of Census), p. 63.

Infant Deaths Per Thousand Live Births, United States, 1940 to 1975

Year	Infant Mortality Rate
1940	47
1950	29.2
1960	26.0
1970	20.00
1975	16.5

Source: *Statistical Abstract of the United States, 1975*, U.S. Department of Commerce, Bureau of Census, p. 63, and National Center for Health Statistics, Public Health Service, Division of Vital Statistics, 1976.

be met before children can move on to whatever contributions they may make to others and to themselves.

Maslow's theory of "the hierarchy of needs" suggests how the satisfaction of one set of needs leads to successive sets of needs that must be satisfied, in turn, before persons reach their highest potentials.[8] (See Figure 3–1). In Maslow's view, once their biological needs are met, individuals must become safe from harm. If they reach some measure of security, they can begin to offer and receive love, to show an abiding concern for mutually supportive relationships with other persons. If these stages are reached, then the next set of needs emerges in terms of esteem, respect, and appreciation from others and for one's self. It is not until these successive needs are met that persons may be motivated enough to make whatever social contributions they are capable of making. This thoughtful, logical ordering of human needs challenges

[8]A. H. Maslow, "Theory of Human Motivation," *Psychological Review*, 50 (1943), pp. 370–396. Copyright 1943 by the American Psychological Association. Reprinted by permission; also reprinted in Richard J. Lowry, ed., *Dominance, Self-Esteem, Self-Actualization: Germinal Papers of A. H. Maslow* (Monterey, California: Brooks/Cole Publishing Company, A Division of Wadsworth Publishing Company, Inc., 1973), pp. 153–73.

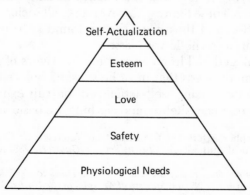

FIGURE 3–1 *The Hierarchy of Needs*

others to check upon its validity or to apply its ideas to their own observations. We cite it here because it helps explain how fundamental needs are transformed into more significant needs and how, in the case of children in lower socioeconomic levels, there can be a thwarting of these needs that can lead to frustrated, angered, depressed, defeated, or counterproductive adults. Maslow's theory may also be applied to other variables such as race, religion, or ethnicity in the lives of children, topics we will explore in greater detail in ensuing chapters.

If our understanding of social class differential opportunities comes close to reality, it follows that *hopelessness* is a familiar state of being for lower class children. This does not mean that all lower-class children feel there are no opportunities or places for them in society because studies, such as that of Simmons and Rosenberg, indicate the contrary.[9] Certain lower-class children believe that they do have a worthwhile future to pursue.

Thanks to glimpses of how other classes live through such media as television, movies, magazines, or newspapers, the very young can have a number of options. For one, they may feel *relative deprivation*, that is, suffering in comparison to what other persons have available to them. For another, they may accept the values of the middle or upper classes, the generalized values of their society, but finding them out of reach by the usual standards, justify alternative means to satisfying them. This is what Hyman Rodman has called "the lower-class value stretch."[10] If money cannot be earned, for example, in jobs or careers that middle or upper-class persons follow, it can still be secured by illegal or extralegal means. One can still "hustle" a living somehow.

Judged by middle or upper-class norms, the very young can and do engage in "irresponsible" behavior. Juvenile delinquency is perhaps the greatest example of this overt conflict between wanting the same sort of things other people have but resorting to unsanctioned means to achieve them. These devil-may-care attitudes can be seen in such acts as the juvenile terrorizing of passengers in subways, buses, or other public conveyances, the muggings of strangers in public parks or streets, and the crude graffiti and vandalism in public places. It is displayed in a distrust for police or other authority figures and the creation of mutual-support groups such as roving gangs or mutual-admiration societies known as cliques.

None of the above implies that we approve of such "acting out" of social class patterns, but we are seeking to understand why it occurs

[9]Roberta G. Simmons and Morris Rosenberg, "Functions of Children's Perceptions of the Stratification System," *American Sociological Review*, 36, No. 2 (April 1971), 235–49.
[10] Hyman Rodman, *Lower-Class Families, The Culture of Poverty in Negro Trinidad* (New York: Oxford University Press, 1971), pp. 194–95.

in the first place. It should be understood, however, that in the making of generalizations, there are exceptions to the generalized rules.

Major cities in America, for example, have become alarming places that call for prudent, vigilant, and secure measures if people are to continue to live in them. The causes of this growing sense of insecurity are the failings of various social systems to deliver on their promise that individuals may achieve personal goals in some approved fashion. In terms of control theory, systems cannot "control" those they dissatisfy and so judge certain deviancies from norms as evidence that some persons are "out of control." Hope that everything will work out well does not come readily to lower-class children when they see their own parents or relatives constantly defeated in their efforts to improve their lot in life.

The exceptions, of course, must also be recognized. One type would be those men and women who did emerge from abject poverty into positions of respect, power, and self-actualization. We would point to entertainers such as Eddy Cantor, Danny Thomas, Danny Kaye, and Jerry Lewis who have linked their names and careers to the support of suffering or deprived children. These individuals did not forget their humble beginnings. Another type would be those who started life as children in fairly comfortable or even luxurious circumstances of privilege and encouragement. Ghandi, Franklin Delano Roosevelt, Martin Luther King, John and Robert Kennedy come readily to mind as persons who had privileged opportunities from their earliest days but who nevertheless were sensitive and responsive to the needs of the less privileged.

In these instances, the sources of change came from *outside* the disprivileged classes under discussion. By this we mean that changes made on behalf of the lower classes came from those in the middle or upper classes. The changes from those living within lower classes were often minimal or characterized by extreme violence such as the eruptions in such major cities as Los Angeles, Newark, Cleveland, Detroit, and Washington, D.C. The "War on Poverty" can now be judged more clearly with the passage of time, and its attempts to provide the means for upward social mobility for those in the lower classes did not really attack the conditions of poverty themselves.[11] It, too, was a measure from outside the target populations and fell short of its objectives.

Unemployment on a large scale seems to be emerging as another manifestation of the shortcomings of the social class system within the

[11]See Barbara Preston, "Statistics of Inequality," *Sociological Review*, 22, No. 1 (February 1974), 103–118, and Louis A. Ferman, ed., "Evaluating the War on Poverty," *The Annals of the American Academy of Political and Social Science*, Vol. 385, (September 1969).

United States of America. Restlessness, anxiety, and lack of a sense of direction among the unskilled, undereducated, and discouraged unemployed are threats to the social order that can become explosive. A call, for example, has gone out for a national policy for full employment, but it waits upon decisions in the field of political-economic policies before it could be implemented.[12] In the meantime, lower-class children will continue to be socialized in ways that can damage their lives and the lives of all they encounter.

LIFE STYLES OF CHILDREN
IN UPPER, MIDDLE, AND LOWER CLASSES

Sociologists and other social scientists have devoted many years of research to describing the actual conditions under which persons live at different social class levels. Much of what we know about children in upper, middle, and lower classes is based upon their contributions.[13] Our debt to them is large.

It is easy to point out that the state of our knowledge at any one point in time is limited. The defects of studies can be magnified by the generalizations derived from them. These defects usually are held to be limited sampling, faulty research design, minimal information, questionable tests of statistical significance, reliability, validity, and overall failure to secure definitive data.

Nevertheless, in what follows, it is worthwhile to portray the nature of the lives of children at various social strata as fully as possible. Where possible, we will try to point out the exceptions to the word portraits we draw.

Upper-Class Children[14]

Upper-class children belong to a select circle that confers upon them certain advantages and disadvantages. The advantages result

[12]Helen Ginsburg, "Needed: A National Commitment to Full Employment," No. 40, Sidney Hillman Reprint Series (New York: Sidney Hillman Foundation, 1976, from *Current History*, August 1973).

[13]See for example, Ruth S. Cavan, *The American Family* (New York: Thomas Y. Crowell Company, Inc., 1969), Chap. 4, "Social Classes, Ethnic Groups, and Mobility," Chap. 5, "Upper-Class Families," Chap. 6, "Middle-Class Families," and Chap. 7, "Lower-Class Families."

[14]See James T. Adams, *The Adams Family* (Boston: Little, Brown and Company, 1930); Cleveland Amory, *The Proper Bostonians* (New York: E. P. Dutton & Company, Inc., 1947); August Hollingshead, *Elmtown's Youth* (New York: John Wiley & Sons, Inc., 1949); Ferdinand Lundberg, *America's Sixty Families* (New York: Vanguard Press, 1937).

from such resources as accumulated material wealth, comforts, and opportunities for a wide variety of experiences with persons and places. Their disadvantages are increased responsibilities to understand, appreciate, maintain, and intelligently use their social inheritances. Upper-class children must be carefully schooled in the arts of taking one's place in the company of the privileged few. This calls for a self-discipline that is not easily acquired by the more adventurous, aggressive, self-assertive type of child.

With the exception of factors such as religion that favors large families, there is a tendency to produce relatively few children per family unit. Regardless of religious background, it is the quality of life for children that appears to take precedence in the value systems of most upper-class families.

For the most part, these children would have considerable freedom to enter various occupations or careers, but in the end, they would essentially have engaged in some form of horizontal mobility in which they emulated the careers of their forebears. Being at the top of the social classes leaves only one other alternative to follow—downward vertical mobility or a "falling" from the high positions enjoyed by their families of origin. Some upper-class children will do precisely that, but most efforts guard against this choice. In the main, the symbolic estates so carefully developed for generations will be theirs to pass on to their children.

Patrilineage or the male line is usually given priority among upper-class persons; consequently the arrival of at least one male heir to carry on the family name or fortune is an occasion for rejoicing. Girls, of course, are welcomed, but their essential function has been that of lending grace, beauty, and expression of upper-class qualities to a given household. Indeed, upper-class families are frequently judged by the ability of their women to handle their social and economic advantages with tact, charm, and dignity. Their public image affirms the favorable or unfavorable public relationships of their respective family lineages.

Both sexes, however, will associate most directly with their upper-class peers and more indirectly with their subordinates. Accordingly, their socialization is taken up in large measure by interaction with carefully screened employees who will help provide seclusion, privacy, and shielding from outsiders while also performing their duties in terms of socializing their young charges in the habits, skills, knowledge, and activities that will enable them to move smoothly among their upper-class peers.

Because upper-class families are at the very pinnacle of society, economically and socially, the use of parental supplements in the form of nurses, servants, governesses, guards, chauffeurs, tutors, and companions is quite commonplace. Upper-class parents may act as overseers and determiners of policy, but much of their influence is indirect. That the emotional life of a child can become closely tied to these parental supplementary figures instead of their parents who are preoccupied with other matters should come as no surprise. Children of royal families, for instance, have formed some strong attachments to their nurses and governesses. Children of Southern planters in the antebellum, colonial plantations likewise developed strong attachments to their "mammies." Servants, too, were confidants of upper-class children who felt free to ventilate their feeling-states to them rather than to parents who remained at distance, engrossed in nonchildish concerns.

The economic well-being and, hence, the high prestige enjoyed by children of the upper classes originated in the work, accomplishments, and reputation of past relatives. Like Moslems who face Mecca, it is understandable why upper classes revere those who have gone before them. A variety of heirlooms from these ancestors are visible evidence of their significance in the lives of their descendants. Portraits, records of achievements or exploits in collections of art, books, citations, medals, and personal effects as well as large land holdings in their name remind upper-class children of the persons who made their present status possible. Whereas other classes may be disinterested and tend to disassociate themselves from kinship networks, genealogical studies hold great interest to upper classes. Through elaborate tracings and record retrievals, one may claim descent from an illustrious line of distinguished men and women. Their reflected glory brightens the lives of those now living, and their exploits and philosophies are subjects of much discussion as upper-class children grow up. Now and then some scoundrel might be found "hanging from a family tree," but the passage of time may transform what was ruthlessness into courage, strength, and admirable cunning.

The health of upper-class children is carefully guarded by the best possible medical attention, with illnesses, accidents, and physically harmful possibilities kept to a minimum. This same attention to health care applies to all other upper-class family members. Thus, while upper-class children may have few siblings, they are more likely to have numerous older relatives about them because their survival into advanced age is maximized by receiving the best medical care possible. Under such circumstances, the wishes of family elders play a larger part in the socialization of upper-class youngsters than in other classes.

With the lowest divorce and desertion rates of all socioeconomic strata, there is a stability to upper-class family life that sustains its influence. Given greater investments in family property and considerable insulation from the more precarious and rapid changes of the outside world, upper-class children are more likely to know chiefly one place of residence. Moving about from home to home, from neighborhood to neighborhood, from community to community, or from state to state either in upward or downward mobility would not be the typical experience of upper-class children. Their parents are neither climbing nor falling off social ladders but are already comfortably stabilized at the top. Upper class children would not be uprooted and required to adjust to a variety of unpredictable neighbors or neighborhoods as are middle class children whose parents may be upwardly or downwardly mobile. Exceptions, of course, can be found in the extensive travel of upper-class children who can enjoy experiences in different cities, regions, or countries, but who always have the comfortable security their station in life affords.

Proper manners are also hallmarks of upper-class socialization. Courtesy, respect, and dignity are held out as worthy objectives. One is taught to be charitable and considerate to persons in all walks of life. Upper-class children must learn to be refined or guarded in their dress, tastes, and speech. The finesse, tact, and polish of being a gentleman or a lady are held up as qualities to be developed and preserved. These inner controls are possible because energies are not expended in gaining external controls over one's life as is the case for both middle and lower-class persons.

The precise number of social classes in American society has never been determined despite concerted efforts to distinguish between various social strata. The usual practice is to speak broadly of a *trichotomy* of upper, middle, and lower classes. W. Lloyd Warner and his associates, however, have subdivided the three major categories into "uppers" and "lowers."[15] Thus, one may speak of a sixfold classification consisting of upper-uppers and lower-uppers, upper-middles, and lower-middles, and upper-lowers, and lower-lowers. Cuber and Kenkel contend that there are numerous social classes between extremes with almost hair-like distinctions separating them so they see social classes as being on a continuum.[16] Undoubtedly the Warner system serves the broader purposes of social classification for many sociologists.

The lower-upper class families have arrived close to the top echelons of their society but not quite far enough to be considered within the ranks of the upper-uppers. This holds significance for lower-upper class children because it will be through them that lower-upper class families may eventually become upper-uppers. Those in lower-upper families may provide just enough support to win their children entry

---

[15]W. Lloyd Warner and Paul S. Lunt, *The Social Life of a Modern Community* (New Haven: Yale University Press, 1941).

[16]John F. Cuber and William F. Kenkel, *The American Class Structure* (New York: Holt, Rinehart and Winston, 1957), and in John F. Cuber, *Sociology, A Synopsis of Principles*, 6th ed. (New York: Appleton-Century-Crofts, 1968), p. 404.

into upper-upper ranks, but they themselves will not enter. Like Moses who was permitted to observe the Promised Land from afar but was denied the opportunity to enter it, so lower-upper family members may be highly aware of upper-upper classes but can only hope to be identified with them through their children. Lower-upper class children may be sent to exclusive schools or academies that will help establish friendships and associations with upper-uppers that could "pay-off" later on. The ultimate triumph, of course, would be marriages of lower-upper class men and women with upper-upper class spouses.

Lower-uppers are interesting, also, because they frequently have more wealth than upper-uppers. Their wealth, which is of more recent vintage, stems from economic good fortune and skillful financial maneuverings based upon huge capital investments. Perhaps the wealth was won through the development of a new product or service, from real estate holdings that increased in value, or from promotion or election to high political office; whatever the reason, their wealth is "new." The term *nouveau riche*, the newly rich, is an apt description of lower-uppers.

Their children will consequently enjoy the latest advantages and innovations that society can provide. Their parents and relatives may purchase an estate, mansion, castle, summer home, or other facility usually associated with upper-upper class life styles. Their homes would be furnished with the most modern devices, aids, decor, or furniture designed for personal satisfaction and comfort. In all probability, the homes of lower-upper class children may be relatively new in comparison to those of upper-upper class children. Ostentation or lavish display of wealth, however, is more likely to be in evidence among lower-uppers. In their zeal to imitate upper-uppers, unless guided by trained taste or advice, their ability to command wealth may exceed acceptable limits. Reserve, simplicity, and elegance are not easily achieved or maintained by the newly wealthy.

In the end, the lives of lower-upper class children are rich and full, but the one remaining upward social step may elude them. Further, we should note that uncertainty is not characteristic of either upper-upper or lower-upper class socialization. Upper classes know what they want to achieve in their children and quite consciously go about doing so. Such is not quite the case for middle-class children.

Middle-Class Children

The center of society is represented by what may be called "the people in-between," those persons who are neither wealthy nor poor, the middle classes. Their lives are quite different from the spacious, comfortable, decision-making styles of the upper classes. They also stand apart from what some have called "the huddled masses" of the disprivileged lower classes. Now and then upwardly mobile members of the lower classes enter the middle classes and so replenish their numbers, but these, too, find that they are only halfway up the social ladder.

The dominant motif of the middle classes is *to get ahead*, to try to surpass the achievements of one's mother or father. This does not mean that middle-class children are to enter the upper classes, but it does mean that they are to improve their economic and social conditions whenever and wherever possible. They are to do so by the rules of middle-class morality. Middle-class children will be urged to keep improving their lot in life and not to become self-satisfied. The formulas to follow consist of hard work, industrious attention to the work at hand, and the harnessing and application of individual energies and capacities to achieve self-assigned goals.

While upper classes have a fairly clear objective of maintenance and possible entry into upper-upper classes through marriage, middle-class persons are less clear as to the appropriate strategies of child rearing. Accordingly, middle-class parents exhibit a keen interest in those matters that may help them maximize the capacities of their children. It is middle-class parents who are the chief supporters of child study groups, avid consumers of how-to-rear-your-child books, and tuned to the achievement of interpersonal harmony. In their view, one should be "open to new ideas," should try "to win friends and influence people," and should "strive, serve, and succeed." In general, middle-class children are urged to become self-reliant, to study diligently, to be loyal workers, to carefully set aside a portion of their earnings for the future, to defer gratifications, and to watch for or create opportunities for greater wealth, comfort, and social power.

Middle-class children are taught to be cooperative, to share, to take turns during play or games, to be considerate of the rights of others. The good middle-class child is obedient to authority and self-controlled in the absence of authority. Fighting, hostility, or overaggressive tendencies are discouraged except in the case of self-defense. To enforce one's will upon another by physical force is considered a lower-class approach and not appropriate for middle-class standards. This middle-class stance pervades much of American life, but it is particularly noticeable when it comes to foreign policies. "Good neighbor" policies, foreign aid programs, detente, and statements about "operating from positions of strength" all carry with them an aura of vigilance, a concern to live and let live, and a reluctance to move too quickly to naked force. Instead, persuasion, tact, and the demonstration of good will are favored to reach international accord.

Aggressive acts that clearly threaten American security are the only acts that can tip public support in favor of outright war. The sinking of the Lusitania and the bombing of Pearl Harbor were said to have provoked America's entry into two major world wars. On a smaller scale, but in highly significant confrontations, crossing the 38th parallel in Korea, the placement of missiles in Cuba, and the moves of North Vietnamese soldiers into South Vietnam were events that legitimized the reactive-fighting that followed. These were all quite in line with the restrained resistance to aggression so carefully taught to middle-class children.

The work ethic is a virtue also upheld to middle-class children. Each family member is to do his or her share: fathers, in terms of being the chief bread winner; mothers, to be economical in their expenditures or to supplement husbands' incomes; and children, to take on some responsibilities such as lawn care, watching over smaller brothers and sisters, or acquiring some sense of how money is earned through a paper route or helping out neighbors with their needs. Later on, when we discuss child-oriented systems, we will note how this same work ethic is promoted through the enterprises of the Junior Achievement Program, the selling of Girl Scout cookies, or the paper drives and car washes of various organizations.

Through hard work or effort, the main goal is to achieve some form of economic independence. Perhaps the greatest symbol of this relative freedom from economic obligations is home ownership. The purchase and maintenance of a small but comfortable home will probably be the largest single financial transaction of middle-class lives. To be one's own landlord, even if the grounds are modest in their proportions and the dwellings unpretentious, is the source of deep, abiding satisfaction for middle-class persons. The rest of the world may be transient, uncertain, and troubled, but at least the middle-class family can have a place of comparative security and contentment.

There is an inverse relationship between social class and numbers of children per family unit; the higher the social class, the fewer the number of children per family, or the lower the social class, the greater the number of children per family. As the popular saying has it, "The rich get richer and the poor get children." From our perspective, we would note that often those who can least provide for children have the most, and those who can provide the most for children have the least.

Middle-class children are to be found midway in this picture by having neither too few nor too many brothers and sisters. Most commonly, middle-class children have one or two siblings with whom to share their formative years. Ordinarily there is enough economic ability on the part of their parents to provide a comfortable living, but because economic resources are somewhat limited, there may well be competi-

tion for the benefits among the siblings. What cannot be secured economically is more than made up in noneconomic rewards of
understanding, warmth, and loving care to individual needs.

Equalitarian sharing calls for deference to the needs of others, and
this is another hard-won lesson for middle-class children. To be thought
of as snobbish, exclusive, or standoffish is not an admirable characteriza-
tion for middle-class persons. Yet there remains some desire to be
unique or different from all others. The solution for middle-class children and for their parents is to establish a small circle of friends or a
clique that effectively cuts off other persons judged to be less compatible. If we could express this middle-class morality, we would suggest
that it professes a love for humanity in the abstract, but in reality
confines its interest to mutual support among relatively few, like-
minded people.

Lower-Class Children

To begin life at the bottom of the social class system means to be
close to the problems of fundamental survival. This is the lot of lower-
class children who have problems with basic needs such as food, shelter,
and clothing. Further, there is less security against physical harm which
results in a personality patterning best described as vigilant toughness.

To sit down together and to discuss problems calmly is the way of
middle-class persons. To settle matters quickly by a show of force, by
crude language, or by violent action is more in keeping with lower-class
life styles. Like their parents or elders who seem to respect only superior muscle, brawn, or threats, lower-class children rather swiftly acquire a physical and personal aggressiveness that is not easily dismissed.
Wife beatings, child beatings, fist-fights, and vulgarity are too evident
to be ignored in the socialization of lower-class children.

It is the lower-lower classes that have probably received the most
attention from students of social stratification. The absenteeism of fathers and the subsequent matricentrality seem to be the most salient
features that affect children's lives. Desertion, imprisonment, unemployment, and early death from hazardous occupations account for
some of the missing fathers and the maximizing of contacts with mothers or mother figures. Reckless and his associates pointed out some years
ago that these mothers or mother surrogates were major factors in the
insulation of their children from delinquency in high delinquency
neighborhoods.[17] That other mothers or mother substitutes were less

[17]Walter C. Reckless, Simon Dinitz, and Ellen Murray, "Self Concept as an Insulator Against Delinquency," *American Sociological Review,* 21 (December 1956),
744–46.

successful in steering the children clear of the antisocial atmosphere of the street-peers is also evident.

Scarcity of economic resources means that everyone is to do their share in lower-lower class families. Not only are adult men and women to bring whatever they can into a household, but so are the children. A lower-class father once remarked during a court case, for example, that his eleven-year old son was "no good" because he "hadn't brought a penny into our family from the day of his birth!" If legitimate means cannot be found to increase incomes, then there is no question that illegitimate or illicit means will be found.

The harsh realities of lower-class life demand some relief, and the most frequent form this takes is escapism. Since one cannot actually remove one's self from ever-present degradation and misery, one can blot it out through alcoholism, drugs, sexual escapades, or flights of fancy and loose talk.[18]

SUMMARY

Children participate in only a small portion of their society by virtue of their placement within socioeconomic levels or social classes. They may be dimly aware of other social strata and can be said to be "relatively deprived" or "relatively advantaged" in comparison to other children. The gradations of social classes are subtle intangibles, but they become real enough to keep one segment of society rather isolated from all other segments. These different levels of power, privilege, and prestige mean that all children are not granted equal opportunities in life but are afforded, instead, differential opportunities to develop their personal capacities. The myths of the open-class society in America are exposed by the studies of social scientists and reveal a mixed pattern composed of elements of open-class, estate, and castelike systems.

Mobility vertically and horizontally is subject to the nature of the social class mix within particular societies. Some children have greater or lesser chances to be more socioeconomically advantaged than their parents, but the destiny of most children seems to be to stay well within their classes of origin. Upper-class children need only hold on to the social status attained by their parental generation and be cautioned against failing to live up to adult expectations. For middle-class children, there are greater distances to move upward and so they are urged

[18]The film "The Quiet One" is a classic portrayal of escapism in action, distributed by Compass Film Service, P.O. Box 43, Genesee, New York.

to perform effectively through self-assigned goals. Lower-class children, however, are the most vulnerable of all children and so are encouraged to acquire whatever skills they can in order to survive in a highly threatening environment.

In this necessarily brief description of the impacts of social stratification on the lives of children, the recurrent theme is loud and clear —*human beings create their own environment.* It follows that those qualities that restrict, confine, or crush the spirits of the very young need to be re-examined and removed.

TWO

Changing
societal issues
and
childhood

4

Children and sexuality

From the moment of conception when a single X or Y spermatozoon unites with an X ovum, the double X or XY zygote begins a life whose sex is established. Moving through successive stages, embryonic and fetal, it finally enters the world as a boy or girl infant. The birth of a male or female child sets in motion a host of reactions and actions by adults allegedly well prepared to receive and deal with either sex.

Internal and external organs, male or female, are normally in place, and their fundamental reproductive functions will manifest themselves more dramatically in adolescence, in the form of seminal emissions or the menarche, the first menstrual period. The primary organs, testes or ovaries as well as penis or vagina, are usually taken as prima facie evidence that children are either male or female and will, soon enough, exhibit additional secondary characteristics associated with their respective gender, skeletal formation, muscular development, voice range, or facial hair.

Thus far, the biological data indicates that there is a dichotomy of sex on a gross level, that a given child is either a male or a female, and that these two sexes will play distinctive, complementary, supportive roles in a heterosexual society.

This simplistic portrayal of "the facts of life," however, ignores the complicated genetic codes, the biochemical conditions, or the physical-physiological circumstances of hermaphroditic children. Further, the socialization practices and objectives of men and women living together harmoniously vary tremendously, producing a confusion and uncertainty that troubles untold numbers of persons.

For years, it was relatively easy to agree with the Freudian dictum that anatomy was destiny. Such is no longer the case. Whereas, in the past, there were a few voices raised in protest to sexual assignments and sexual ascriptions, the outcries have become increasingly vocal, strident, and frequent.[1] Nature and nurture do not always mesh as smoothly and as efficiently as many were once led to believe. The traditionalist perception of sex as an either male or female proposition represents *only one view and not the only view* of males and females.

Mounting pressures demand that the dominant positions of males and the subordinate positions of females be re-examined. The ancient, long-standing, unremitting stance that the sex of children is the single determinant in placing them irrevocably into one of two distinctive worlds, masculine or feminine, is being questioned. It is no wonder that persons are puzzled, uncertain, and indecisive about even casual meetings between the sexes. Laurel Walrum has, for example, classified the types of reactions when male and female strangers reach an unopened door at the same time.[2] Some are confused; some test the situation; others decide to compete for entry or defer on humanitarian grounds; and still others rebel and do as they please.

Our concerns in this chapter are threefold. First, we need to examine sexism, the social biases that promote one sex over another. Second, we need to discuss sex roles and sex-role taking. Third, we need to discuss sexual expression. All three are significant matters that affect the socialization of children. They weigh heavily in the decisions of children's caretakers concerning how to proceed and what to stress when sexual factors are involved.

[1]See for example, June Sochen, *Movers and Shakers, American Women Thinkers and Activists, 1900–1970* (New York: Quadrangle/New York Times Book Company, 1973); Robin Morgan, ed., *Sisterhood is Powerful, An Anthology of Writings from the Women's Liberation Movement* (New York: Random House, 1970).

[2]Laurel R. Walrum, "The Changing Door Ceremony: Notes on the Operation of Sex Roles in Everyday Life," *Urban Life and Culture*, 2, No. 4 (January 1974), 506–15.

SEXISM

With a few notable exceptions, most societies have been characterized by the dominance of males over females. Kephart, among others, finds biological foundations for the dominant male and submissive female syndrome in the animal kingdoms of crustaceans, amphibians, reptiles, birds, and mammals.[3] Within our own species, the physical, mental, and emotional makeup of females, for instance, is said to be "body-bound," biologically predetermined, and so justifies the social ascriptions of women as bearers and rearers of children, maintainers of homes, and helpmates to men. Alleged to be docile and vulnerable because of their skeletal-muscular-organic structures and weakened by such processes as menstruation, pregnancy, and lactation, females are justifiably protected, guarded, or carefully watched. In short, their sexual makeup is said to support the social and cultural rationales that consign them to a secondary place in society in relationships with males.

To be sure, in this traditional perspective, females have a place in the world and that place is to be found in domesticity, in matters surrounding the maintenance of homes and families. Females are to find satisfaction in *nurturance*, in food preparation, in keeping domiciles clean and organized, in caring for the young, the old, the sick, or the injured, or in catering to the needs of males for release from sexual, emotional, and physical tensions. When women did move out of their homes, they were given access primarily to those occupations that were extensions of their former sheltered or domestic lives. Such occupations as teaching, nursing, clerical work, librarianship, social work, decorating, or waitressing are or have been predominantly female. Females are simply not males and so *must* be treated differently is the gist of the argument.

These are the models that are or have been set before children. That they see them daily, that they mimic them, or that they take their cues to behavior from them is to be expected.

Unconscious Sexism

Conscious sexism is roughly equated with what we have described. It is the subtle, the finer nuances, or the unconscious sexism that needs attention because these reinforce the assignment of females to social inferiority. These are matters that are not causative, but they do reflect

[3]William M. Kephart, *The Family, Society, and the Individual,* 3rd ed. (Boston: Houghton Mifflin Company, 1972), Chap. 2, "Biological Foundations of the Family," pp. 15–48.

and reaffirm the foregone social conclusions that males shall dominate and females shall be judged by male standards.

LANGUAGE. The repository of human heritages, the very means by which human beings may symbolically communicate with each other, language is replete with examples of the unconscious neglect of females. No less a child authority than Benjamin Spock, the renowned author of *Baby and Child Care* that has sold in the millions, has acknowledged his unconscious sexism in the earlier editions that established his fame. No longer, he is on record as saying, will he refer to a girl baby as "him."

When reference has been made to all human inhabitants, the term that was used was "mankind." All persons, male and female, have been held to be created in the image of men. The basis for this, of course, rests upon religious documents, consciously or unconsciously, written by males, interpreted by males, and enforced by males. Anthropology, a field closely associated with sociology, used to be defined as "the study of mankind and his works." Some wag could not resist appending to the definition" . . . also embracing women."

It has been commonplace to use such words as fireman, policeman, chairman, repairman, mailman, manpower, manhandle, manslaughter, fellowship, or brotherhood when women were also involved. The use of such familiar expressions as "every man for himself," "my righthand man," "man the lifeboats," "give a man a chance," and "we agreed to a man," even when the participation and presence of women was obvious, again demonstrates the ways in which women were pushed into the background, made invisible or persons of little or no consequence.

Animals that attack humans were typically said to be "maneaters" even if they sometimes dined on females. When there was a search for suspected or known criminals, a "manhunt" was alleged to have begun even if the one for whom the authorities searched was a female. Even the lowly cover of a sewer has been labeled "a manhole cover."

When and if a woman was in a position of some importance, persons have felt obliged to preface their statements by observing that the individual is "a woman judge," "a woman truck driver," "a woman scientist," or "a woman pilot." Such references reflected the assumptions that *everyone knows* that these occupations are normally *masculine* jobs. When and if the reverse occurred, that is when men entered fields traditionally the province of women, it was held necessary to describe the person as "a male nurse," "a male clerk," "a male secretary," or "a male teacher."

These examples of linguistic assumptions of social reality might appear to be insignificant trivia. We are saying that they represent the accumulative mirroring of long-standing sexism that bears upon the way children are reared and prepared for adulthood.

MASS MEDIA. Technological devices have been developed to facilitate the rapid dissemination of ideas, data, and perspectives to huge audiences. These mass media include books, films, radio, television, magazines, newspapers, records, tapes, and last but not least, advertisements.[4]

A steady barrage of messages has been purveyed by the mass media, particularly in the recent past, that have largely had the effect of reinforcing or sustaining traditional images of dominant males and subordinate females. Women are portrayed as mainly concerned about finding, attracting, and holding on to men. Their fulfillment is largely derived from using their "feminine attributes or wiles" to get their way. Women are allegedly creatures who are pleased when their dishes shine, their deodorants work, their hair falls neatly into place, their panty hose does not sag, their husbands are promoted to positions of prominence, or their children brush their teeth. Such images held up to children so continously cannot fail to be effective in shaping decisions about ways and means to prepare them for their adult roles of the future.

It should be clear that the mass media are not being criticized by these observations as causal factors in initiating sexual biases. Rather, they are feedbacks to persons who are presented with what they have taken for granted. In the recent present, however, the messages have changed somewhat; there is a countercurrent of protests, cries of outrage, and reasoned, eloquent, and empirically supported evidence that women as well as men have dignity and worth.[5] What has been called women's studies, women's liberation, or women's rights has attacked conventional wisdom and transmitted information of desirable changes to those who are receptive.

Our concern remains the socialization of children, and so we look to the philosophies, images, attitudes, models or ideas propounded to children. Tibbets, for example, in studying children in the first four elementary grades found that both boys and girls believed that men

---

[4]See for example, Joseph E. Dispenza, *Advertising the American Woman* (Dayton, Ohio: Pflaum Publishers, 1975).

[5]See for example, Seymour M. Farber and Roger H. L. Wilson, eds., *Man and Civilization: The Potential of Woman* (New York: McGraw-Hill Book Company, 1963); Lucille Duberman, *Gender and Sex in Society* (New York: Praeger Publishers, 1975).

should be lawyers, astronauts, pilots, judges, farmers, clowns, police officers, taxi drivers, baseball players, veterinarians, firefighters, and train engineers. Girls, by contrast, felt that women should be nurses, secretaries, cooks, ballet dancers, baby sitters, and housecleaners.[6] Further, Tibbets found that these same youngsters most often favored their own sex as playmates and supported the idea that there should be a division of labor in terms of traditional tasks for men and women in their own households. The study is one of the most current researches available and does indicate the continuation of stereotypic roles for males and females for some time to come despite the protestations of those who hold differing views.

O'Kelly also found that children's television programs purveyed that same traditional sex-role images, presenting males in exciting, interesting, challenging tasks and females in the subservient roles of wives, mothers, secretaries, and airline hostesses.[7]

Busby did a content analysis of children's cartoons and found that sex-role stereotyping could be found embedded in these entertaining and effective animated picture-stories.[8] Male figures were identified as those having financial responsibilities for homes and their families while female figures were overwhelmingly portrayed as weaker, less capable, prosaic beings whose major concerns revolved around their homes, children, or husbands.

Kutner and Brogan studied university students and found that, even in this mature stage of their lives, male students knew significantly more slang and shared more humor that denigrated females than the female students shared among themselves or turned against males.[9] The contentious wit not only exploited the advantageous social statuses of males but amounted to a "sexploitation" in which females were treated as faceless nonhumans whose bodies were far more important than their personalities or capacities for social contributions.

Lastly, the work of Chesny-Lind who examined the records of the Honolulu Juvenile Court covering a forty year period dating back to 1929 is pertinent.[10] The traditional consensus that females are far more

[6]Sylvia-Lee Tibbetts, "Sex-Role Stereotyping in the Lower Grades: Part of the Solution," *Journal of Vocational Behavior*, 6, No. 2 (April 1975), 255–61.

[7]Charlotte G. O'Kelly, "Sexism in Children's Television," *Journalism Quarterly*, 5, No. 4 (Winter 1974), 722–24.

[8]Linda Jean Busby, "Defining the Sex-Role Standard in Network Children's Programs," *Journalism Quarterly*, 5, No. 4 (Winter 1974), 690–96.

[9]Nancy G. Kutner and Donna Brogan, "An Investigation of Sex-Related Slang Vocabulary and Sex Role Orientation Among Male and Female University Students," *Journal of Marriage and Family*, 36, No. 3 (August 1974), 474–84.

[10]Meda Chesney-Lind, "Juvenile Enforcement of the Female Sex Role: The Family Court and the Female Delinquent," *Issues in Criminology*, 8, No. 2 (Fall 1973), 51–69.

conforming than males and, if they deviate from these expectations, are more likely to be treated with leniency than males was not sustained in her study. Instead, she found that females were prominent in their nonconformity to norms and that female offenders were more severely penalized than their male counterparts.

Like glaciers that melt, crack, and imperceptibly move, the time-honored traditions of male or female-appropriate behavior do change but very slowly. The Institute of Life Insurance and Health Insurance Institute, for instance, have conducted surveys of attitudinal changes since 1970, and their *Youth 1974* survey documents that traditional ways of handling male-female relationships remain fairly intact but are being modified.[11] Whereas previously wives deferred to their husbands in deciding questions of purchasing life insurance, planning vacations, buying a car, or making investments, fully two-thirds of the youthful respondents favored equal decision-making powers affecting the futures of the men and women concerned. The findings suggest that an attitudinal change is taking place but that it will take a generation or more to implement these attitudes held by the children of today.

SEX ROLES AND SEX-ROLE TAKING

The birth of a child usually provides the biological evidence, as we have noted, that a child is either a male or a female. With the development of amniocentesis, the process in which a sample of amniotic fluid containing cells that confirm the sex of the fetal body can be drawn, expectant parents need not wait for the delivery of their child to learn if it is male or female. Whichever procedure is used, the sexual labeling sets into motion a ready-made set of social and cultural expectations from which relatively few children can escape. A male or female given name is typically assigned for life along with a male surname because of our patrilineal traditions. The child of designated sex will then be clothed in pink or blue, given or withheld from trimmings of ribbons or lace, given appropriate toys or diversions, and frequently handled, addressed, or treated in the ways in which adults have been taught to respond to males or females.

What is paramount in this context is what has been called the *sex of assignment*.[12] Far more important from our perspective than a given set of biochemical or anatomic-physiological evidence are the ways in

---

[11] *Youth 1974* (New York: Institute of Life Insurance and Health Insurance Institute, 1975).
[12] John Money and Anke A. Ehrhardt, *Man and Woman, Boy and Girl* (Baltimore: John Hopkins, 1972).

which the evidence is interpreted. Sociologists, at least, are more prone
to support the contention that how situations are defined is more meaningful than what the situations really are. It is the definitions imposed
upon children that take precedence and become real in their consequences. Such a perspective is supported in discussions of to which sex
a child is said to belong and what training or preparation he or she
should receive in order to enter maturity.[13]

Arguments about sex-role differentiation have been advanced
along many fronts, genetic, biochemical, physiological, anthropological,
historical, and sociological. Otto Klineberg, far ahead of his time, considered some of these arguments on justification for treating males and
females differently and found them rather questionable.[14] Ashley Montagu also startled many in the academic world with his bold assertions
that women were naturally *the superior sex.*[15]

Montagu's reference, of course, was in terms of the sheer survival
power of females in comparison to males. Mortality rates for males, for
instance, far exceed that of females starting with the moment of conception and continuing throughout the life cycle.[16] While the conception rate is known to be about 120 males conceived for every 100
females, the weaker XY combinations begin dying in utero so that some
nine months later, at the time of birth, the ratio is approximately 105
males delivered for every 100 females. The infant mortality rates (IMR)
of male infants exceeds that of females and the death rates continue to
diminish the ranks of males in far greater numbers than females for
each successive year of life.[17] Cohort analysis, the survival of persons for
each 100,000 individuals born alive, shows that females outlive males
at every age despite their mutual birthdates.[18]

When men are said to be "weaker" and women are said to be
"stronger," or "superior" as Montagu has expressed it, there is a storm
of protest. Those who object point out that males become taller, heavier, more muscular than females in every known society. Thicker bones,
greater food consumption, and quicker energy production provide the

[13]See Letha Scanzoni and John Scanzoni, *Men, Women and Change, A Sociology
of Marriage and Family* (New York: McGraw-Hill Book Company, 1976), Chap. 2,
"Becoming Men and Women," pp. 14–53.
[14]Otto Klineberg, *Social Psychology* (New York: Henry Holt and Company, 1940),
Chap. 10, "Sex Differences," pp. 265–81.
[15]Ashley Montagu, *The Natural Superiority of Women*, rev. ed. (New York: Macmillan, 1968).
[16]See *Life Tables*, II-Sec. 5, *Vital Statistics of the United States, 1971, 1972, and
1973*, (Washington, D.C.: U.S. Department of Health, Education, and Welfare,
Public Health Service, Health Resources Administration, National Center for
Health Statistics).
[17]*Ibid.*
[18]*Ibid.*

physical aggressiveness and strength that would seem to justify and explain why males are dominant over females.

What has been conveniently overlooked, of course, is that advancing and available technologies have helped nullify whatever biological advantages or disadvantages one sex or the other may have. If there are arduous tasks called for the expenditure of great muscular strength, there are numerous machines, devices, and procedures that can and will perform the work at the touch of a button or the flip of a switch. To be sure, hard physical labor still exists for many males and for many females in our society and in countless other societies, but what is happening is the increasing availability of "mechanical slaves" to do the necessary work. What has been called "work" for both males and females increasingly consists of relatively light physical labor such as shuffling papers, using a phone or car, generating or retrieving information, or speaking to clients, patients, customers, personnel, or staff members. To continue to insist that biological differences unalterably requires that males and females be schooled in contrasting life styles is a statement in cultural lag. Social procedures have simply fallen behind rapidly changing technical skills and achievements, and people are reluctant to change.

Masculinity, Femininity, Unisex, or No-Sex

It is one thing to try to justify differential sex roles through innate sexual differences, but it is another to inculcate personality attributes in male or female children. *Masculinity* is the set of qualities alleged to belong to males, and *femininity* is the set of qualities alleged to belong to females. *Unisex* is the blending of alleged masculine and feminine characteristics within the personalities of males or females. *No-sex*, in this context, refers to efforts to get away from historic and conventional ideas concerning the appropriate personality of persons of either sex and to deal instead with those traits that have little or no relationship to one's gender. We incorporate masculinity, femininity, unisex, and no-sex in this discussion because, depending upon what persons believe them to be, boy and girl babies are programmed accordingly.

Robert Scott, for example, has discussed how social definitions of biological or physiological conditions are able to achieve intended results. Scott's concern is over the rigidities of those who seek to rehabilitate the blind.[19] His analysis in *The Making of Blind Men* is to the effect that, given the factor of sightlessness, blind persons are trained, coerced, or pressured into positions of dependency. Those blind persons

[19]Robert A. Scott, *The Making of Blind Men: A Study of Adult Socialization* (New York: Russell Sage Foundation, 1969).

who objected received negative sanctions and those who were compliant were positively rewarded. The parallel to the socialization of male and female children is striking. Children are urged, through encouragement or discouragement of certain behavior to move toward preconceived ideas of how males and females are to act. Such social imprinting leaves unmistakable marks that endure for most of a lifetime.

The evidence from ethnographic studies, long known to students of anthropology, is that masculinity and femininity as defined by our society and culture is only one definition out of many. Margaret Mead, for instance, has observed that those qualities Americans claim are characteristic of one sex or the other are precisely the opposite in other sociocultural situations.[20] Among one Philippine tribe, it was conventional to assume that no man could possibly keep a secret. The Manus believed that only men enjoy playing with infants. Todas felt strongly that work around the home was far too sacred to be given over to women. In New Guinea, when Mead presented dolls to the children, it was the boys who played with them and not the girls.[21]

The Arapesh insist that women's heads are stronger than men's and consequently find it quite understandable that women should carry heavier loads than men.[22] It is a protective gesture on behalf of "weaker" men. Some years ago, one of the authors had a firsthand observation of such a definition in the Fijis. A young girl, who was carrying out her daily chores of gathering firewood, lost her life in a nearby ravine when she slipped back on the damp rocks carrying a log on her back. To see a newspaper headline in contemporary American society that proclaims "Log-Carrying Girl Loses Her Life!" would be unthinkable in terms of normative expectations. The point, of course, is that adult men and women determine sex-appropriate personality qualities and raise their children in accordance with arbitrary standards.

The customary way of looking at masculinity and femininity is to view them as a distinct dichotomy. (See Figure 4–1)

Such a perspective, however, emphasizes gross, strongly contrasting personality elements and unequivocably assigns them to *either males or females.*

In Figure 4–2, however, we see another way of looking at personality factors, a continuum of qualities that do not necessarily belong to one sex or the other. It is, in our judgment, a far more objective descrip-

[20]Margaret Mead, *Sex and Temperament in Three Primitive Societies* (New York: William Morrow & Co., 1935), p.xix.
[21]Margaret Mead, *Growing Up in New Guinea* (New York: William Morrow Company, Inc., 1930), Mentor Book Ed. (New York: The New American Library of World Literature, Inc., 1961), p. 96.
[22]Mead, *Sex and Temperament.*

FIGURE 4-1 *The Dichotomy of Masculinity and Femininity*

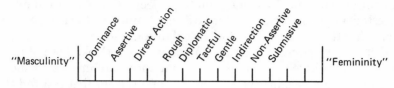

FIGURE 4-2 *The Continuum of So-called Masculinity and Femininity*

tion of social definitions than that so frequently defended in dichoto-mizing male and female attributes.

What has been evident for some time is the mixing of so-called masculine and feminine qualities in the personality organization of many individuals. The dichotomization of the sexes is thus abandoned in favor of a blurring, blending, or sharing of personality elements among males and females that has been labelled *unisex*. The wearing of long hair by males and the wearing of jeans by females are probably the most commonly cited features of the unisex image. The entry of girls into formerly exclusive boys' domains has made headlines in our times. Soap Box Derbies, Little Leagues, Pee Wee Football, or Boy Scouts have begun to include girls in their activities. Boys, on the other hand, have turned to such interests as teaching, nursing, cooking, child care, or ecology. There is a mutual interest in comfortable, practical, individualistic, colorful clothing or personal adornment. There are frank, open exchanges among male and female adolescents on a variety of subjects formerly discussed only in utmost secrecy among trusted persons of the same sex.

The whole pattern of unisex or the sharing of personality qualities among males and females is, of course, not a revolutionary change. There was a time when men wore lace, powder, and wigs and practised the arts of gentleness. The term, gentleman, comes down to us from such a source. It is interesting to note the resentment implied in a recent women's rights publication entitled *The Lace Ghetto*[23] in which the vignettes suggest the exclusive assignment of females to a decorative, but segregating, status in American society. Many have forgotten that one of the earliest movies ever made in America, *The Squaw Man*, was based upon the willingness of American Indians to allow role-reversals for men who did not relish the idea of becoming fierce warri-

[23]Maxine Nunes and Deanna White, *The Lace Ghetto*, New Women Series: 3 (Toronto: New Press, 1972).

ors or hunters. Indeed, there have been some who have been shocked by the "unladylike" Joan of Arc who defied authority, wore armor, and led soldiers into battle.

Once the distinct barriers that separate the sexes are breached and the blending of characteristics has begun, as we have indicated, it does not take too much imagination to project a future that some have suggested might be called a "no-sex" environment. Such a prospect means that the sex of a given individual in some social status is held to be of little or no consequence and so it may be overlooked or not taken into account. Orwell's novel *1984*[24] contained a reference to such a possibility in his imaginative description of a society that insisted that men and women should be active in an "Anti-Sex" organization that stressed devoting one's self to "Big Brother." Marabel Morgan's *The Total Woman*[25] seems to be a part of the reactions against such a no-sex policy by calling for a return to the more established and familiar use of feminine wiles to get one's way.

Changes in sex roles affect the rearing of children. If it is accepted that males and females are to be kept apart, then preparations along these lines are set in motion. If, on the other hand, the blending of alleged masculine and feminine attributes, as in unisex, or the rejection of sex as a major factor, as in no-sex, are held to be acceptable, then children's training reflects these objectives. In any event, there seems to be a threat to some persons, to some faction or other, no matter what course of action is followed. For such a reason, we have placed this facet of socialization among the *sensitive* areas, the *unresolved* issues, confronting those responsible for the raising of children in an unsettled society.

SEXUALITY

While we have been stressing sexism and sex-role taking as they affect children, we have not dealt with sex itself or its affirmation in sexual actions. This we do, albeit briefly, in this section of the chapter.

Modesty

Modesty, of course, is something that has to be learned by boys and girls. As infants or small children, they do not enter the world with preconceptions about what is deemed immodest and what is modest.

[24]George Orwell, *1984* (New York: Harcourt Brace, 1949).
[25]Marabel Morgan, *The Total Woman* (Old Tappan, N.J.: Fleming H. Revell, 1973).

As a spoof, a wag once launched a campaign to put dresses on mares and cows and pants on stallions and bulls to spare them embarrassment when they appeared in public. The proposal was taken seriously by some because there is a strong feeling that exposure of sexual organs is somehow indecent, immodest, immoral, and downright disgusting. The photographic and explicit book *Show Me*[26] was an exercise in straightforward sex education, resented by some and approved by others.

Entering the world naked, exposed, and unashamed, children learn to be clothed, covered, and ashamed, a reversal that is a part of what is called "sex education" in a given society. It is the shame or guilt associated with sexuality that has attracted the most concern among sex educators.

Toilet Training

Quite obviously, the intake of food and liquids calls for their absorption by the body and the elimination of waste products through bowel or bladder movements. This perfectly normal and healthy process of intake, absorption, and elimination is accomplished, however, under the rules of societies and cultures in which children live. Toilet training is usually not begun too early for infants because the conscious control of body functions requires abilities to attain greater sphincter muscle control. The most common approach is acceptance, some would say resignation, of infant "soilings" by anticipating them and using such devices as diapers to absorb them.

There has been much social psychological discussion about the significance of toilet training upon the whole personality of a child but, more to the point, is the manner, speed, and scope of the toilet training that reflects acceptance or rejection of a child by its caretakers. *Attitudes* reflected in overt behavior are far more salient than debates about whether or not one particular socialization practice is better or worse than another. It is true, of course, that once toilet training has been successful, children have taken an important step in socialization.

There is one thesis concerning toilet training that perhaps merits more than passing comment. It is the rather drastic reversal of attitudes that must be accomplished by persons concerning their own sexual organs and the sexual organs of others. During toilet training and for all their childhood, children are carefully taught that the sexual organs are to be kept clean. The association, however, with the elimination of waste products is rather fixed in the minds of the young. Later on, in adolescence and adulthood, when sexual activities are initiated and

[26]Will McBride and Helga Fleischauer-Hardt, *Show Me! A Picture Book of Sex for Children and Parents*, English Ed. (New York: St. Martin's Press, 1975).

sustained, it is not necessarily easy to begin regarding the organs usually associated with urine and feces henceforth as clean and immaculate. The notion that sexual organs are "dirty" or are to be the locii of modesty and the reasons for privacy during elimination is not readily dismissed. The bane of sex educators for years has been the inability of many to disassociate, disavow, or disclaim the years of training that sexual organs are unclean.[27]

The Pleasure Principle and Sexuality

The relief of bowel or bladder tension in elimination is normally pleasurable. The relief of sexual tensions is also pleasurable, a discovery that comes soon enough for most persons. The often accidental discovery by children that the rubbing or stimulation of sexual organs is pleasurable often begins the earliest manifestations of erotic satisfaction for individuals. Self-stimulation or masturbation by the very young was viewed with horror not so many years back.[28] However, most of these imaginative and deliberately negative judgments have now been discarded. Insanity, impotence, acne, and a host of other dire results simply do not materialize as a direct result of masturbation. Again, more important, are *the attitudes toward sexuality.*

Perhaps we should make another point regarding the sexual organs or sexuality in association with the pleasure principle. The sexual organs and their attendant systems are often referred to in terms of being the *reproductive* systems of males or females. To be sure, the joining of male and female sexual systems brings children into the world. The reproduction of the species is fundamental for survival. However, as we have noted, sexual stimulation and relief from tensions is generally a pleasurable act. We should, of course, acknowledge the inadequacies, the failures, the frustations, and the inadequate responses of certain men and women that occur in later life.[29]

What we are saying is that sexual expression is learned, and the distinction between sexual *reproduction* and sexual *pleasure*, while acknowledged and known by most persons, is often publicly denied or underplayed. If sexual intercourse or release from erotic tensions were generally painful, such activities would not be so eagerly sought. Nevertheless, we continue to refer to our sexual systems as our reproductive systems and not our *pleasuring* systems. Reuben's distinctions concern-

---

[27]Abram Kardiner, *Sex and Morality* (New York: The Bobbs-Merrill Company, Inc., 1954, Charter Books Ed., 1962), p. 129.

[28]B. G. Jefferis and J. L. Nichols, *Light on Dark Corners, A Complete Sexual Science* (Toronto, Ontario: J. L. Nichols and Company, 1895), p. 227.

[29]See William H. Masters and Virginia E. Johnson, *Human Sexual Inadequacy* (Boston: Little, Brown and Company, 1970).

ing "repro-sex" and "fun-sex" closely follow this same line of reasoning.[30]

It is imperative, of course, that we at least mention that one need not be flippant or treat sexuality too lightly. Depending upon one's reference group, there is deviant behavior in homosexuality, voyeurism, forcible rape, pedophilia, exhibitionism, fetishism, incest, sadism, masochism, and bestiality that has brought pain, sorrow, and degradation to many lives.[31] The roots of some of this deviate sexual behavior do lie in childhood. What has been overlooked, as exchange theorists would tend to stress, is that the pleasures of one or more individuals are not necessarily the pleasures of others. Indeed, the pleasures of some have brought pain to others. What has been forgotten is reciprocity. When persons are not treated as persons but as *things*, physical pain and social difficulties do occur. This is what Kirkendall found in his Oregon Studies.[32] This is what Kephart had in mind when he suggested that the pleasures of one individual, one group, or one society might be superseded by more harmonious procedures in which individuals, families, and societies are considered and benefited.[33] Concern, affection, gentleness, and abiding responsibility for the well-being of sexual partners are also teachable goals in the training of children.

SUMMARY

The long-standing view that the presence of two sexes demands two distinct ways of treating males and females is being questioned. In the promotion of sexism, the idea that one sex is superior to another, in the social ascriptions that require distinctive roles for each sex, and in the expression of sex itself, those who rear children find support for the ways in which they prepare the young for adulthood. That these established ways are being challenged because of their failure to develop well-adjusted, personally happy, and socially effective men and women has profound effects upon what present and future socialization practices will become.

While sexism that favors the dominance of males over females has been consciously promoted, the unconscious or more subtle ways, par-

[30]David Reuben, *Everything You Always Wanted to Know About Sex, But Were Afraid to Ask* (New York: David McKay Company, Inc., 1969), pp. 44–46.
[31]See Kenneth L. Jones, Louis W. Shainberg, and Curtis O. Byer, *Sex* (New York: Harper & Row, Publishers, 1969), Chap. 3, "Deviate Sexual Behavior," pp. 27–37.
[32]Lester A. Kirkendall, *Premarital Intercourse and Interpersonal Relationships* (New York: The Julian Press, Inc., Publishers, 1961).
[33]Kephart, *The Family, Society and the Individual.*

ticularly the use of language, lend strong support for its continuance. Further, the mass media have reinforced sexism with considerable effect. Studies made to date affirm that children learn the social expectations of female submission and male dominance quite early in life.

The rationale for distinctive sex roles for which children are to be prepared is often based upon the natural, biological, fundamental differences between the sexes. Far more significant, however, are the interpretations or social constructions that people have developed to justify their sexual ascriptions of appropriate behavior for boys and girls. Masculinity and femininity are social products that do not preclude the possibility of blending, blurring, or shading them in the personalities of male and female children. Even more radical than unisex is the "no-sex" concept that sexual makeup need not be taken into consideration in the training and development of children.

When it comes to sex itself, there is even more sensitivity. Toilet training and modesty are two of many specifics in dealing with the sexuality of small children. By underestimating the pleasure principle in sexuality, children's caretakers have created more problems than they have resolved. What seems to be needed is concern for the pleasure and well-being of *all* persons and not *some* persons.

5

Children
and
religion

There is an old maxim that counsels not to discuss religion, politics, or the economy if one seeks to retain amicable relationships for very long. Yet these matters are too vital in the life of human society and too close to the main concerns of persons to be ignored. In America at least, open and continued discussion of sensitive matters is a part of the fabric of life. It was G. K. Chesterton who championed objective study of sensitive issues by noting, "There is the thought that stops thought. That is the only thought which ought to be stopped."[1]

When we label religion as "sensitive," we affirm the distinction between the cognitive and the affective components of religion. On the one hand, there is knowledge of historical events, logical ordering of information, and thoughtful reasoning-interpreting of information. On the other hand, there is deep emotional involvement, the excitement of spiritual dedication, and the fervor of convictions that moves persons to take action in the name of religion.

[1]David E. Engle, "Objectivity in the Teaching of Religion in Public Schools," *Religious Education*, LXXI, No. 1, (January–February 1976), 90.

Just what actions have people carried out in the name of their religious faiths? There have been cruel and barbarous "holy wars" directed against "infidels" from outside one's faith, as in the Crusades, and there have been the torture and suffering of "heretics" who were less convinced than "true believers" within a faith, as in the Inquisition. There have been centuries-old schisms over church doctrine and policies as in the case of Roman Catholics and Protestants. There have been the animosities of anti-Semitism in which Jews have been excluded from the company of Christians. Finally, we may note the vigorous competition among various religions to bring converts into their religious fold.

All religious action is not necessarily vicious, negative, or directed against opponents. We would be remiss if we did not also point out the positive, the helpful, the generous acts of religious people. Their religious fervor and dedication spur them on to relieve pain, sorrow, and tragedies that befall everyone, friends and foes, the nearby neighbor and the distant stranger. Drawing upon religious wellsprings, many persons have been encouraged to cope with their own limitations, trials, or tribulations. Out of sheer religious compassion, persons have reached out to aid the helpless, to share generously their limited personal resources with others, and to demonstrate the need for respect and courage when one is rejected or deprived.

Just how, then, should we treat the relationships between religion and children, knowing that religion seems to bring out both the worst and the best in people? We consider first the nature of religion, its tremendous diversity, and its involvement in society. Next, we examine functions of religion to bring both children and their caretakers under social control. We then consider the tensions between religions and secular education. Lastly, we discuss the ability of religion to help children confront the reality of death in terms of both themselves and their loved ones.

RELIGION AND SOCIETY IN TENSION[2]

What is Religion?

It would be helpful if we make as clear as possible what we mean by "religion." At least, the referent upon which we rely will enable others to understand why we select certain matters for emphasis and tend to neglect or underplay other aspects.

[2]See Charles Y. Glock and Rodney Stark, *Religion and Society in Tension* (New York: Rand McNally & Company, 1965).

Religion, in our view, deals with *a community of believers, those bound together in a shared faith that provides meaning and guides to appropriate conduct.* Religion explains to them why they and others think, act, feel, and behave as they do. It helps them through life crises and, particularly, to confront pain, disappointment, and death. Lastly, it transforms their lives enough to gain a special perspective of how their lives can make more sense amidst a host of baffling, overwhelming forces that are far beyond their control.

Diversity of Religious Views

There would be no major problem for children or for those who socialize them if there was unanimity, universal agreement, or undivided opinion concerning religious ideology, organization, ritual, attitudes, or behavior. Such a fantasy seems to be the vision that the religiously faithful have. If all others believed as a particular community of believers do, then all would be well. These idealistic hopes, however, vanish before the realism of tremendous religious differences. The idea of a harmonious human family does have its appeal, but the hard facts are that religious differences abound, and religious discord and dissensus are closer descriptions of reality.

In pluralistic American society that is alleged to be dedicated to religious freedom, the problems generated by religious differences would seemingly be resolved by each set of believers going their own way, neatly sidestepping those issues that could otherwise bring about confrontations.

Troubles endure, nevertheless, because religious diversity itself generates dilemmas of its own. While certainly not an exhaustive listing, how shall Baptists, Black Muslims, Episcopalians, Hare Krishnans, Islams, Jews, Lutherans, Methodists, Mormons, Presbyterians, Roman Catholics, and Seventh Day Adventists be supported to bring their children into their respective faiths? Which religions should predominate, and which religions should either be ignored or undervalued? How can a government that draws its strength from all its citizens satisfy religious freedoms without favoring or sponsoring one religious view over another? Within a single faith, there are denominations, branches, wings, or sects that promote special emphases. These, too, compound the problem because the selection of one emphasis tends to be judged as automatically discounting contrasting persuasions.

Sacred and Secular Religions

Another difference that sorely troubles people is the difference between that which is sacred and that which is secular. Nottingham wrestles with this distinction in her sociological analysis of religion.[3] Emile Durkheim's observation that primitives distinguish between the ordinary events of life and the extraordinary or supernatural events of life is cited as evidence of the separation between that which is secular or profane and that which is sacred or supernatural. Religion, in the Durkheim sense, emerges from efforts to deal with the supernatural, to come to grips with the overwhelming power of uncontrollable forces, to stand in awe of the unexplainable.

If we, however, persist in our view that religion consists of a community of believers, we must also include secular faiths along with the sacred faiths. As Nottingham correctly observes, "Communism is also a faith, a faith in the Marxian dialectic as something that will work itself out and produce a classless society—a kind of heaven on earth, supposedly—independently or even in spite of the political or economic means used."[4]

Other secular faiths might be capitalism, nationalism, humanism, or scientism. These faiths revere the power of personal gain, the destiny of a particular cultural heritage, the dignity and worth of all women and men, or the orderly discovery and use of verified knowledge. Auguste Comte, it will be recalled, once hoped that sociology would produce scholarly "priests" whose wise counsel would direct human society into an era of peace and accord. While such a vision was abandoned and laid to rest, the dedication and high hopes of some sociologists suggest that the discipline will yet yield "a better world" than currently exists, at least from their point of view.

American Civil Religion

Because we deal mainly with American children, we can profitably consider how deeply entangled sacred and secular religions really are. Robert Bellah's article on "Civil Religion in America" began a prolonged literary debate among religious scholars that still continues.[5] Bellah forthrightly recognized that America's political life is historically intermingled with Judeo-Christian religions without endorsing any single sacred faith such as Judaism, Catholicism, or Protestantism. Rather, as Bellah portrayed the civil religion of America, there seems to be generalized acknowledgment that an omnipresent, omnipotent, omniscient God watches over America during its greatest trials such as the

---

[3]Elizabeth Nottingham, *Religion, A Sociological View* (New York: Random House, 1971), pp. 13, 25–26.

[4]*Ibid*, p. 26.

[5]Robert N. Bellah, "Civil Religion in America," *Daedalus*, 1966, reprinted in *The Religious Situation-1968*, ed. Donald R. Cutler (Boston: Beacon Press, 1968), pp. 331–56.

American Revolution, the Civil War, and the numerous struggles to encourage world peace.

This close identification with the sacred does seem to contradict the determination of the American nation to separate "church" and "state" as set forth in the First and Fourteenth Amendment to the United States Constitution. Despite numerous attempts to breach "the wall of separation" between one established faith and the government of all American citizens, the "separation" has been maintained with considerable fortitude but not without serious criticism.

The criticism emerges out of the strong religious convictions of many Americans who find it difficult to set aside their religious predilections in the course of their daily lives. Their political philosophies in terms of conservatism or liberalism tend to be affected by their particular religious faiths. Their business or economic dealings also tend to mirror their religious affiliations. To an even greater extent, their religious identifications are tested and made evident when the education of their children is involved.

Without seeking to deny, undermine, or denigrate specific faiths, the federal, state, and local governments are also hardpressed to separate the sacred from the secular. The Supreme Court invokes the blessings of God at the opening of each day's session. Both the United States Senate and House of Representatives open with daily prayers. Each President has asked for the protection and guidance of God upon his assumption of the Presidency. Since 1865, American coins have carried the motto, "In God We Trust." Chaplains of the major faiths are officers in the military services. Holidays such as Veterans Day, Thanksgiving, and Christmas have direct religious connections. As most students of sociology are familiar with the nature of social institutions such as religion, family, polity, education, and the economy, the efforts to keep them in separate and distinct compartments are doomed to failure.

Religious Conservatism or Liberalism

Michael Argyle's classification of denominational differences summarized some of the ways in which religious identity affects one's approach to secular affairs.[6] He places the Roman Catholics, Lutherans, and some Episcopalians and Anglicans as "conservative" religionists. They display a high rate of public worship and have a rather low rate of private worship. Their clergy are powerful and held in high regard. Their services are formal and ritualistic. The "liberal" religionists, by contrast, include the Unitarians, most Jews, Quakers, and some persons

[6]Michael Argyle, "Denominational Differences," *International Encyclopedia of the Social Sciences,* 13 (1968), 422–23.

with no particular religious affiliation. Their services are less ritualistic and less well attended. Their concerns focus more on understanding, intellectual inquiry, and reasoning than upon emotional appeals. Argyle places the Protestant churches such as the Presbyterians and the Methodists closer to the conservative side of the religious continuum, but one step toward greater liberalism. Church attendance is lower than the Roman Catholics, and individual clergy have devoted followers but less formal power over secular affairs. Sects are placed by Argyle closer to the liberal religions with their rejection of church organization and their informal, more emotional services.

It was Eugene Schoenfeld's thesis that the dominant values of love and justice in religious teachings are behind the tendencies of some people to move toward either a liberal or a conservative approach to secular affairs.[7] Schoenfeld points out that love can be said to be the dominant value in Christianity and that this love suggests the appropriate response to make when people find themselves in some sort of social difficulty. The response would be characterized by efforts to treat the pains that people suffer. This is a most generous and honest way of dealing with human anguish, but it fails to attack the causal factors that brought about the human suffering in the first place. Kind treatment amounts to dealing with the symptoms of social inadequacies but does not prevent the possibility of more people experiencing similar difficulties in the future. In secular affairs, this is translated into political conservatism, because the sources of social problems are frequently neglected or overlooked.

Justice is one of the dominant values of Judaism. Justice calls for guarding against the abuse of power through some appropriate allocation of resources among people. This social justice recognizes that the way men and women organize themselves generates social problems and that these social systems can be amended or changed. By taking preventative measures, the sources of human suffering are cut off, and superficial treatment is significantly reduced. In secular affairs, such an approach tends toward political liberalism.

We should note, of course, that love is not an exclusive value of Christianity any more than justice is an exclusive value of Judaism. Love and justice are merely two of the many major values to be found in the Judeo-Christian heritage. While there are theological, ideological, and historical differences among religions, far too often, the *common ground* they share is overlooked. (See Figure 5-1.)

---

[7]Eugene Schoenfeld, "A Preliminary Note on Love and Justice: The Effect of Religious Values on Liberalism and Conservatism," *Review of Religious Research*, 16, No. 1 (Fall 1974), 41–46.

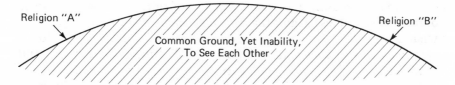

Religion "A"

Common Ground, Yet Inability, To See Each Other

Religion "B"

FIGURE 5-1 *The Common Ground of Religions*

DEVELOPMENT OF MORALITY IN CHILDREN

Children, at least from a sociological perspective, are not born as moral, immoral, or antimoral creatures. Rather, they are *amoral* beings. They have no preconceived, innate ideas that human behavior or interaction with other persons is acceptable under specified conditions. They neither seek to misbehave nor to attack the moral codes of their caretakers. Children stand outside moral codes and are introduced to them as they grow up. Morals are learned, acquired, or gained through socialization. Thus, moral development is central to the religious training given to children. Through their religious experiences, it is hoped that the very young will come to know more about themselves and how they might relate to others.

Lawrence Kohlberg, among others, has theorized that the development of moral character in children occurs in progressive stages.[8] Further, Kohlberg has indicated that this moral development is closely associated with bringing children under social control. In the end, if the moral training has been successful, the social controls are internalized enough to enable the person to exercise self-control.

The sixfold stages of Kohlberg consist of the following:

Stage 1. Obey rules to avoid punishment.
Stage 2. Conform to obtain rewards . . .
Stage 3. Conform to avoid disapproval . . .
Stage 4. Conform to avoid censure by legitimate authorities and resultant guilt.
Stage 5. Conform to maintain the respect of the impartial spectator judging in terms of community welfare.
Stage 6. Conform to avoid self-condemnation.[9]

The conceptualization of moral development in children occurring in a step-by-step fashion may or may not be correct, but the logical

[8]Lawrence Kohlberg, "Development of Moral Character and Moral Ideology," *Review of Child Development Research*, Vol. 1, eds., Martin L. Hoffman and Lois Wladis Hoffman, (New York: Russell Sage Foundation, 1964), pp. 383-431.
[9]Ibid, p. 400.

ordering of increasing ability on the part of children to know the mores of their society does suggest that the very young do become exposed to what is expected of them and adapt themselves accordingly. Children can be said to be constantly refining and adjusting their behavior and judgments as they grow older from the crude perceptions that misbehavior brings swift punishment to the more sophisticated decisions to gear one's actions to specific situations because of prior learning.

Identification with religion, most likely the religion of their parents, places children squarely on the path of moral development and social control. At least this is the alleged motivation of the religiously faithful in bringing their young "into the fold." Desired objectives include the ability to take the needs of others into account, to gain a certain sense of humility in the face of overwhelming forces or conditions, and ultimately, to be able to arrive at some world view or philosophy of life that provides meaning for existence.

While these moral goals may be held up as ideals, there is obviously a "falling short" of these ideals in reality. Some might well argue that religions are failures because the world of socialized adults is far from utopia. Others, however, affirm that it is not so much religions that have failed people as it is people who have failed religions. Many ask how their society or the world became so tragically entangled or divided. The answers, of course, go back almost to antiquity when such moral codes as that of the "Golden Rule," treating others in the way individuals would like to be treated, were promulgated.

Religious training should aid the moral development of children, but the greatest teachers of all, from our perspective, are the *models of morality* set before children. What kind of parents, citizens, or religiously faithful are grownups? Their deeds are far more impressive than their creeds when their children acquire their moral codes. We would tend to support the eloquent challenge of Dorothy Gross when she wrote:

> Neither punishment nor permissiveness nor preaching leads to sound moral development. Only one path remains, that of *exemplification*. (Italics ours) But it is not enough to practice honesty and fairness in one's own family or neighborhood or classroom. The world must be one's family—the world of long -and short-hairs; the world of suburbanites and welfare receivers; the world of addicts and prohibitionists; the world of atheists and fundamentalists; the world of radicals and rightists; the world of college professors and truck drivers; the worlds of Women's Liberationists; of students, of homosexuals, of union members, of Jews and

blacks and Chicanos, and even, upper-class whites. Can we stretch our minds and attitudes to include all?"[10]

The Effects of Religious
Training on Individual Morality

Many apparently believe that religious training encourages moral conduct of the highest order, namely a concern for the well-being of others. When this thesis was tested in 1928 by Hartshorne and May with some eleven thousand children, the evidence did not support the thesis.[11] They did not find a positive correlation, for example, between Sunday School attendance, knowledge of the Bible, and honest behavior. In the years that have followed the Hartshorne and May study, literally hundreds of studies confirmed that church attenders were, on the average, more racially and ethnically prejudiced than nonchurch people.[12]

There remains, however, some counterevidence that religious training does help bring about desirable moral character. Campbell and Fukuyama, for instance, in 1970, studied the moral changes in persons in terms of the four ways through which people relate to their faith, namely through its organization, religious knowledge, belief, and its religious practices. They found, except for belief, particularly in reference to racial treatment, the other three relationships did make a statistically significant difference in bringing about moral changes.[13]

Joseph Fichter, a religious scholar of considerable repute, remains convinced that religious training for children does bring about the development of moral character.[14] Fichter contends that while education can provide technical, secular knowledge and community life can teach social virtues, it is religion that can encourage children to adopt values and to find real meaning in their actions. In Fichter's view, the force of community life has declined for children because social roles are fragmented and persons drift into secondary group accommoda-

[10]Dorothy W. Gross, "Comment on Watergate: Implications for Moral Development," *Childhood Education*, 50, No. 1 (October 1973), 56. Reprinted by permission of Dorothy W. Gross and the Association for Childhood International, 3615 Wisconsin Avenue, N.W., Washington, D.C. Copyright © 1973 by the Association.

[11]Hugh Hartshorne and Mark May, *Studies in the Nature of Character*, Vol. I (New York: Macmillan, 1928), 407–14.

[12]See S. Ellis Nelson, "Sanctification Sociology," *Religion in Life*, XLI, No. 3 (Autumn 1972), 305.

[13]Thomas C. Campbell and Yoshio Fukuyama, *The Fragmented Laymen* (Boston: Pilgrim Press, 1970).

[14]Joseph H. Fichter, *Community, Education and Religion* (New York: State University of New York, Albany, 1972).

tions. It becomes the responsibility of education and religion to serve together as character-builders so that moral human beings can be developed.

The scholarly thinking is thus divided and inconclusive. On the one hand, there are studies and analyses that point to the inability of religious training to achieve its objectives in terms of high moral conduct. Jarvis, for example, has suggested the hypothesis that much of the religious content employed in the various religious schools are beyond the conceptual level of children.[15] O'Neil and Donovan are, in similar fashion, highly critical of what they find in formal religious training centers.[16] On the other hand, there are children who are touched affirmatively by their religious training. These children do not necessarily move smoothly through their religious training in some steadily progressive manner. Along with Argyle, we would suggest that the pattern is cyclical or intermittent.[17] Perhaps the children do take an unrealistic view of religious teachings. Their prayers reflect belief in a "servant" God who will gratify their immediate needs. Later on, however, as they grow older and encounter greater exposure to views other than those of their early childhood, they may offer considerable resistance to their earlier religious trainings. They may rebel and alienate themselves from their earliest religious exposure. Some children, of course, enter into no such conflict with their parents, relatives, or friends.

One need wait upon greater maturity before they can anticipate a "return" for those who have "strayed." For young adults, there is a need to be preoccupied with finding one's way in a secular world. Religious participation consequently declines or suffers. But the coming of children turns parents toward the religion of their own childhood, at least to the one with which they are most familiar. If the return of the children and the reawakening of long-forgotten religious lessons have a beneficial, gratifying effect, the chances are that these parents will remain fairly steadfast in their faith for the remainder of their lives. If, however, there was high doubt as to the value of religion in a person's life, the later years will not necessarily see a return to faith but will show, instead, a consistent rejection of religious teachings.[18]

[15]Peter Jarvis, "Religious Socialization in the Junior School," *Educational Research*, 16, No. 2 (1974), 100–06.
[16]Robert O'Neil and Michael Donovan, *Children, Church and God, The Case Against Formal Religious Education* (New York/Cleveland: Corpus Books, 1970).
[17]Argyle, *International Encyclopedia of Social Sciences*, p. 426.
[18]See Marvin R. Koller, *Social Gerontology* (New York: Random House, 1968). See also, studies of Albrecht, Barron, and Orbach reported in *Handbook of Social Gerontology*, ed. Clark Tibbitts (Chicago: The University of Chicago Press, 1960), pp. 739–42.

RELIGION AND EDUCATION IN TENSION

There is perhaps no greater playing out of the differences between the sacred and the secular in American society than in the issue of the separation of church and state. In a sense, children are the pawns in this interface between formal religions and formal educational training. Their parents make the fundamental decisions as to what constitutes an appropriate mix of secular training and spiritual, emotional, moral concerns. By seeking to accomplish both secular and sacred educational goals, parents and their children run squarely into the determination of the American society to carry out a policy of building a wall of separation between religious faiths and public, tax-supported education.

A Brief Historical Background on Separation of Church and State

Having emerged from a European background in which religious freedom was stifled, those who came to the American colonies were determined to follow their religious convictions without fear of interference or suppression by political authorities. By 1789, the U.S. Constitution was in effect, but it was not amended with its vital Bill of Rights until 1791. The First Amendment declared that laws respecting the establishment of religion or the prohibition of the free exercise of religion could not be enacted. Later, the Fourteenth Amendment extended this policy of the separation of church and state to the respective states. Thomas Jefferson is said to be the author of the "wall of separation" although, being both a religious gentleman and a great scholar, he favored both private and church schools for the young as well as a free, tax-supported system of public schools.

By 1830 the American system of public schools, tax-supported but nonsectarian, was rather firmly established. This did not mean, however, that efforts to test that "wall" or to build "bridges" over it were not made. Indeed, a series of cases have been carried to the Supreme Court for purposes of testing the constitutionality of specific laws or regulations that may or may not be in violation of the separation of church and state policy.[19]

[19]Useful sources include, Donald E. Boles, *The Bible, Religion, and the Public Schools* (Ames, Iowa: Iowa State University Press, 1965); Theodore R. Sizer, ed., *Religion and Public Education* (Boston: Houghton Mifflin, 1967); Herbert M. Kliebard, ed., *Religion and Education in America, A Documentary History* (Scranton, Pennsylvania: International Textbook Company, 1969); Niels C. Nielsen, Jr., *God in Education* (New York: Sheed and Ward, 1966); John H. Laubach, *School Prayers, Congress, the Courts, and the Public* (Washington, D.C.: Public Affairs Press), 1969.

Selected Cases Concerning
Public and Private-Parochial Schools

While we cannot deal comprehensively with each instance of alleged violations of religious freedom in the education of children, we
can identify a few of the more significant cases.

In 1930, *Cochran* v. *Louisiana Board of Education,* the issue was
the use of tax funds to purchase text books for children enrolled in
either public or private-parochial schools. The Supreme Court held that
this policy was acceptable because it was designed for the benefit of the
children and not to promote a particular religious dogma.

The child-benefit theory was again followed in the 1947 case of
Everson v. *the Board of Education.* The Court ruled 5 to 4 that public
funds for the transportation of children to parochial schools are constitutional.

However, when other issues were raised, the Court began to render decisions of unconstitutionality because the wall of separation between religion and state was endangered. In the *McCollum* v. *Board
of Education* case in 1948, the issue was released time for religious
study during public school hours with parental consent. The Court
ruled that such practice is in violation of the Constitution because,
among other matters, it used public buildings paid for by public funds
and employed public school teachers in religious instructions.

The *Engle* v. *the Board of Regents of New York,* 1962, dealt with
what came to be known as "the Regents' Prayer." The Board of Regents
had ordered the recitation at the beginning of each school day of a
generalized, nondenominational prayer. It read: "Almighty God, we
acknowledge our dependence upon Thee, and we beg Thy blessings
upon us, our parents, our teachers, and our Country." Later attempts
to secure approval included not requiring all students to recite the
prayer but to remain silent if they wished or to leave the room. Nevertheless, the Regents' Prayer was held to be in violation of the First
Amendment. This decision provoked an outpouring of rage that spoke
of removing God from public schools and called attention to the hypoc-
risy of lawmakers who engaged in public prayers but who denied them
to little children.

A similar public outrage came in 1963 when the Madylyn Murray
case protesting the public recital of the Lord's Prayer was upheld by the
Supreme Court. It was also in 1963 in the *Abington* v. *Schemp* case that
the opening of each school session with the reading of ten verses of the
Holy Bible without comment from the teacher was held to be unconstitutional.

More recent cases, in the 1970s, such as *Walz* v. *Tax Commissioners, Lemon* v. *Kurtzman,* and *Early* v. *Di Censo,* dealt with the prob-

lem of aiding religious schools through various tax policies. These policies allowed tax credits, tax forgiveness, or tax exemptions for those parents whose children attended nonpublic elementary and secondary schools. In each situation, the Court stood firm and held that excessive tax entanglement in religious education was unconstitutional.

Charles Whelan has pulled together what he sees as the areas in which there can be one of three decisions. The first would be policies that were clearly constitutional. The second would be those procedures that would be unconstitutional. The third area would be the "gray," uncertain, doubtful practices that may or may not be upheld as constitutional.[20]

Those likely to be held as constitutional would include real estate exemption for school property; use of buses, books, school lunches, and health services; secular, neutral, nonideological services, facilities, or materials to all school children; dual enrollments or shared time; and government payments for record-keeping or for the provision of standard textbooks required by law.

Those procedures that would be unconstitutional include such things as purchase of secular services and teachers' supplemental salaries; tuition payments not based on need and not restricted to the cost of secular education; and any assistance that requires an audit of nonpublic school books to classify all expenses as either secular or religious.

Finally, Whelan believes the doubtful areas to consist of instruction in nonpublic schools by public school teachers; tax benefits limited to nonpublic schools, teachers, students, parents, or sponsors; educational payments based on real need; educational programs that focus upon children with special needs whether rich or poor; sharing of facilities by public and nonpublic schools; and lastly, educational vouchers for children in both public and religious schools.

As we indicated earlier, this topic of religious training of children can and does arouse intense emotional reactions. In the 1975 Kanawa County, West Virginia textbook controversy, parents, ministers, and public officials were locked in battle over the use of certain textbooks by their children. The objections included claims that the public schools were teaching atheism and ridiculing God as a superstitious myth. Demonstrations, boycotts, bombing, sniping, and even a prayer for the early death of a Board member who favored the use of certain textbooks intensified this situation. Undoubtedly, for some time to come, the interface between religious training and public school training for children will be a battleground.

[20]See Edward R. D'Alessio, "Public Policy Implications for Public Assistance to Non-Public Education," *Religious Education,* LXX, No. 2 (March-April 1975) 181–82.

ON DEATH AND DYING

Religion serves to provide meaning to life, but it serves to provide meaning to the end of life as well. Each religious faith has its own way of confronting the inevitable death of persons and so attempts to comfort, explain, and encourage its adherents to live steadfastly and considerately. Christianity, for example, has offered much solace and great satisfaction to its followers through its teachings of life after death. Judaism, by contrast, recognizes death as part of the "plan" of the Creator; it concentrates more upon the living, the ongoing lives of generations who are to remain inspired and faithful to the awesome powers of a Supreme Being. Deuteronomy 30:19 forthrightly states ". . . I have set before thee life and death, the blessing and the curse; therefore choose life, that thou mayest live, thou and thy seed . . ."

A number of observers have pointed to the rather strange turnabout that came to those who were concerned with children. For many years, it was customary to avoid references to the beginnings of life, particularly when they involved the sexuality of adults. Interestingly enough, these same adults did not hold the same attitude toward the ending of life and regaled their young with vivid tales of death, dying, and eternal punishment or reward for one's deeds on earth. The saving of souls from eternal damnation was a favored topic to be dwelt upon at length before willful children.

In the more recent past, it became fashionable to discuss more openly, honestly, and forthrightly the nature of human sexuality with small children. At the same time, it was deemed appropriate to shield children from grasping the reality of death that comes inevitably to everyone. Death denial was the mode among adults and consequently was applied to their children as well. Because death did come to older grandparents, uncles, aunts, friends, or pets, some explanations had to be fabricated. These were usually euphemisms such as "going to sleep," "taking a long journey," "passing on," "being rewarded for one's deeds on earth," "laid to rest," "joining the angels," "returning home," or "gathered unto his or her parents." Small wonder that children became confused, worried, or fearful when they began to apply such explanations to their own lives. Some have been known to refuse to go to sleep. Others wondered out loud why good deeds meant that one died. Still others, knowing that some loved person or animal has "gone far away," would ask when the person or animal might return.

Venturing a guess about the present, we would judge that it is increasingly acceptable to discuss *both* human sexuality and death with small children. A part of this newer approach is the rapid growth of the field of thanatology, the study of death, among mature students. An extensive literature on this subject has begun to accumulate.[21]

It is important to recognize that religious faith has always been sensitive to the needs of its followers to confront pain, suffering, and death itself. For many, it has comforted and eased the loss of loved ones. In the main, it has sustained the bereaved and encouraged the living to continue. Whether or not religion has truly reached into the inner consciousness of children and those who guide them in religious teachings remains unknown. Constanzo, a religious scholar, has pointed out the great difference between what religions have taught or avowed and what their followers truly believe. Constanzo wrote, ". . . in the context of religious education, . . . sotto voce . . . obedience to one's own personal conscience is not always and necessarily in conformity with the publicly avowed dictates of its religious profession."[22]

With Constanzo, we would surmise that religious explanations do not provide the comforting balm and satisfactory support to those who suffer the deaths of relatives, friends, and associates no matter how well done. Most important of all, when it comes to facing one's own death, there remains a modicum of doubt that everyone is fully prepared. Because adults have given evidence of lack of comprehension of their own deaths, it follows that their skills in convincing young children that dying and death are of minimal concern are also inept. To be sure, there is still much to be done when it comes to enabling young children to draw upon their religious training when considering their own deaths.

SUMMARY

Religion is an emotion-laden area in societal life that can bring foward some of the most vicious animosities or the most generous and gentle acts of which human beings are capable. Essentially, religion is a social product that emerges through a community of believers whose shared faith provides meaning to life and offers guides to appropriate

[21]See for example, Geoffrey Gorer, *Death, Grief, and Mourning* (New York: Doubleday & Company, Inc., 1965); Elisabeth Kübler-Ross, *On Death and Dying* (New York: Macmillan, 1969); John Hinton, *Dying* (Baltimore: Penguin Books, 1967); Earl A. Grollman, ed., *Explaining Death to Children* (Boston: Beacon Press, 1967); Robert Fulton, ed., *Death and Identity* (New York: John Wiley & Sons, Inc., 1965); Barney Glaser and A. L. Strauss, *Awareness of Dying* (Chicago: Aldine Publishing Co., 1965); David Sudow, *Passing On, The Social Organization of Dying* (Englewood Cliffs, New Jersey: Prentice-Hall, Inc., 1967); Douglas Kimmel, "Dying and Bereavement," in *Adulthood and Aging* (New York: John Wiley & Sons, Inc., 1974).

[22]Joseph F. Constanzo, S. J., *This Nation Under God, Church, State and Schools in America* (New York: Herder and Herder, 1964) p. 437.

conduct. Children are usually exposed to a single religious set of beliefs and practices rather than objectively introduced to the tremendous diversity of religious perspectives that really exist. Even within the confines of a single faith-system, children are also directed to attend to a particular version, denomination, branch, or wing that promotes items of special importance. While religions are generally concerned with the sacred or extraordinary, contemporary urban-industrialized life styles have developed secular religions as well. These, too, are stressed for young children who are schooled in their importance. It has been suggested by Robert Bellah, for instance, that a generalized "American Civil Religion" has been promoted for American citizens.

The close relationship between the sacred and the secular is further evident in the tendencies of certain religions to be either conservative or liberal in nonreligious matters such as economics or politics.

The diversity of religions, however, from our perspective, may be overemphasized or overdrawn. What is often forgotten is the common ground upon which most religions stand.

Children are particularly introduced to religions to aid their moral development. Through religious training, they move through successively refined stages or steps of social conformity from obedience out of fear of external punishment to self-control through sophisticated internalized controls that are self-imposed. The models that are set before them by adults are, again from our perspective, the most significant in their adaptation to religions. Studies are divided and inconclusive as to whether or not religious training does in fact bring about the desired moral character attributed to it. If religion is to make its mark upon children, the usual pattern seems to be one of childlike acceptance followed by doubt, confusion, or alienation as other views are promoted. Religious belief will then return in maturity if it is to ever manifest itself.

Perhaps the greatest tensions for children being introduced to their society occur when religious training and secular education are brought face to face. For Americans, the principle of separating religion and political-economic organization has been the chief guide to handling sensitive religious diversity. This separation, however, is challenged frequently in the courts and has led to untold moral outrage and indignation when specific cases were decided one way or another. We see this interface between children's religious training and their public school training as a continued battleground for many years to come.

Lastly, we considered briefly the topics of death and dying. If religion provides meaning to life, it must also provide meaning to the ending of life. For children who have just begun to live, the prospect of ending it is most confusing and puzzling. Euphemisms that deny the reality of death are frequently brought into play for both young and old. We noted, however, that the older tabus concerning human sexuality and death are slowly giving way to a newer approach of confronting these realities and learning to cope with them. The inescapable is now identified, and religious explanations are openly discussed and debated. We noted further that official pronouncements or stances by a particular religion do not necessarily coincide with the private, personal views of religious adherents. For children to begin to understand that life has its limitations for them, too, is a most sobering lesson to learn. It is, nevertheless, a part of their growing up to fulfill their lives as men and women.

6

Children and racism

Perhaps the most tragic feature of American history has been the prolonged and continuing struggle for the dignity, freedom, and rights of different races. It began with the earliest contacts of European "whites" with Amerinds, the American Indians along the coastal shores of the New World, continued with the importation of black African slaves, and manifested itself repeatedly as Mexicans, Chinese, Japanese, Korean, Vietnamese, Filipinos, Hawaiians, or Samoans encountered Americans during economic-political excursions involving peaceful exchanges or full-scale wars. It is "tragic" because the rejection of people by reason of physical features occurs in a land and among people who pride themselves on respect for persons and the encouragement of their potential abilities.

The begrudging assimilation of people of nonwhite origins into American culture and society diminishes America in the eyes of a world population that is overwhelmingly nonwhite. The problem is further compounded by attempting to keep those who are already "in" the society as alienated as possible from the society.

To find smoldering resentment that now and then breaks out into open and massive violence should come as no surprise. One does not have to be a race relations specialist to be aware of the fear, mistrust, apprehension, and misunderstanding that motivate the "flights from contact" that white majorities have chosen to take. But, most of all, there must be concern about "the little victims," the children of all races in America who are marked for life by their early socialization in *racism, the contention that one race or another, one people or another, is either superior or inferior by reason of genetics to any other race or people.*[1] In their socialization lie the seeds of generational perpetuation of racial myths that will continue to blight lives far into the distant future.

BLACK AMERICANS[2]

It would be worthwhile to examine in detail the many racial minorities within contemporary American society because each provides a unique and instructive pattern of racism in action. Those who have an abiding interest in these minorities should consult the numerous excellent sources available to them.[3] For our purposes, we will confine our attention to black Americans because they constitute some 90 percent of the nonwhite population in the United States. Much of the literature on racism has direct reference to black-white relations and somewhat parallels the treatment accorded other nonwhites in America. As little as possible, then, will be lost by focusing most of our discussion on black Americans.

White Racism

The usual practice has been to identify a social problem with the name of those who suffer from it. Thus, it has long been customary to refer to "the black problem" in America. However, the reverse strategy

[1]Howard James, *The Little Victims* (New York: David McKay Company, Inc., 1975). See also, William Ryan, *Blaming the Victim* (New York: Random House, 1971).

[2]See Alphonso Pinkney, *Black Americans,* 2nd ed. (Englewood Cliffs, N.J.: Prentice-Hall, Inc., 1975). For a psychological view see E. Earl Baughman, *Black Americans, A Psychological Analysis* (New York: Academic Press, 1971).

[3]See for example, Bill Hosokawa, *Nisei: The Quiet Americans* (New York: William Morrow & Company, Inc., 1969); Matt S. Meier and Feliciano Rivera, *The Chicanos: A History of Mexican Americans* (New York: Hill and Wang, Inc., 1972); Nathaniel N. Wagner and Marsha J. Haug, eds., *Chicanos, Social and Psychological Perspectives* (Saint Louis: The C. V. Mosby Company, 1971); Dee Brown, *Bury My Heart at Wounded Knee: An Indian History of the American West* (New York: Holt, Rinehart and Winston, 1970); Theodore W. Taylor, *The States and Their Indian Citizens* (Washington, D.C.: Bureau of Indian Affairs, 1972).

of identifying the perpetrators rather than the victims of discrimination is most telling. This was precisely what the editors of *Ebony* magazine did when they published their August, 1965 issue under the title of "The White Problem in America."[4]

It is worth repeating that the problems of youth are really the problems imposed upon them by the nonyoung. The problems of the poor are really the problems created by those who have wealth. The problems of displaced persons are the problems brought into being by those who have a place. The problems of the old are problems that are caused by the nonold. Discrimination against women results from the actions of males. So it is that the multiple and complicated problems of black Americans in the backwaters of America are the responsibility of the whites in the powerful mainstream of American society. It was the Kerner Report, the report of the National Advisory Commission on Civil Disorders in 1968, that pointed out the racial divisiveness of America. Without equivocation, the commission noted "that white institutions created it, maintained it, and white society condones it."[5]

There are those who would rather stress the responsibility of blacks to meet the standards of, at least, white middle-class Americans. Blacks, they observe, are not helpless innocents who cannot change their circumstances. When they have demonstrated their abilities, *then* they will have access to all that America has to offer. This rationale is comforting to those who have already "arrived" in America, often by reason of hard work and diligence. But the rationale crumbles when racism is at the heart of the issue. When blacks do make the effort, the visible race issue is still present. There remains the fear of retaliation, the subtle resentment of competition and displacement, the uncomfortable feeling of exclusion because one is simply not with his or her "kind." The experiences of a lifetime are not erased by good intentions. Because the socialization begun in childhood and sustained through adulthood has consistently favored racism, even the prospect of a world in which racial differences are held to be inconsequential is difficult to envision.

Reverse Racism

Perhaps the best way to begin to understand what racism is and what it achieves is to experience it for oneself. When the tables are

---

[4]Editors of *Ebony, The White Problem in America* (Chicago: Johnson Publishing Company, 1966). See also, Marcel L. Goldschmid, ed., *Black Americans and White Racism, Theory and Research* (New York: Holt, Rinehart and Winston, Inc., 1970).
   [5]*Report of the National Advisory Commission on Civil Disorders* (New York: The New York Times Company, 1968), p. vii.

turned and majorities are confronted with rejection, displacement, separatism, discrimination, and frustration, there are cries of outrage.[6]

The status quo is unchallenged when minorities are exploited; little remorse or opposition was elicited in response to the limited economic opportunities of blacks. However, when special privileges, headstarts, raised quota hirings and the like began after centuries of neglect, the question raised by formerly privileged whites was precisely the question asked by disprivileged blacks all along, namely, why distinguish between people on the basis of their physical features alone?

Black Power

For many years, the relationships between blacks and whites were studied in terms of integrating blacks into white society. That objective has never been abandoned, only slowed and sometimes discouraged by such procedures as closed and open housing, closed and open unions, closed and open private and public schools, closed and open churches, and closed or open access to occupations or careers.

What is different in our times is that the younger generation of racial leaders has stressed a new concept that if blacks are to improve their circumstances, they must take responsibility for themselves on their own terms. Out-group sympathy and support are welcomed from whatever quarter, but in-group pride, solidarity, and power were held to achieve much more for blacks than spiritual defeatism and acceptance of nonblack standards. "Physician, heal thyself," an ancient admonition, takes on new significance when applied to "black power," "black pride," "the black experience," "black soul," and "black brothers and sisters." These philosophical underpinnings raise a new image of American blacks based on self-help toward self-imposed goals. It is a racial separatism made real and logical after the alienation long imposed by nonblacks.

C. Eric Lincoln has chronicled how, for example, Black Muslims used this rhetoric in the origin and development of their faith.[7] Perhaps no more eloquent spokesman and example for this self-pride strategy among blacks could be found than the martyred Malcolm X who rose from an unhappy childhood to a life of charismatic leadership.[8]

[6]An excellent debate occurred among Edgar F. Borgatta, Troy Duster, Suzanne Keller, James J. Kilpatrick, and others in "Affirmative Action-Reverse Discrimination?," *The American Sociologist*, 11, No. 2 (May 1976), 62–93.

[7]C. Eric Lincoln, *The Black Muslims in America* (Boston: Beacon Press, 1961). See also, Stokely Carmichael and Charles V. Hamilton, *Black Power, The Politics of Liberation in America* (New York: Random House, 1967).

[8]Alex Haley and Malcolm X, *The Autobiography of Malcolm X* (New York: Grove Press, 1966).

Violent or Nonviolent Racial Strategies

Judging from a great social distance, many have mistakenly assumed that there is some monolithic unity among black Americans concerning objectives and how to achieve them. In reality, however, black Americans differ in terms of social classes, regions, rurality or urbanity, generations, religion, families, and personalities just as white Americans or any other large segment of the population. That they would differ on goals and their accomplishment should come as no surprise. Within this heterogeneity, leadership and strategies differ markedly. There are those who call for immediate action and those who advise caution. There are those who call for revolution and those who believe that evolution will ultimately resolve the unrest and malaise. Some would work within the system, while others advocate work "outside" the system.

For those concerned about lives and property, the issue is whether social changes will be made violently or nonviolently. Certainly, black-white relations have been characterized by both violence and nonviolence and, realistically, some mix of the two is likely to occur.[9]

In our concern over how children are trained to deal with racism, we quite obviously would opt for nonviolence much in the manner of the dream of Dr. Martin Luther King, Jr.[10] Like his model, Mohandas Karamchand Gandhi, who favored nonviolence but who, ironically, died through the violence of an assassin, so lived and died the revered Dr. King. Known to many as "the Black Prince of Peace," Dr. King often spoke of the time when children of all races could peacefully fulfill their lives. This can come about only when children are able to observe all about them adult examples of mutual human concern.

The Irrationality of Racism

Racism, in sociological terms, is categorical thinking, the labelling of persons on the basis of arbitrary criteria. John Howard Griffin demonstrated its effects when he contrasted the treatment he received as a white reporter in the early years of the civil rights movement of the 1960s and the treatment he received when he passed himself off as a black through an unprecedented experiment involving both the inges-

[9]See for instance, Louis H. Masotti and James R. Corsi, *Shoot-Out in Cleveland, Black Militants and the Police: July 23, 1968,* A Report submitted to the National Commission on the Causes and Prevention of Violence, May 16, 1969, Civil Violence Research Center, Case Western Reserve University (New York: The New York Times, 1969).
[10]Martin Luther King, Jr., *Where Do We Go From Here, Chaos or Community?* (New York: Harper & Row, 1967).

tion of chemicals and external cosmetic changes.[11] A similar technique has been used by advocates of open housing by documenting the differential treatment experienced by white and black couples of identical social class levels when they attempted to buy homes in various neighborhoods. The acceptance of whites and the rejection of blacks solely on the basis of race since there were no other significant differences in social or personal qualities exemplifies the absurdity of racial labels. Unfortunately, American history is filled with untold numbers of cases that tell the same story of personal humiliation and categorical rejection on the basis of race.[12]

The Changing of a Label: Negro is Defamatory, Black is Beautiful

One of the interesting changes that has occurred in the decade between 1960 and 1970 has been the determined move to shed the label *Negro* in favor of a more respectful term, *black*. The change came through the concerted effort of those who pointed out that Negro was a white term for persons of African origin, those brought as slaves to America's shores. It was not a term used by indigenous Africans to describe themselves.

For a time, there was debate about referring to those who originated in Africa as *Afro-Americans.* It seemed to be appropriate because it has been traditional to speak of "hyphenated Americans" who came from numerous European ethnic origins. While the Afro-American label has some support, the name *black* has won the greater approval and support.

Black displaced the defamatory "Negro" because it did not, as some observed, carry with it the connotation of "*ne*gative *gro*wth" or a failure to improve living conditions, but rather a pushing back of an important segment of American citizenry on the basis of their genetic makeup. Instead, freedom schools were opened to children to instruct them that they are "black and beautiful," "black and proud," or "black citizens" who have all the rights of citizens in a free nation-state. Some would call this brain-washing or propagandizing. Others, however, would disagree and would call this work with impressionable youngsters an attempt to balance out through education the centuries of self-hatred, self-rejection, and self-defeat brought about by mindless custom.

[11]John Howard Griffin, *Black Like Me* (Boston: Houghton Mifflin, 1961).
[12]A useful bibliography can be found in William Loren Katz, *Teacher's Guide to American Negro History* (Chicago: Quadrangle Books, 1968). See also, E. Earl Baughman, and W. Grant Dahlstrom, *Negro and White Children, A Psychological Study in the Rural South* (New York: Academic Press, 1968).

Self-Attitudes of Children

When the original edition of this text first appeared in 1964, we charged that "children are being raised under a cloud of race-thinking."[13] We anticipated a certain amount of protestation over our sweeping generalization but were prepared to stand our ground on the basis of factual data. The passing of over a dozen years did not bring one objection. Instead, there has been dramatic silence.

Perhaps a textbook declaration has little or no significance as authors may reluctantly admit. The thesis we would like to believe explains the silent reception of what we took to be a shocking statement of fact is that the observation was irrefutable, allowing, of course, for the usual exceptions that are understood when generalizations are formulated.

Prejudices are, of course, undeterred by factual evidence. In point of fact, they are not necessarily based upon straightforward, rational reasoning. Rather, they are ingrained, carefully taught, indoctrinated by repeated references to invidious distinctions such as poor academic performance, inadequate care of personal property or appearance, illegal or criminal activities, immorality, uncleanliness, or lack of accepted manners. When these same characteristics are found among whites, they are not attributed to fixed racial traits but rather to various environmental factors that are amenable to social or personal changes.

People have simply decided that there are distinctive races with immutable characteristics. No amount of scientific data, no matter how overwhelming or voluminous, can, by itself, rationally be expected to divest persons of their irrational, emotional, internalized prejudgments that one race or another is inferior to whites.[14] Nevertheless, there is a patient willingness on the part of authors, teachers, research specialists, and students to demonstrate ultimately that racial prejudgments are without foundation. There remains the hope that sooner or later people will come to understand that people of different races are all part of the human family and manifest all the strengths and weaknesses of human beings.

The place to begin, of course, from our perspective is the socialization of children. In this early stage of life, children acquire the guiding attitudes that direct much of what they will accomplish as adults. The most meaningful attitudes of all are the attitudes that individuals ac-

[13]Oscar W. Ritchie and Marvin R. Koller, *Sociology of Childhood* (Englewood Cliffs, N.J.: Prentice-Hall, Inc., 1964), p. 250.
[14]See Stanford M. Lyman, *The Black American in Sociological Thought* (New York: G. P. Putnam's Sons, 1972), pp. 131–32; Norval D. Glenn and Charles M. Bonjean, eds., *Blacks in the United States* (San Francisco, California: Chandler Publishing Company, 1969), pp. 458–66.

quire concerning themselves. Certain self-attitudes prepare persons to take positive, constructive steps to accomplish their goals, or, conversely, set the stage for self-defeat and abject failure because they fail to provide the motivation to move toward worthy goals.

A number of studies, using doll-preference techniques, affirm the damage being done to small children when they show a marked aversion to figurines of their own racial appearance and a decided approval of stereotypic versions of white boys and girls.[15] Rita James Simon, for instance, using baby doll figures, pictures, and family figures of different skin colors, found that black-American, Korean, and Amerind children adopted by white families consistently exhibited white racial preferences rather than selecting dolls or figures closer to their own physical features.[16]

THE CHARACTER-BUILDING INSTITUTIONS AND RACISM

Schools

In the historic decision of the Supreme Court in the 1954 case of *Brown* v. *Topeka Board of Education,* the long-standing principle of "separate, but equal" school facilities for white and black children was set aside.[17] Perhaps the most telling argument that convinced the Supreme Court to reverse former decisions to segregate white and black school children was the irreparable harm that was done to small children by this procedure.

One hope held by those who seek to raise children to fully participate in American society is that this can be accomplished through the public schools. In this educational setting the principles of American democracy could be taught and exemplified. It could not be done by requiring a white child and a black child to attend different schools and so learn that some people are "more equal" and "more free" than others.[18]

[15]Jeanne Begles and Anies A. Sheikh, "Development of Self-Concept in Black-White Children," *The Journal of Negro Education,* 43, No. 1 (Winter 1974), 104–10, and Doris Wilkinson, "Racial Socialization through Children's Toys, A Socio-historical Examination," *Journal of Black Studies,* 5, No. 1 (September 1974), 96–108.

[16]Rita James Simon, "An Assessment of Racial Awareness, Preference, and Self-Identity Among White and Adopted Non-White Children," *Social Problems,* 22, No. 1 (October 1974), 43–57.

[17]Reported in detail in Kenneth Clark, *Prejudice and Your Child* (Boston: Beacon Press, 1955).

[18]Robert L. Crain and Carol Sachs Weisman, *Discrimination, Personality, and Achievement, A Survey of Northern Blacks* (New York: Seminar Press, 1972), pp. 154–78.

Now, well over two decades later, the integration of public schools is still not a fact but remains a bitterly fought issue involving busing for racial balances, use of private schools to evade public controls, and the fight for "quality education" within local neighborhoods.[19]

A study available in 1976 commissioned by the Department of Health, Education, and Welfare reveals that racially imbalanced schools decreased in southern and border states during the 1970s but increased steadily in the Northeast and Midwest.[20] Western schools changed very little in the 1970s.

In the 1974–1975 school year, roughly six of every ten black students in the midwestern states and northeastern states were attending "intensely segregated" schools in sharp contrast to the schools of the South in which slightly over two of every ten black students were attending segregated schools. A notable change has occurred since 1964 when about 98 percent of black students in the South were attending all-black or mostly black schools. The one region that was traditionally regarded as the center for segregated schools has within a single decade become a pioneer for desegregation. What is ironic is that the northerners who used to decry the segregation of blacks and whites in public schools now find themselves embroiled in embittered battles over schools with some 90 percent or more of racial minority enrollments. Children cannot help but learn something about themselves and the world in which they live when they see white adults demanding that they be left undisturbed in their support for racial separation and divisiveness.

Families

Families constitute the initial agencies of socialization for children. Further, they not only begin the lifelong process of socialization, but they sustain it over time through the schools, churches, voluntary groups, and friends with whom they associate. There is considerable academic debate as to whether or not families are as influential in the lives of children as has been held in the past. We shall reserve that debate for the next chapter, when we discuss families in the lives of children in general. In the context of racial issues, the specific impacts of families are more to the point because we wish to address ourselves particularly to black families.

[19]Everett F. Cantaldo, Michael Giles, and Douglas Gatlin, "Metropolitan School Desegregation: Practical Remedy or Impractical Ideal?," *Annals of the American Academy of Political and Social Science,* 422 (November 1975), 97–104.
[20]Data compiled by the Department of Health, Education and Welfare, Gary Orfield, Brookings Institute, Chief Investigator, June 1976, Washington, D.C.

In 1965, what came to be known as the Moynihan Report on black families in America was issued.[21] The report portrayed black families as "a tangle of pathologies" in which children were hopelessly enmeshed. The emphasis was placed upon absentee fathers who left behind matrifocal, matriarchal, extended families of low income with an overburden of children.

Little black girls were somewhat advantaged in this setting because they would acquire models of adult motherhood and womanhood with responsibilities both in and out of families. The little black boys, however, were alleged to be guaranteed a type of demasculinization by their mothers, grandmothers, sisters, and female kin by virtue of the missing father syndrome. Their only recourse was believed to be alienation from their dominating mothers and grandmothers by following their street peers in escapades calculated to show their real manhood. The pattern was thus self-perpetuating because females learned how to maintain a strong mother-child bond whereas males learned to take a more casual interest in families and to find their sense of self-worth in a tough, precarious, and male-oriented street society.

The Moynihan Report provoked a series of monographs, studies, and publications that strongly objected to the serious flaws in its stereotypic analysis of black family life.[22] One major objection argued that the stress on low-income, poorly housed, crowded, welfare dependent, mother-centered, inadequately educated, overburdened families neglected the majority of black families who were quite different. As many studies have since shown, black families, in the main, consist of husband-wife equalitarian families and range from middle-class to upper-class lifestyles. Another objection stated that the Moynihan Report placed black families as the source of a host of problems that flowed from a struggling and weakly knit family unit when, in reality, the type of family with which Moynihan was concerned was an understandable adaptation to extenuating circumstances. Rather than weak, this type of family organization was strong in the face of conditions not of its making. Finally, and perhaps most important of all, the Moynihan Report failed to recognize that black families are the products of a conscious or unconscious racist society that generates the very conditions which Moynihan found so deplorable.

Two studies will suffice to represent some of the literature that offered substantial rebuttals to the controversial Moynihan Report. One

[21]Daniel P. Moynihan, *The Negro Family, The Case for National Action* (Washington, D.C.: U.S. Government Printing Office, 1965).
[22]See particularly, Andrew Billingsley, *Black Families in White America* (Englewood Cliffs, N. J.: Prentice-Hall, Inc., 1968). See also, Jessie Bernard, *Marriage and Family Among Negroes* (Englewood Cliffs, N. J.: Prentice-Hall, Inc., 1966).

is the study of Louis Kreisberg which is data-based. The other is the more logical-theoretic analysis of Robert Hill.

THE KREISBERG STUDY.[23] Kreisberg relied upon interviews with a cross-section of families in low-income public housing projects and their surrounding neighborhoods, interviews with a panel of applicants for such housing, and observations of participant observers living in the housing projects themselves. Kreisberg was interested in determining if there was, indeed, a self-perpetuating "culture of poverty" or if there was a situational explanation in which existing circumstances allowed or prevented movement away from poverty-ridden characteristics.

In brief, Kreisberg's data led him to reject the culture-of-poverty explanations for black family life and supported the contention that the difference between the poor and the nonpoor were matters of degree. Even then, the poor and the nonpoor families were not very far apart on a number of indices. If circumstances outside the study families were changed such as employment opportunities, increased incomes through tax allowances, and improvements in sanitation safety and housing, possibilities for children's chances to move out of ghetto conditions would be greatly enhanced.

THE HILL STUDY.[24] Based upon the operational definition of family strengths as presented by Herbert Otto in his article, "What Is a Strong Family?,"[25] five qualities were held to be evidence of family development, stability, and survival. These were:

1. Strong Kinship Bonds
2. Strong Work Orientation
3. Adaptability of Family Roles
4. Strong Achievement Orientation
5. Strong Religious Orientation

While found among white families, these criteria for a strong family applied equally well to black families that had adapted to the racial oppressions of the larger society. Black families, more so than white families, took in greater numbers of minor children as well as the elderly. Many of these were out-of-wedlock children who were not as readily adopted by outsiders as were white children. Three-fifths of the

[23]Louis Kreisberg, *Mothers in Poverty, A Study of Fatherless Families* (Chicago: Aldine Publishing Company, 1970).
[24]Robert B. Hill, *The Strengths of Black Families* (New York: Emerson Hall Publishers Inc., 1972).
[25]Herbert A. Otto, "What Is a Strong Family?" *Marriage and Family Living*, 24 (February 1962), 72–80.

black poor work in comparison to one-half of the poor whites. Attitudes among blacks favored going to work rather than relying upon welfare.[26]

Two-thirds of the wives in black husband and wife teams work out of necessity compared to only half of the white wives, but did not surpass the income of their husbands. Further, the black husbands held on to their jobs for longer periods of time than the white husbands in similar circumstances.

In black families, the sharing of tasks was commonplace. Women did shoulder the responsibilities of maintaining homes while working outside their homes whenever possible.

Wives were not necessarily deserted by their husbands but were separated because there were economic advantages through, for example, eligibility for support payments. However, some 70 percent of black families were found to be husband-wife families. What has been well publicized in the mass media is the presence of some 28 percent female-headed families among blacks in comparison to 9 percent female-headed families found among whites.

Finally, Hill found ample evidence that tremendous numbers of black families held high aspirations for their children and encouraged their motivations for upward class mobility.[27] The preponderance of data weighs in favor of a strong religious orientation. The inspirational and pragmatic leadership of black ministers on both the local and national levels explains in many ways the fortitude with which black families have confronted their special problems.

On all counts, black families have far more strengths than their well-publicized weaknesses. Black children may be deprived at the lower income levels in material comforts, but the deprivation cannot be said to extend to their morality, motivation, and movement toward positive goals.

RACIAL DISCRIMINATION

The classic and benchmark study of black-white relations in American society was made in 1944 by Gunnar Myrdal, a scholar given carte blanche to assess the interracial situation as it then stood.[28] Myrdal offered what appeared to be an ambivalent picture of the discrimina-

[26]Hill, *Strengths of Black Families*, pp. 4, 9.
[27]Ibid, pp. 27–32.
[28]Gunnar Myrdal, with the Assistance of Richard Sterner and Arnold Rose, *An American Dilemma: The Negro Problem and Modern Democracy* (New York: Harper and Brothers, 1944), pp. 60–61. Reprinted by permission.

tory practices then extant by means of which whites held blacks away from full participation in American society.

The theory was his conceptualization of "a rank order of discrimination" in which some discriminatory practices were held by whites to be more important than other discriminatory practices directed against blacks. There were:

Rank 1. Intermarriage or coitus between black men and white women

Rank 2. Social etiquettes such as in dancing, eating, drinking, swimming, conversations, or friendships

Rank 3. Public segregation such as in schools, churches, or public transportation

Rank 4. Political disfranchisement

Rank 5. Legal discrimination through law enforcement agencies such as police, courts, or in legal representation

Rank 6. Economic discrimination including ownership of land, homes, credit, jobs or careers, and access to public welfare.[29]

This rather dismal picture of discrimination, however, contained room for encouragement because this rank order of discrimination was also noted by Myrdal as just the reverse order of concern by blacks. What this meant was that the acts of discrimination of least concern to whites were of most concern to blacks. What was of most concern to whites was of least concern to blacks. Accordingly, if there were going to be pressures to bring about changes, these pressures would be exerted by blacks in their own order of priorities, and these were precisely the matters on which whites were most likely to give ground or offer concessions.

We have the perspective now, some thirty or more years later, to judge the wisdom of Myrdal's theory. Historical events have occurred that tend to support his thinking. This is not to say that discrimination has vanished from contemporary America but rather that the walls of discrimination have been under attack and have, in many instances, been breached.

Economic conditions are still poor for the largest proportion of blacks, but there have been economic gains by many black individuals or black organizations. Legal decisions have been made that widen the opportunities for blacks although, in far too many cases, the openings are begrudging, minimal, and slow to be implemented. Nevertheless, with both economic and legal support, blacks do vote in increasing numbers and have political "clout" that political leaders must take into account.

[29]Ibid, "Rank Order of Discrimination," (pp. 60–61). Reprinted by permission of the publisher.

Public segregation has been broken down through massive efforts in the 1960s civil rights campaigns, but the battle is far from over in the mid-1970s. The public schools appear to be at center stage with children the pawns in the maneuvering of adults. De facto segregation appears to have greater effect than de jure desegregation. There have been calls for *resegregation,* but these represent the ebb and flow of the clash of social values to be expected in a pluralistic society.

Finally, not only in good sportsmanship, but in numerous personal contacts there are many more black-white friendships and close comraderies in which social etiquettes are not so much racial as they are common courtesies to be extended to all friends and associates.

Lastly, miscegenation laws are now held to be unconstitutional, and black-white sexual relationships are regarded as private matters and less subject to public comment. Interracial marriages, however, are still quite minimal, some 1 or 2 percent of all marriages in the United States, attesting to the power of traditional mores.[30]

This last discriminatory arena, the fear and rejection of amalgamation by whites, is of particular interest because it has considerable relevance for children. For one thing, as has been pointed out by many observers, if whites were consistent about their fear and abhorrence concerning black-white mixtures, they would have drawn the sexual barriers much clearer. Instead, their most important discriminatory action did not exclude the possibility of white men taking sexual advantage, licit or illicit, of black women. The progeny of these sexually exploitive acts would have the same racial composition as the offspring of black men and white women joined in legally sanctioned, nonexploitive marriages.

Further, the universal rule that people "mix" when they meet, regardless of the subordination of one people by another, is substantiated by the countless numbers of racially mixed children who were born throughout the history of black-white contacts. The sexual contacts occurred in Africa, during passage to America, during slavery and post-slavery days, and up to the present time. Brewton Berry has been interested in these racial hybrids or "mestizos," and his *Almost White*[31] describes the lives of children who were neither black nor white but "in between" the races, "marginals" in Stonequist's terms[32] who may or may not "pass" racial barriers.

[30]Thomas P. Monahan, "An Overview of Statistics on Interracial Marriage in the United States, with Data on Its Extent from 1963–1970," *Journal of Marriage and the Family,* 38, No. 2 (May 1976), 223–31.

[31]Brewton Berry, *Almost White* (New York: Macmillan Company, 1961).

[32]Everett V. Stonequist, *The Marginal Man, A Study in Personality and Culture Conflict* (New York: Charles Scribner's Sons, 1937).

The black-white child in America, at least, is labeled "black" whereas in other societies, such as Brazil, black-white children have been received as "white."[33]

The possibilities for ambivalence, a desire to be accepted by persons of both races, are quite strong in racially mixed children. Over a half-century ago, Langston Hughes expressed this ambivalence succinctly in his conciliatory poem, "Cross."[34]

CROSS

My old man's a white old man
And my old mother's black.
If ever I cursed my white old man,
I take my curses back.

If ever I cursed my black old mother,
And wished she were in hell,
I'm sorry for that evil wish
And now I wish her well.

My old man died in a fine big house,
My ma died in a shack.
I wonder where I'm gonna die
Being neither white nor black.

One of our own university's students has adopted the name of "John Grey" to explain to whomever would listen that the lives of racially mixed children are more a product of social and cultural definitions than a matter of genetic pooling. In fact, John Grey has gone about the nation to use his own racially mixed ancestry as "a bridge of understanding" so that others may learn that their racial perspectives deeply affect the lives of innocent children.

Socialization Practices

The study of socialization practices with regard to black children invariably leads to consideration of social class variables. As we have noted, black children are reared at every social class level, and this cross

[33]Donald Pierson, *Negroes in Brazil, A Study of Race Contact at Bahia* (Chicago: The University of Chicago Press, 1942).
[34]Copyright 1926 by Alfred A. Knopf, Inc. and renewed 1954 by Langston Hughes. Reprinted from *Selected Poems,* by Langston Hughes, by permission of Alfred A. Knopf, Inc.

section of race with variant socioeconomic life styles complicates attempts at some generalized picture that applies to all black children. Instead, there is a tendency to focus upon black children in the lower classes and rather neglect or underplay black children in the middle and upper classes.

Andrew Billingsley has visualized the social class settings of black children as a pyramidal figure with approximately 10 percent in the upper classes, 40 percent in the middle classes, and 50 percent in the lower classes.[35] (See Figure 6-1.)

While there is room for argument about these proportions,[36] Billingsley does support the need to take social class into account in any assessment of how black children are handled.

In the Billingsley schema, there are two subtypes among the upper class, three within the middle class, and three more within the lower class. The distinctions that separate them are not necessarily

[35]Billingsley, *Black Families in White America*, p. 123.
[36]See Gerald R. Leslie, *The Family in Social Context*, 3rd ed. (New York: Oxford University Press, 1976), p. 323.

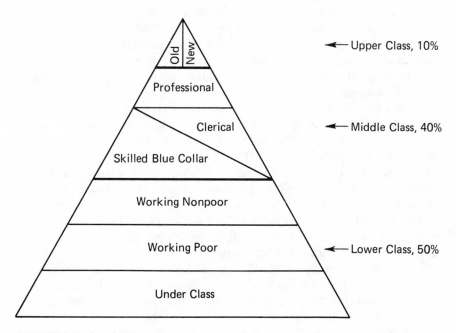

FIGURE 6-1 *Social Classes Among American Blacks*

clearcut but do make a difference in how particular families conduct their affairs.

The "old" upper-class black families are those whose status and accomplishments date back many generations, some before the Civil War. The "new" upper-class black families are those in which the key members have risen to prominence within a single generation.

The professional, clerical, and skilled blue collar black families of the middle class have relatively modest incomes compared with those of upper-class families, but their overall incomes provide living styles that are quite similar. In general, these middle-class black families do less well than their white counterparts because the incomes are usually lower, their job security is not as assured, and their wives work out of necessity outside their homes.

The working nonpoor work at hard, steady jobs, usually protected through union contracts. The working poor, however, never quite make enough to rise above the established poverty level. The underclass family heads are those with the minimal marketable skills, often school dropouts, who can find work only now and then. They are so far down the social scale that Billingsley views them as "outside" the social class system. Although these families receive the maximum attention when black families are discussed because of their multiproblem nature, they comprise only 15 or 20 percent of all black families and are certainly not representative of black families in contemporary American society. They are significant, however, because they represent how our social systems can generate deprivation among so many in an otherwise affluent society.

Within this social class context, Billingsley sees three different ways black families socialize their children. There are those that function adequately, those that function less adequately, and those that function inadequately. Those that function adequately protect their children, show concern for their well-being, encourage them to develop their capacities, help them meet normal expectations, and show them how to use the existing institutions to their own advantage.[37] Those that function less adequately are not consistent and will succeed and fail as favorable and unfavorable conditions occur. They move in and out of welfare and their children may be in or out of trouble. The struggle for respectability, conformity, and achievement does not come easily. Those who function inadequately neglect their children or are without resources to protect their children from the vicissitudes of poverty. These children are the most vulnerable to such troubles as delinquency, deviance, and dependence. Rather than being a part of

[37]Billingsley, *Black Families in White America,* pp. 144–45.

society, they are, in Billingsley's terms, "deserted" by their society.[38] Failure to include them within the social structure produces the results we have noted.

In our own view, much of the resentment against racial segments of the American population results from social and economic differences or social class distinctions. The negative reactions are a response more to different social class styles than to race differences alone. If this is true, there is room for optimism because social class differences can be reduced or changed if our society chooses to move in that direction. The vicious cycle of racism that causes the discrimination that leads in turn to insufficient economic and social resources that feeds back on itself can be broken. The place to begin is with socioeconomic conditions, and the motivation should come from seeing the disturbed or shattered lives of children who are products of that system. Along with Eric Hoffer, we agree that there is "ordeal" in change, but it must come because we cannot mar the lives of children forever without grievous consequences.[39]

SUMMARY

Focusing upon black children, we have examined the impacts of racism, the contention that one race or people is either superior or inferior to any other race or people by reason of genetics. We found that black children were "the little victims" of the perpetuation of racism by the white majority. When the tables are turned through special privileges going to blacks, the reverse racism arouses cries of outrage and indignation on the part of whites.

A variety of strategies provides the background against which black children have been reared. Integration into the mainstream of American society has long been the major effort of black leadership. Separatism is another strategy and seeks in-group pride and solidarity through self-help and self-imposed objectives. Militants counsel violence, and moderates counsel nonviolence.

[38]Ibid, p. 144.
[39]Eric Hoffer, *The Ordeal of Change* (New York: Harper & Row, 1963). Other sources of value are Robert Staples, "Towards a Sociology of the Black Family: A Theoretical and Methodological Assessment," *Journal of Marriage and Family*, Decade Review Pt. 2, 33, No. 1 (February 1971), 119–38; Reynolds Farley and Albert I. Hermalin, "Family Stability: A Comparison of Trends Between Blacks and Whites," *American Sociological Review*, 36, No. 1 (February 1971), 1–17, and Anthony R. Harris, "Race, Commitment to Deviance, and Spoiled Identity," *American Sociological Review*, 41, No. 3 (June 1976), 432–42.

Above all, a self-respect, a self-pride, is sought among the black minority. Black children have shown a self-hate, a self-rejection, a self-negation that demonstrates how deeply the poisons of racism penetrate the personality and guarantee the perpetuation of sustained racial discriminatory practices.

Looking for help from two character-building institutions, schools and families, we found little comfort in the evasive efforts to circumvent the newer policies of equal opportunities for all citizens. We did find that most black families were dedicated to the well-being of their children, but those in the lowest socioeconomic levels could not overcome the exigencies of impoverishment, neglect, and rejection.

We did see that the walls of racial discrimination had been and continue to be breached. In the lives of racially mixed children, we found some who could bridge the chasm between blacks and whites.

In the social class differences among black families, we found another glimmer of hope that the future can be happier for both black and white children. We noted that much of what passes as racism is linked to social class differences and that these differences are not immune to appropriate social changes, difficult as they may first appear to be.

THREE

Social institutions and childhood

7

The initial and initiating groups

Of all the major social institutions, the family has long been considered the initial and most basic influence on the lives of children. Other institutions representing education, religion, politics, or economics would, soon enough, make their influence felt, but the family was unquestionably the dominant system that shaped children's destinies.

In our times, this sociological truism has been called into question. Rather than accepting families as the primary locus of children's socialization, there is serious debate as to just how important families are in the welter of competing groups for the growth and development of young lives.

Seeking objectivity, we need to examine the antifamily factors as well as the profamily factors if we are to determine for ourselves which way the generational tides seem to be flowing.

The antifamily factors can be subdivided into external and internal forces that call for radical changes from long-established, traditional family ways. On the other hand, the profamily forces refuse to be stampeded into some promised, utopian wonderland in which children may be reared with joy, ease, and pleasure unbounded. For our own part, we wade into the troubled waters of American family life with the, hopefully, innocuous observation that children at least begin their lives in family settings or the remnants of family settings. Thus we see families as the *initial* groups that bring children into life and sustain them in their formative years. As children grow up, there is undoubtedly a sharing of the responsibilities of socialization with nonfamily agencies, but there is usually a continual turning back to families to reinforce the intimate bonds that link children with parents and related kin. Just how much more attractive and forceful nonfamily agencies are differs with individual lives but, in the main, family bonding is a powerful lodestone that gives direction and substance to most lives.

ANTIFAMILY FACTORS

Competing Institutions

Families may occupy the lion's share of children's attention, but they also operate in a matrix of other institutions that can and do diminish familial inputs. Formal schools, for example, will require the daily attendance of children beginning usually around age five. Thus, seven-twelfths of the twelve years of childhood are tied to formal training by nonfamily authorities. These may or may not support whatever families want to see emphasized in their offspring. Employment and business conditions may seem remote from the lives of children, but they touch them closely in terms of the preoccupation of fathers and mothers with earning a livelihood, with housing and neighborhood patterns, and with supplying the funding for food, clothing, recreation, transportation, and medical care. We have already seen the economic system at work in terms of social classes, and we have yet to examine just how much economic exploitation plays a part in children's lives. We will also look more closely at the politicalization of children in the chapters that lie ahead.

Probably the greatest competitor of all is the mass media. The vast literature of books, magazines and newspapers undoubtedly leaves its mark upon children. Radio, tapes, records, and films also leave an unmistakable imprint upon young children. Last, but not least, is the queen of them all, the lure of the television tube that occupies one of the most prominent positions in the homes of the nation. Television, like other mass media, seems to be a mixed blessing with vast amounts of "wasteland" interspersed now and then with tremendous achievements of drama, artistry, beauty, enchantment, and challenge. What should not be forgotten, however, is that families do have the power of turning off or on various programs or inputs. The flick of a dial remains at the control of families if they care to take the responsibility of making choices. The same applies to the books they read, the newspapers they buy, or the films they attend. Indeed, there is a time interval in the early evening called "the family hours" during which time certain programs will be encouraged and others delayed or discouraged. As some have expressed it, families may allow their possessions to possess them or they may possess their possessions.

One other development that seems to be emerging is the growth of family surrogates, family substitutes, or family adjuncts that are alleged to be necessary in a world of multiple demands upon the time, energy, and ability of adults. Day care centers, for example, are already in operation, but are in short supply and out of economic reach for families in which both mothers and fathers must work outside the home and away from their young children. Parents have been described as rank amateurs who need to be replaced by professional parents. They may merely need the reassurance that their child-rearing decisions are sensible, as Benjamin Spock has done, or they may need licensing to bring children into the world. But there is serious contention on the part of those who are most concerned about the physical, psychic, and social damage being done to children that children's caretakers be prepared professionally for the arts and science of children's socialization. The Israeli kibbutz is one possible model for the twenty-first century, and communal styles are another possibility.[1] In this context, parenting is seen as a fulltime profession in which adults earn their living in services to and with children. This is not too far removed from the socialist-communist procedures of molding future citizens to serve the greater society. In the capitalist-individualistic mode, however, it remains to be seen whether some quasi-family forms would be better suited to the professional parenting movement than some adaptations yet to be made to our changing family systems.

Competing Groups

PEERS OR COEVALS. What has been taken as the classic statement on parent-youth conflict was made by Kingsley Davis many years ago.

---

[1]See for example, Dan Leon, *The Kibbutz: A New Way of Life* (Oxford, England: Pergamon Press, 1969); Edwin Samuel, *The Structure of Society in Israel* (New York: Random House, 1969); Marvin Sussman, ed., *Non-Traditional Family Forms in the 1970's* (Minneapolis: National Council on Family Relations, 1972); Rosabeth Kanter, *Commitment and Community: Communes and Utopias in Sociological Perspective* (Cambridge, Massachusetts: Harvard University Press, 1972).

His article entitled "The Sociology of Parent-Youth Conflict" stressed the inevitability of parent-children clashes because of the rapid rate of changes that have occurred between the generations, the acceleration of socialization for children and the deceleration of socialization for their parents, the lag between the cultural content that guided the life of parents and the new cultural content of their children's lives, the physiological decrements of parents and the physiological gains or increments of their children, the practical realism of adults and the untested idealism of youth, and the collision between parental authority and youthful searches for autonomy. Complicated further by conflicting norms, competing authorities, few explicit directions as to how to exercise parental authority, concentration of need fulfillment within a very small circle of relatives, open competition for socioeconomic status outside family circles, and the rising sexual tensions of preadolescents and adolescents, the conflict between parents and children in Davis' view is inescapable.[2]

Conflict theory is further supported by the shifting of loyalties from family figures to peers or coevals. Peers are those who occupy the same status or position and have supposedly experienced common treatment, thus creating a common bond of understanding, empathy, and comraderie. Coevals are persons of the same or similar age, contemporaries who share generational experiences. While these terms could be applied to persons of all ages and with commonalities, their usage has been specifically applied to preadolescents, adolescents, and postadolescents, those who are in the process of moving out of childhood but who have not quite moved into adulthood. Peers or coevals are pertinent to our discussion because they may or may not detract from the earlier training given to children living with their families. The issue becomes one of determining to which reference group one attributes one's values and cues to behavior.

Some research favors the growing influence of peers or coevals as children explore the larger world outside their family circles. It could be said that numerous children are socialized more by their coevals than by their parents, particularly where parents have defaulted or directed their attention away from their children. In play groups, friendships, or larger crowds of children, boys and girls begin their initiation into nonfamily worlds. We suggest that these *initiating groups* are not so much detractors or supporters of familistic inputs

[2]Kingsley Davis, "The Sociology of Parent-Youth Conflict," *American Sociological Review*, 5, No. 4 (1940), 523–34; also reprinted in Mahfooz A. Kanwar, ed., *The Sociology of Family, An Interdisciplinary Approach* (Hamden, Connecticut: Linnet Books, 1971), pp. 106–21.

as they are testing grounds in which attitudes, values, and behavior learned in families are compared, contrasted, tried out, or modified.

The studies we have seen do affirm that in terms of learning how to live among one's peers, there is support for an adolescent subculture or life style that often differs strikingly from what parents might prefer.[3] But these same studies also show that peer group influence is transient, a passing phase in which children continue their moves toward adulthood. It is the adult world that beckons and not the world of the adolescent who is still undergoing metamorphosis. The weight of the evidence, then, is not that peers fix the directions in which children will fulfill their lives, but rather that parents and families are far more significant that they have heretofore been given credit.[4]

THE SOCIALIZERS AND THE SOCIALIZED. Exchange theory with its emphasis upon reciprocity is supported, for example, by Harriet Rheingold in her thoughtful essay on how infants socialize their parents.[5] The usual direction of influence is from parents to children, and this is the way most socialization processes are conceived. But interaction also occurs between children as initiators of action and parents as recipients of this action. While parents manipulate children, it should also be noted that children manipulate their parents. In the case of infants, as Rheingold observes, the manipulation is nonverbal, body language that signals approval or disapproval, reward or punishment. In crying, infants signal their distress and call for relief. The powerful aversion of adults to infantile crying brings about the search for reasons for the discomfort and for its prompt relief. In the smile of infants, reward comes to its caretakers. In the gurgles, cooing, and rudimentary vocalizing of infants as well as the recognition and grasping for familiar faces or hands, mothers and fathers receive encouragement to continue to work in behalf of their children. In a very real sense, children are the

[3]James Walters and Nick Stinnett, "Parent-Child Relationships: A Decade Review of Research," ed. Carlfred B. Broderick, *A Decade of Family Research and Action* (National Council on Family Relations, 1972), pp. 99–140; Boyd R. McCandless, "Childhood Socialization," ed. David A. Goslin, *Handbook of Socialization Theory and Research* (Chicago: Rand McNally and Company, 1969), pp. 807–10; Jerome Kagan and Robert Coles, eds., *Twelve to Sixteen: Early Adolescence* (New York: W. W. Norton & Company, Inc., 1972); E. E. LeMasters, *Parents in Modern America*, rev. ed. (Homewood, Illinois: The Dorsey Press, 1974), "Parents, Mass Media, and The Youth Peer Group," pp. 157–70.

[4]Ian P. Chand, Donald M. Crider, and Fern K. Willits, "Parent-Youth Disagreement as Perceived by Youth, A Longitudinal Study," *Youth and Society*, 6, No. 3 (March 1975), 365–75.

[5]Harriet L. Rheingold, "The Social and Socializing Infant," ed. David A. Goslin, *Handbook of Socialization Theory and Research* (Chicago: Rand McNally and Company, 1969), pp. 779–90.

teachers and parents are the students. It is the children who let their parents know when they have succeeded and when they have failed.

WOMEN'S RIGHTS AND THE RIGHTS OF OTHERS. The child-centered family has come under increasing attack by reason of the rising expectancies of women to be taken seriously as total human beings. One runs the risk of severe criticism if one upholds the traditional nuclear family in which fathers go to work to support families that consist of dependent and mutually-tied mothers and their children. James Caroll, for instance, drew the wrath of women when he published an article on "The Inevitability of the Nuclear Family."[6] The rejoinder by Kathryn Corbett pointed to women's rebellion against traditional, subordinate wife and mother roles that are changing society and the old order.[7] Corbett observed that dependable birth control methods have resulted in fewer children and that these few children are far too important to trust their lives to nuclear families that are more noted for their failures than for their successes. Children, she felt, should be entrusted to the larger "society," a practice similar to the professional parent movement we have already discussed.

PRONATALISM AND ANTINATALISM. The very beginnings of life are under serious criticism as the twentieth century draws to a close. The pronatalist and antinatalist groups are locked in combat, and the outcomes are vital to the fortunes of children.

The popular press turns out cogent publications such as *The Baby Trap*,[8] *Mother's Day Is Over*,[9] and *The Case Against Having Children*.[10] For the past twenty-five years, the United States has witnessed a marked decline in birth rates. (See Figure 7–1.) The death rates, by contrast, have been fairly low and steady over the same period of time. Accordingly, natural increase, the excess of births over deaths, is slowing down. At the same time, medical and social sciences have achieved the prolonged survival of older persons so that those who formerly focused upon the very young find that it is equally sensible to concentrate upon the elderly.[11] Life cycle specialists are keenly aware that in

[6]James W. Caroll, "The Inevitability of the Nuclear Family," *Humboldt Journal of Social Relations*, 1, No. 1 (Fall 1973), 60–65.

[7]Kathryn L. Corbett, "Rejoinder," *Humboldt Journal of Social Relations*, 1, No. 2 (Spring-Summer 1974), 146–47.

[8]Ellen Peck, *The Baby Trap* (New York: Bernard Geis Associates, 1971).

[9]Shirley L. Radl, *Mother's Day Is Over* (New York: Charterhouse, 1973).

[10]Anna and Arnold Silverman, *The Case Against Having Children* (New York: David McKay Company, Inc., 1971).

[11]Marvin R. Koller, *Social Gerontology* (New York: Random House, 1968).

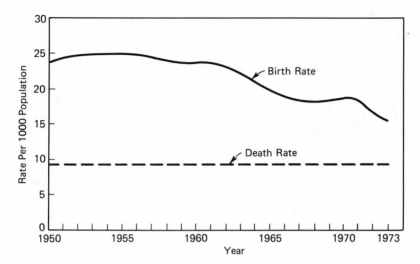

FIGURE 7-1 *Birth and Death Rates: 1950-1973*

Source: *Statistical Abstract of the United States, 1975,* p. 52.

addition to childhood as a vital area to which to direct one's attention, there is much to be gained by the study of scientific gerontology or pragmatic geriatrics.[12]

Fecundity refers to the potential number of children a woman might have. Scientists have estimated that a woman at birth has some half million eggs in her ovaries and that throughout her reproductive life she ovulates, brings to possible impregnation, some four hundred of them.[13] Taking as many intervening variables as possible into account, Eaton and Mayer have calculated that the maximum fecundity of a woman would be about twelve to fourteen live births.[14]

Fertility refers to the actual number of children a woman produces. The record for live births, according to the *Guinness Book of*

[12]Useful sources are Robert C. Atchley, *The Social Forces in Later Life, An Introduction to Social Gerontology* (Belmont, California: Wadsworth Publishing Company, 1972); Douglas C. Kimmel, *Adulthood and Aging* (New York: John Wiley & Sons, Inc., 1974); Rosamonde R. Boyd and Charles G. Oakes, eds., *Foundations of Practical Gerontology,* 2nd ed. rev. (Columbia, South Carolina: University of South Carolina Press, 1973).

[13]Leslie Aldridge Westoff and Charles F. Westoff, *From Now to Zero, Fertility, Contraception and Abortion in America* (Boston: Little, Brown and Company, 1968), p. 12.

[14]Joseph W. Eaton and Albert J. Mayer, *Man's Capacity to Reproduce* (Glencoe, Illinois: The Free Press, 1954).

World Records, was sixty-nine children born to Mrs. Fyodor Vassilet who in 27 confinements gave birth to sixteen pairs of twins, seven sets of triplets, and four sets of quadruplets.[15] Single births, however, are far more common and expected than multiple births.

Birth control or fertility control has been placed increasingly in the hands of women and they are opting for the best possible contraceptive devices or procedures to free themselves from unwanted pregnancies. The efficiencies and side-effects of such items as the birth control pill, I.U.D., or diaphragm are debated, discussed, and evaluated.[16] Contraceptive experimentation continues in the form of implantations to interrupt reproductive processes or surgical operations to sterilize permanently or temporarily vast numbers of people.

Conception control is only part of the broader picture. Interrupting pregnancies so that they are not carried to full term is also involved. The easing of legal restraints against abortion has made this alternative to unwanted pregnancies and children increasingly available. While many rejoice at this triumph of liberalized abortion laws that has been called "the right to control over my body" by many women, there has been a countermove that has mobilized opponents under the banner of "the right to life" movement. The issues over who shall prevail and who shall have to suffer or die are complicated and often charged with emotion.[17] Raymond Adamek has provided a most useful source that summarizes the central arguments of both proabortionists and the right-to-life protagonists in his position paper, "Abortion, Personal Freedom, and Public Policy."[18] From our concern with children, the issue involves the personal freedoms of those who have already been born and are experiencing life versus those who might-be-born and have yet to experience life. In our society that calls for freedom of choice, the moral dilemma has been placed squarely in the hands of thoughtful adults who wish to determine for themselves how they should act under a given set of circumstances.

Much of the pronatalist and antinatalist conflict is related to the much larger and broader perspective of *population control.* This, in turn, is an integral part of growing concern over the environment that

[15]Norris and Ross McWhirter, *Guinness Book of World Records,* rev. and enlarged ed. (New York: Sterling Publishing Co., Inc. 1969), p. 18.
[16]See for example, Donna Cherniak and Allan Feingold, eds., *Birth Control Handbook,* rev. (Montreal: Journal Offset, Inc. February, 1972).
[17]See for example, Dr. and Mrs. J. C. Willke, *Handbook on Abortion, The Case for the Unborn* (Cincinnati, Ohio: Hiltz Publishing Co., 1972). See also, Germain Grisez, *Abortion: The Myths, the Realities, and the Arguments* (New York and Cleveland: Corpus Books, 1970).
[18]Raymond J. Adamek, "Abortion, Personal Freedom, and Public Policy," *The Family Coordinator* (October 1974), pp. 411–19.

our technological, urbanized-industrialized society has brought into being. The rapid dissipation of the limited resources of land, water, and air calls into question whether the population should continue to grow, to "double" itself at shorter and shorter intervals, and eventually create unbearably crowded conditions. Travelers to foreign lands have often been admonished "not to drink the water." Those who come to our shores may have to be instructed "not to breathe the air" if pollution continues apace.

The question of population control is essentially whether or not "people pollution" exists. Unlimited reproduction of children within the finite space and resources of the United States poses a threatening problem to some and a solvable problem for others. A Zero Population Growth or ZPG movement has been underway for some time in the United States if not in many other developing nations in the world. The threat lies in the quality of life possible in a crowded world, and the "solvable" problem rests upon decisions as to what sort of social system men and women decide to develop for themselves. Leslie and Charles Westoff have detailed where Americans stand in the twentieth century and where we may be in the early twenty-first century in *From Now to Zero, Fertility, Contraception, and Abortion in America.*[19] The objective would be to reach a replacement rate of about two children for each married couple.

But there is "a fly in the ointment" and we must credit the insightful exposition of Kingsley Davis, the same Kingsley Davis who provided the classic "Sociology of Parent-Youth Conflict" with which we started this discussion of parents and children.[20] In a closely argued essay, "Zero Population Growth: The Goal and the Means," Davis urges us to consider how the right of couples to have the number of children they want can be defended while the public policy is ostensibly to achieve birth limitation. As Davis expresses it:

> . . . The key lies in our unstated background. Our mores were formed when societies could survive only with a birth rate thrice that required by a modern death rate. Built into the social order, therefore, are values, norms, and incentives that motivate people to bear and rear children. These cultural and institutional inheritances form the premises of our thinking. Respected leaders of society are not about to disavow them, nor is the general public likely to do so. Accordingly, what is strategically required, if one

[19]Westoff, *From Now to Zero.*
[20]Kingsley Davis, "Zero Population Growth: The Goal and the Means," *Daedalus* (Fall 1973), 102, No. 4 Proceedings of the American Academy of Arts and Sciences, Issue on "The No-Growth Society," pp. 15–30.

wants to be a population policy leader, is a formula that appears to reduce reproduction without offending the mores that support it. The formula is to interpret the social problem as an individual one and the solution as a technological matter.[21]

Davis concludes:

> Thus the "population problem" is not a technological problem. It is not something the definition of which is universally agreed upon and the solution to which awaits only the discovery of an effective means. It is not like yellow fever or wheat rust. It is a social problem in the sense that it involves a conflict of wants. People want families and children. If they did not want families and children, it would be technologically easy to satisfy them. But they do want families and children. That being the case, they are not whole hearted about population control. They do not want run-away population growth either, but they want to avoid it painlessly. They want a solution that leaves them the freedom to have five children if they wish. In short, they want a miracle.[22]

Changes and Challenges to Traditional Families

Finally, we need to recognize the tremendous changes and significant challenges being made to traditional family life. These, too, portend a different future for children than we heretofore imagined. Those of us who have worked in the family field for twenty or thirty years are keenly aware of the reversal of attitudes that we have witnessed in our students. At one time, it was taken for granted that those who came to study marriage and family came to learn how to "work within the system," to adopt, to adapt, to adjust themselves to an established, time-tested system. Such is not necessarily the case at the present. It can be likened to entering a class in geology only to find that most of the students are skeptical about rocks or even are antirocks! There is, however, considerable reason for taking this stance.

Concerning "the state of our unions," all is not well. Leontine Young speaks of the American family as *The Fractured Family.*[23] Cuber and Harroff found five recurring configurations of families among the most affluent: the Conflict-Habituated, the Devitalized, the Passive-Congenial, the Vital, and the Total.[24] Far too many operated at a "utili-

[21]Ibid, p. 21.

[22]Ibid, pp. 28–29.

[23]Leontine Young, *The Fractured Family* (New York: McGraw-Hill Book Company, 1973).

[24]John F. Cuber and Peggy B. Harroff, *The Significant Americans, A Study of Sexual Behavior Among the Affluent* (New York: Appleton-Century-Crofts, 1965), pp. 43–65.

tarian" face value level that was moderately acceptable than at a deeper "intrinsic" level that was truly fulfilling. Divorce, desertion, and disillusionment are commonplace events that far too often mask the tragedies of absent or missing fathers and mothers.[25] Jessie Bernard wonders about *The Future of Marriage* when she puts together some of the salient "random events" such as the women's liberation movement, the concept of no-fault divorces, the relaxation of abortion laws, the improvement and spread of contraceptive information to both the married and the unmarried, the push for zero population growth, the proliferation of communes, the rise of adolescent subculture, and the greater toleration of homosexuality.[26] Daniel Yankelovich writes about *The New Morality* of American youth in the seventies.[27] Larry and Joan Constantine have studied group marriages in which three or more persons experiment with living together.[28] Gail Fullerton offers her view of family interaction, conflicts, and alternatives in *Survival in Marriage.*[29] These are not mentioned in a negative sense but are meant to suggest that sober contemplation of American marriage and family life is in order if they are to serve children, their parents, and their grandparents.

There is nothing astoundingly new about the finding of numerous studies that husbands and wives tend to report a steady deterioration of satisfaction with their marriages from the high ecstatic peaks of their weddings and honeymoons to the dull, prosaic, depressed malaise of their midlife.[30] What is relatively new is that research has begun to correlate this disenchantment of married couples with the arrival and socialization of their children. Bernard, for example, notes the way children seem "to whoosh" through their parents' marriage, sorely testing the husband-wife relationship until, at last, they are launched into the nonfamily world.[31] Once the children have grown up and left their parents alone then, as Rollins and Feldman have shown, marital satisfactions improve, rise, and reach new heights quite similar to the

[25]See for example, Reuben Hill and Donald A. Hansen, "Families Under Stress," ed. Harold T. Christensen, *Handbook of Marriage and the Family* (Chicago: Rand McNally and Company, 1964), pp. 782–819; Gerald R. Leslie, *The Family in Social Context,* 3rd ed. (New York: Oxford University Press, 1976), "Divorce and Desertion," pp. 673–717.

[26]Jessie Bernard, *The Future of Marriage* (New York: World Publishing, 1972).

[27]Daniel Yankelovich, *The New Morality, A Profile of American Youth in the 70's* (New York: McGraw-Hill Book Company, 1974).

[28]Larry L. and Joan M. Constantine, *Group Marriage* (New York: The Macmillan Company, 1973).

[29]Gail Putney Fullerton, *Survival in Marriage, Introduction to Family Interaction, Conflicts, and Alternatives* (New York: Holt, Rinehart and Winston, Inc., 1972).

[30]For pertinent discussion on husband-wife satisfaction see Letha and John Scanzoni, *Men, Women and Change, A Sociology of Marriage and Family* (New York: McGraw-Hill Book Company, 1975), pp. 254–360.

[31]Bernard, *Future of Marriage,* pp. 62–63.

earlier period before children ever appeared on the scene.[32] In a more recent reevaluation, Rollins and Cannon believe that much of this U-shaped patterning of marital satisfaction is tied to role strains that are compounded by the presence and care of children.[33] Wesley Burr found much the same thing except that he found that the problems associated with school-age children were the most difficult rather than the adolescent or prelaunching stage when teen-age children were close to the time when they would leave home.[34]

Few would argue that the arrival of children simplifies marriage and automatically strengthens the bonds between husbands and wives. Rather, there is more logic in the *testing* of relationships between men and women who have brought children into this world.

This is the rationale behind Margaret Mead's proposal of a "two-step marriage" in which the first step of friendship, companionship, and personal fulfillment may or may not be followed by a second step of procreating and socializing children under a renewed agreement of strong mutual commitment and resolve to provide a firm foundation upon which children may build lives of their own.

For those who know themselves well enough not to become parents, there are nonprocreational alternatives such as mutual cohabitation, group marriage, or "open marriage" in which extramarital relations are acceptable.[35] These all rely, of course, upon the effective use of contraceptive measures. Homosexual liaisons also should be mentioned in this context because there seem to be increased efforts to bring homosexuality "out in the open" rather than keep it clandestine because the majority approves only of heterosexual relationships.[36]

Motherhood and fatherhood by choice and not by chance is, of course, not yet realized. There are, in reality, numerous accidental, menopausal, illegitimate, unexpected, or unwanted children. These still need love and care in order to flourish. The responsibility for their

[32]Boyd C. Rollins and Harold Feldman, "Marital Satisfaction Over the Family Life Cycle," *Journal of Marriage and the Family,* 32, No. 1 (February 1970), 20–28.

[33]Boyd C. Rollins and Kenneth L. Cannon, "Marital Satisfaction Over the Family Life Cycle: A Reevaluation," *Journal of Marriage and the Family,* 36, No. 2 (May 1974), 271–82.

[34]Wesley R. Burr, "Satisfaction with Various Aspects of Marriage Over the Life Cycle: A Random Middle Class Sample," *Journal of Marriage and the Family,* 32, No. 1 (February 1970), 29–42. See also, Eleanore Braun Luckey and Joyce Koym Bain, "Children: A Factor in Marital Satisfaction," *Journal of Marriage and the Family* 32, No. 1 (February 1970), 43–44.

[35]Nena O'Neill and George O'Neill, *Open Marriage, A New Life Style for Couples* (New York: M. Evans and Company, Inc., 1972); Thomas C. McGinnis and Dana G. Finnegan, *Open Family and Marriage, A Guide to Personal Growth* (Saint Louis: The C. V. Mosby Company, 1976).

[36]See for a useful discussion, "Homosexuality," in Ira L. Reiss, *Family Systems in America,* 2nd ed. (Hinsdale, Illinois: The Dryden Press, 1976), pp. 209–26.

presence falls upon the adults who conceived them. If for whatever reason these adults cannot and will not take appropriate care of their offspring, then the greater society or community assumes the responsibilities. Adoption and foster care are social alternatives that have worked in the past, but even here, conditions can be far from satisfactory. There have been errors in placements, mistreatments, and child rejection. Untold numbers are held to be "unadoptable" because of some physical, mental, or social defects.

PROFAMILY FACTORS

While there have been serious attacks upon nuclear families for years because they have been less than satisfying for many, there remains a vast majority who can and have found satisfaction within fairly traditional structures and processes. Marriages continue in impressive numbers although fluctuations occur as certain conditions develop such as recessions or improved economic opportunities.[37] When men and women do not choose to remain together, they more freely terminate their marriages, but they do not necessarily reject the marriage and family system as it currently stands. These seek partnerships with more compatible persons, having learned what it is they really seek rather than what they thought they wanted at an earlier, less experienced age. Their past quarrels and tribulations emerged from *interpersonal relationships* and not necessarily from "the system" of heterosexual monogamy. If two persons cannot get along together, how then with more complicated, multiperson matrices is there greater guarantee of personal happiness? The answer is determined by the depth or intensity of relationships that people seek. If it is to be shallow, fleeting, or without concern for others, then the variety of experimentation and multipersonal ties is supported. If, however, there is interest in total devotion to each other's well-being, then the heterosexual dyad becomes the key link in marriage and in the children that marriage produces.

The Primary Nature of the Nuclear Family

Charles H. Cooley is credited with the conceptualization of *primary* and *secondary* groups.[38] Primary groups were characterized as involving the whole personalities of their participants and not merely

---

[37]See *Statistical Abstract of the United States, 1975* (Washington, D.C.: U.S. Bureau of Census, 1975), p. 51.
[38]Charles H. Cooley, *Social Organization* (New York: Charles Scribner's Sons, 1915), pp. 23–24.

fragments or segments of personalities as secondary groups do. Primary groups demand and achieve face-to-face relationships over long periods of time, while secondary groups rely heavily upon intervening media such as pictures, letters, advertisements, and formal forms of discourse that are used intermittently. There is a spontaneous, unrehearsed, relaxed informality in primary groups, whereas in secondary groups one behaves among functionaries who follow highly structured, formal, and routine procedures. In secondary groups, one acquires knowledge deliberately or consciously in rather sharp contrast to primary groups in which training is subtle, indirect, or unconsciously given. Primary groups are relatively small while secondary groups can become quite huge.

All these criteria are well met within families which makes them the most vivid and real example of primary groups to be found. In families, interest is fixed upon the overall personalities of each participant and not some portion of their personal attributes such as being a good employee, effective student, or capable professional. In families, members are often brutally frank with each other whereas in nonfamily situations more tact and restraint are observed so that associates or other persons with whom they deal are not offended. Their contacts in families are intimate, eye-to-eye, and not handled by written communications, commercial inducements, or formal publications. Cecily and Albert Dreyer call for more study of the family dinner time as an excellent setting for sociological study of family life[39] just as Bossard and Boll did some years ago.[40]

Obviously, families consume tremendous amounts of time and consequently have tremendous impact upon participants. The exposure to parents, siblings, and other relatives is sustained or prolonged and occupies, in a sense, a lifetime. Whether near and immediate or far away and only remembered, the ties that bind family members last a lifetime. One can have only one set of biological parents or grandparents. Brothers and sisters are *always* brothers and sisters whether they appreciate each other's company or not. Other kinship ties such as being a nephew or a niece, a grandson or a grand-daughter, a cousin, or an uncle or an aunt may be close or distant but are inescapable. If relatives are supportive, congenial, and appreciated, the exchanges and contacts are savored. Even if they are bitter, cold, or unconcerned, the affinity bond is still there despite protests to the contrary.

[39]Cecily Dreyer and Albert S. Dreyer, "Family Dinner Time as an Unique Behavior Habitat," *Family Process,* 12, No. 3 (September 1973), 291–301.
[40]James H. S. Bossard and Eleanor Boll, *The Sociology of Child Development,* 3rd ed. (New York: Harper & Row, Publishers, Inc., 1960), pp. 229–43.

Individuals cannot hide in the small numbers that make up nuclear families. The slightest behavior is subjected to close scrutiny and endless comment. The growing child appears to be under almost constant surveillance, and he or she must answer to family members for errors, or may receive their approval for accomplishments that contribute to family pride.

In sum, families are the *initial* builders of personalities, and their handiwork can be seen in the immediate lives of children as well as in the long-range consequences when they become mature adults.

There is need, however, to understand that families do not operate in a social vacuum. They are a part of a larger system of primary and secondary groups that do function to nullify or blur the impacts of family life.

Clyde Kluckhohn in discussing the infancy and childhood of the Navajo people makes this same point. He wrote:

> The most striking theoretical question which emerges from this consideration of some of the main aspects of Navajo infancy is this: how can this picture be reconciled with the facts of Navajo witchcraft, or the states of morbid melancholia and endemic uneasiness which have been well documented for adult Navajo? How can the anxiety level be so high among a people where infants are nursed whenever they want to be, where childhood disciplines are so permissive, where there is genuine affection for children? If the writings of certain psychoanalysts were literally true (and the whole truth), adult Navajos ought to have calm, beautifully adjusted personalities. In spite of the fact that Navajo infants receive a maximum of protection and gratification, they tend to be moody and worry a great deal when they become adults.
>
> The explanation may rest in part upon the frequent ill health of Navajo children, upon teasing, upon refusal of the breast to toddlers, and upon delays in response to crying or upon other factors (such as genetic ones) that have been overlooked. But the main point is probably not that the theorists are utterly wrong, *but that they claim too much for the earliest years* (italics ours) and do not pay enough attention to later events and to the total situation in which the mature person finds himself.[41]

Families, then, are fundamental to personality formation, but are only the first of a series of primary and secondary groups that will make

[41]Clyde Kluckhohn, "Some Aspects of Navajo Infancy and Early Childhood," *Psychoanalysis and the Social Sciences*, Vol. 1, (New York: International Universities Press, Inc., 1947), pp. 85–86.

critical contributions to life histories. Even in what must be called "nonfamily" associations, there remains some retention of family relationships, some effort to be "like" a family. These quasi-families encourage addressing each other as "brothers" and "sisters" or referring to their "founding fathers" or their "one big happy family." It is pure fabrication to use such terms in nonfamily situations, but it satisfies the longing that many people have for warmth, security, and affection in a world that appears to be cold, insecure, and lacking in consideration for human needs or morale. Despite attack, criticisms, and shortcomings, family life does endure and shows tremendous adaptability because it serves its participants through its vital functions.

Functions of Families in Relation to Children

The functions performed by families in behalf of their children are probably numerous, but in the interest of brevity, it is important to identify, at least, some eight vital functions. These are: (1) to serve as a basic culture carrier, (2) to interpret and simplify a complex world, (3) to discipline, (4) to protect, (5) to give freedom, (6) to problem-solve, (7) to enrich family life, and (8) in sum, to develop personalities. These are to be understood as universal functions, applicable to all families with children, unless otherwise qualified. Furthermore, they are operational particularly within contemporary American society despite claims that modern families are rapidly being "defunctionalized" or losing their functions to nonfamily agencies. In the main, we seek to identify and explain these functions and not to advise children's caretakers how to perform these functions "properly" according to some middle-class norm.

AS CULTURE CARRIER. Culture, an abstraction of all the ways people in a society live, cannot promote itself without appropriate agents. A prime carrier of a particular culture is a family unit within a specific societal context. As we have noted, this is usually the first human grouping into which a child is brought. In the child's most impressionable years, family units are charged with responsibilities for its care and upbringing. As we have also noted, family influences run deep and are felt well into the adult years.

The family serves as society's representative and chief spokesman as far as the child is concerned. It must convey the message that eventually he or she will become part of the larger group and occupy some particular status within it. The family will bring to the child, according to its ability to comprehend, the ways of the society to which it belongs, detail upon detail, item after item, and part by part until much of the fabric of social life is unveiled. Thus the child will be acculturated in much the same style as the people who have come before him or her. If the process fails, falls short in some ways, however, the child runs the risk of becoming a misfit, a threat to human company.

Despite the seeming chaotic state of living that some assign to an industrialized, urbanized, high-energy society such as ours, there are rules to social living. Before participating in the game of life, the child is schooled by his or her family to learn what these regulations are. There are things that one must do and there are things that one must not do. There is a whole language to learn, and the child must become familiar with both its technical aspects and its idioms, the subtle meanings behind words, the masks that sometimes hide more pointed ideas. There is a cultural logic to pursue from first premise to final conclusion. There is a cultural philosophy to develop that gives both rhyme and reason to an otherwise confusing world. There are kinship ties to understand so that one knows just how one stands in relationship to others. There are cultural implements to use that can be of considerable help or which can become exceedingly dangerous to the careless user. There are dangers to avoid and there are worthy cultural goals to pursue. These are some of the major cultural items that the family carries from its greater society and attempts to introduce to its children.

AS INTERPRETER. Families select only portions of a culture to convey to their children and consequently neglect other elements that could have been emphasized. In a sense, the family serves as a screen that allows through only those portions of its culture that it deems worthy of attention or that it is capable of passing along. In this manner, the family does bias the information it conveys to help shape the child. Families may offer the fine, the spiritual, or the noble. They may, on the contrary, expose the child to the worst, the vulgar, or the most unworthy portions of its culture. These value-laden terms, of course, are judged from the point of view of those who participate directly in a given culture and not from the perspective of outside observers. By this conscious or unconscious selective process, families explain to children their cultural universe.

Children have been called walking question marks. The answers to their questions will be based on the family's knowledge or understanding of the particular subject. If family members are prejudiced or ignorant about certain matters, it is within this context that the child comes to view the world. If, on the other hand, the family participants are well informed and objective, a calm, adequate, thoughtful interpretation of the question is given. It is difficult to visualize circumstances in which a culture reaches a child untouched, unhampered, or unaltered by the processes of family communication. Like newspapers, families twist the news to the consumer to fit their preconceived views. The presentation of all the facts in a given case without bias of any sort is an ideal condition that is rarely, if ever, achieved. Families may not be trying deliberately to distort cultural characteristics, but unconsciously, by use of individualistic and highly selected examples, this is what occurs. Children, then, see the cultural world through the eyes of their family.

AS DISCIPLINER. Unfettered freedom to do as one pleases does not exist. To create an ego which has no regard for other egos guarantees a collision course with others with dire results. Families have some responsibilities to control children, to restrain natural urges and outbursts, and to rein in behavior that can only lead to conflict with others in the society.

Certainly one does not break a young colt to harness immediately. There must be a time for kicking up one's heels, for sheer energy expansion, and for letting adults carry the serious social burdens. To place a heavy weight on a fragile back can only serve to break or harm it unduly. But, as a young one gains strength, there does come a time for understanding that carefree days are over.

So it is with children. They are judged to be entitled, and most cultures regard it as their birthright, to be freed for a time of responsibility, to be allowed to play and to seek only fun. In time, children do grow up and must put aside childish behavior and childish goals. Surely they will rebel as discipline intrudes upon their pursuit of pleasures. But society will have its way, and the family is the initial group to apply fairly strong measures, if necessary, to prepare children for adulthood.

Discipline connotes for some a harshness and cruelty to the defenseless. Discipline can, however, be gentle, persuasive, firm, fair, sensible, and consistent. Its virtue lies in the strength of persons who can act in concert. It exerts pressures in socially approved directions so that paths are cleared and society can be ongoing. It pools energy rather than disperses it. Persons learn to discipline themselves by choice if they are ever to live effectively with others. Self-discipline in harmony with a person's sociocultural environment is the ultimate goal and is not easily or automatically reached.

AS PROTECTOR. Unfortunately, there are potential dangers that await children who may stray or venture away from the guardianship of their families. Some societies live under more precarious circumstances than others, but in all of them, there still lurks serious trouble for vulnerable, naive, unsuspecting children. One of the most life-supporting functions that families perform is to guard children from harm until they command both strength and judgment to cope with potential threats.

There was a time when it was taken for granted that female children would be overprotected in rather great contrast to the underprotection accorded male children. The solicitous care given females accounted for their more gentle nature, social responsiveness, keener interest in interpersonal harmony, and rejection of brutal, coarse, or cruel aspects of human treatment. Male aggressiveness, rough-and-tumble behavior, direct manners, and seeming unconcern for social niceties were understandable derivatives of their relative independence.

How much of this remains in the present is not really known, but in the unisex-equality syndrome, we would surmise that there is mounting pressure to shed the overprotective treatment of women and the underprotective treatment of men. More likely, what exists in the present is a mixture of the newer efforts to avoid sex-typing by opening up opportunities for young girls and women and for liberating young boys and men from treating females as fragile, dainty, dependent, subordinate beings.

Parents, as well as many others, are puzzled as to which tactic or strategy to adopt when it comes to their female and male children. Until the time comes when American society, if not the world, becomes totally committed to male and female equality, there is guaranteed dissonance between the sexes over the extent to which sexual differences must be taken into account and the extent to which they can be ignored.

AS FREEDOM-GIVER. In providing protection, there is some intrusion upon personal freedom and, in American society at least where personal freedom is prided, parents are caught between controlling and restraining their children and attempting to maximize their opportunities for personal freedom. Numerous children have been quick to pick up the promise of personal freedoms and have taunted their elders with "It is a free country, isn't it? Why can't I do as I please?"

The problem, in our view, involves the failure of so many Americans to grasp the dual nature of freedom with both negative and positive features. Americans have tended to stress *negative freedom* that calls for no prohibitions upon personal conduct. With the Declaration of Independence now moving into its third century of existence, there is the bold assertion that is a "self-evident truth" that persons are entitled to "life, liberty, and the pursuit of happiness." The Bill of Rights later asserted that individuals must not be stopped from such "inalienable rights" as assembling, reading, petitioning, worshipping, or bearing arms. All too vivid in our memories are the cries of outrage that came when the massing of civil rights advocates in the 1960s and the Vietnam protesters of the 1970s was held by some government officials as unlawful.

Positive freedom, however, means encouraging persons to develop their capacities and their abilities to achieve some worthy goals. Positive freedom is supportive and enabling.

Public schools, for instance, are in keeping with positive freedom. They are allegedly designed to bring out the best qualities of children so that they may grow emotionally, intellectually, and socially. At the college level, state supported schools invite young adults to enter fields of their choice at the least possible expense. There is discipline, self-control, and dedication in the process, but it is discipline and control that is freely chosen.

Translated for parents, positive freedom means that parents will not only say that they will not stop their youngsters from reaching for their goals, but they will help them achieve their goals to the best of their abilities. The help, which may be financial or emotional support, is the fuel that motivates the young into constructive actions. Not everyone will achieve their desired goals, but they must match their capabilities with their objectives and, if they fall short or fail, must seek the appropriate usage of their respective talents or limitations.

AS PROBLEM-SOLVER. There would be no problem if there were clearcut guidelines as to how to act under every condition, but such is far from the case when it comes to the day-to-day decisions concerning children that must be made by parents. What is "proper"? What is "fair"? What is "the right thing to do"? Parents must play their parts by ear, so to speak. Although too many operate on impulse, mood, or sheer chance, others take their roles seriously and carefully weigh the evidence before deciding what should be done in a specific situation.

The seemingly trivial decisions to speak to children in certain tones of voice, to allow or to refuse to allow certain actions, to punish or reward behavior, to extend or withhold love, to shame or appreciate, to listen or not listen to explanations are long remembered in the memories of young minds. Most parents must act on occasion with minimal information at hand and are consequently prone to make split-second decisions on matters of grave importance to their children. It is not an enviable task, but one that is carried out daily by parents whether they like it or not. Parents have asked themselves, "Where did we go wrong?" The answer may lie in the incident that they held to be trivial but which turned out to be momentous and filled with significance in the lives of their children. Even the decision not to decide remains a decision nevertheless.

AS ENRICHER OF FAMILY LIFE. For many people, the struggle to make a living disallows living itself. But for the many who are above the poverty or subsistence levels, there is an important function in making family life as interesting, exciting, stimulating, challenging, and pleasing as possible.

Young adults contemplating marriage and their future families ask, "What is there for couples to talk about for so many years? What is there for couples to do together for two, three, four, or five decades?" They visualize a dull, routine, prosaic existence that "turns them off."

There is no quick, easy answer to such questions. For one thing, there are routines or solutions to problems that work for some couples and not for others. For another, there are individual and couple-oriented alternatives in abundance, and we would be in error to suggest only a few and not even mention other possibilities. We remember John Cuber's definition that "happiness is what happy people have," and what thrills some couples leaves others completely cold. Our only concern is that children be privileged to experience as varied, as stimulating, as interesting family experiences as possible under the leadership of thoughtful and sensitive parents. Failure in these measures means that both parents and children will seek satisfaction in nonfamily areas or have already done so.

AS PERSONALITY-DEVELOPER. Personality is the subjective reflection of all that goes into a person's makeup, namely one's physical qualities, emotional state, and social experiences. Sociologists have been close to the truth when they have called families "the cradles of personality," in our terms, the initial entities that mold each person's special combination of overt and covert characteristics. Some have wisely observed that when you touch a child, you touch their parents. The marks may or may not be visible or manifested at some specific point in time, but they are there nevertheless. Some would go as far as saying that family experiences penetrate so deeply that they can never be erased. It is this personality that is formed within the first twelve years of life that becomes the chief function of families.

There is something to be said for what some sociologists call "the placement function" of families in which they provide entry into the social class system of their society. As we noted in our discussion of social classes, lifetime moves may be vertical or horizontal, and a prime factor in these moves is the particular personality organization of the individual. Just what personality attributes should be encouraged and which should be discouraged depends largely upon how families view their larger society. If families see their society as competitive, then they may strive to inculcate aggressiveness, self-confidence, and decisiveness. If they interpret their society as essentially a cooperative one, then they may promote the corresponding qualities of conciliation, consideration, generosity, self-effacement, and the like. It remains deep within the personality, however, that families make themselves felt in the lives of their children. This is the heritage families bequeath to their young regardless of their social class status.

SUMMARY

The families in which children begin their lives are no longer assumed to be the primary source of the influences that mold the remainder of their lives. Indeed, there seems to be an array of competing groups, institutions, movements, and social forces that we have identified as antifamily factors. We have held that families are, at least, the initial groups that give children life and provide the earliest and most sustained contacts and inputs during the most impressionable years.

Competing institutions like formal schools may or may not reinforce what families desire in their children. Mass media, particularly television, crowd family life into social corners and offer programmed enticements that may or may not be in the best interests of children as far as their parents are concerned. There is a growing movement to provide professional parents who are paid for their services and expertise while parents who are preoccupied with other matters turn away from their children to labor in the economic vineyards.

Peers or coevals, too, provide generational refuge from parents who have been more influenced by the past than they are by the present. Loyalties and behavior cues come from these peers and coevals rather than parents or other family members. The ideas and values presented first by families are tested in reality with peers and coevals. While the adolescent period is particularly marked by peer group influences, studies indicate that these influences are a passing rather than an enduring phase in the lives of individuals. Children moving out of their childhood may try out their wings a distance from their family nests, but they soon return to continue their movement toward independence and adulthood.

It is important to remember in connection with socialization that there is considerable reciprocity between those who are socializers and those who are being socialized. We demonstrated this exchange theory in terms of the nonverbal influences infants have upon their parents.

In this chapter, we noted that women's rights have become another source that requires a change in the stance that families are primary in the lives of children. We discussed how pronatalism and antinatalism are counterforces that have much significance in the years that lie ahead. We tended to agree with Davis when he pointed out the inconsistency of calling for population control while retaining the older mores of choosing the numbers of children families will bring into the world. Finally, we observed the serious criticisms of traditional nuclear family living and the mounting interest in experimentation. Children do put a strain upon husband-wife relationships and upon entire families, but the strains are not enduring, and men and women achieve renewed heights of satisfaction in their more mature years.

Turning to profamily factors, we suggested that interpersonal relationships were more important to consider than the "systems" in which these relationships occurred. Compounding relationships were far from guarantees of satisfaction, and many seem to be attracted to them based more on what they may derive from them rather than what they can contribute to others.

We noted that families were living examples of primary groups who can and do affect the lives of their participants. There are other primary groups that continue the socialization process, but families enjoy the advantages (some would negatively say risk the disadvantages) of initiating the processes.

The central functions of families remain relatively intact although they are carried out in different ways than in the distant or recent past. In behalf of children, families serve as culture carriers, interpreters of that culture, discipliners, protectors, givers of freedom in both the negative and positive sense, problem resolvers, enrichers of family life, and, finally, basic molders of personality attributes. As Mark Twain once observed about the premature announcement of his death, families are not yet extinct despite announcements that they are in disarray or dying.

8

Education

or

miseducation of children

The normative expectations are that formal education will follow after families or family substitutes have had rather exclusive opportunities to raise children to about five or six years of age. From five or six years of age to about seventeen or eighteen, schools build upon the foundations of personal qualities laid down by families in their respective children. Families and family backgrounds are never far removed from the compulsory schooling their children receive and, indeed, serve to sustain or hamper whatever input formal schooling provides. Nevertheless, the efforts of schools to affect the lives of children merit our attention in their own right.

We are concerned about the whole range of formal educational experiences from nursery and kindergarten levels through college and postcollege levels, but because we focus upon children twelve years of age or younger, we concentrate our attention upon the elementary levels in this chapter. There is a distinction between public and private schools that reflects social class, religious, ethnic, and regional differences, but we will be focusing on the public schools up to and including the first six grades. These elementary levels are especially important because the maximal proportions of youngsters are enrolled in them. Table 8-1 shows that while the kindergarten level enrolls about 87 percent of eligible children, the elementary grades approach 99 percent of eligible children or higher. It is not until the junior and senior high school levels that enrollments begin to fall in terms of percentages of eligibles. Those past high school mainly take the option of not enrolling in college, and as age increases, the percentage of those who continue their formal college and post-college education decreases.

The most recent available data shows that elementary schools deal with some 30 to 34 million children out of the total 58 to 59 million persons enrolled in elementary, secondary, and higher education facilities throughout the United States of America.[1] Some 1,317,000 elementary classroom teachers, public and private, perform their professional duties in 62,749 public schools and 14,372 private schools.[2] As Table 8-2 shows, these are mainly women teachers although the numbers of men teachers have grown markedly. The sheer magnitude of the elementary school numbers involved suggests that we exercise some caution in our macrosociological analyses, but it is of paramount importance that we grapple with some of the criticisms that have been leveled at "the school years" of children. Our aim is not so much to resolve the issues to everyone's satisfaction, as it is to provide a sociological perspec-

---

[1]*Digest of Education Statistics, 1975 Ed.* (Washington, D.C.: Department of Health, Education, and Welfare), p. 6.
[2]Ibid, p. 11.

TABLE 8-1 **Percentages of Eligible Age Categories Enrolled in Formal Schools, The United States, October, 1974**

Years of Age	Percentage Enrolled in Formal Schools
5	87
6	98.7
7–9	99.1
10–13	99.5
14–15	97.9
16–17	87.9
18–19	43.1
20–24	21.4
25–29	9.6
30–39	5.7

Source: *Digest of Education Statistics, 1975 Edition,* Washington, D.C.: Department of Health, Education, and Welfare, p. 9.

TABLE 8-2 Elementary School Teachers, Public and Private, Including Kindergarten, By Sex, 1929-30 and 1973-1974

Academic Year	Numbers of Men	Numbers of Women
1929-1930	68,705	633,819
1939-1940	70,187	569,860
1949-1950	58,407	607,258
1959-1960	124,566	828,865
1969-1970	191,024	1,080,443
1973-1974	213,123	1,114,857

Source: *Digest of Education Statistics, 1975 Edition,* Washington, D.C.: Department of Health, Education, and Welfare, p. 10.

tive so that the points of contention can be seen more clearly and can, hopefully, be dealt with for the benefit of young children.

CRITICISMS OF CONTEMPORARY EDUCATION

Equality or Inequality of Educational Opportunity

Once public education was established as one of the major responsibilities of local and state governments so that children from all social classes, from all walks of life, could acquire at least the rudiments of knowledge that would serve them in adulthood, a Pandora's box was opened. The common public school supported through public taxation did not become a great "leveler" or "equalizer" of opportunity as some believed it would be. Instead, public schools continued to reflect the diversity, the complexity, and the inequality of life styles in the larger society. Indeed, some have charged that public schools work consciously or unconsciously to magnify social inequities and so become part of the problem they were allegedly to resolve. Race, ethnicity, religion, rurality or urbanity, sex, and the overriding social class variables are not nullified, modified, or counterbalanced as much as they are reinforced, sustained, or enlarged upon by the public schools. It is a serious charge and one that has troubled and continues to trouble sensitive, concerned, dedicated professional educators.

Studies in major cities such as Chicago, New York, and Detroit confirmed the hypotheses of long-run discrimination in terms of facilities, investments, and staff.[3] What came to be known as the Coleman

[3]Chicago Urban League, *An Equal Chance for Education* (1960); Patricia Cayo Sexton, *Education and Income* (New York: Viking Press, 1961).

Report was commissioned by the U.S. Congress in 1965 to assess the full magnitude of inequalities by surveying 600,000 children in grades one, three, six, nine, and twelve.[4] Some four thousand schools were involved in the study and documented what was already suspected, namely, that racial, ethnic, or economic discrimination existed and was supported in the public schools. The gaps were not as large as some critics believed between lower and middle-class children when it came to school facilities, but what did manifest itself was the discrepancy in performance on achievement tests between privileged and disprivileged children that grew even larger as they stayed in school up to and including the twelfth grade. Minority children were about two or three years behind white majority children at the junior and senior high school levels.

As Ernest Campbell put it, "One must indeed be remarkably insensitive to the nature of learning to miss this basic point: those whose nonschool environments are least equipped to provide or support meaningful educational experiences are placed in schools that provide the least stimulating interpersonal environments for learning, whereas those whose home environments most typically provide knowledge and encourage curiosity attend schools that provide interpersonal environments more appropriate to educational tasks."[5]

Rather supportive of the views we expressed concerning the importance of families in children's lives, Christopher Jencks observed in his perceptive book, *Inequality, A Reassessment of the Effect of Family and Schooling in America,* "Unless a society completely eliminates ties between parents and children, inequality among parents guarantees some degree of inequality in the opportunities available to children."[6] While some measures suggest that family backgrounds account for some 20 to 40 percent of the income differentials that occur among educated persons, Jencks calculates more conservatively that some 15 percent of income differences among educated persons may be attributed to family backgrounds.[7] Genetic factors, cognitive skills, and other variables account for the ultimate income differences when children become adults.

Nevertheless, Jencks does reject "the factory model" of schools that convert an "input" like the raw materials of childhood into the finished product of employable adults. Rather, Jencks states that his

[4]James Coleman, et al., *Equality of Educational Opportunity* (Washington, D.C.: U.S. Government Printing Office, 1966).

[5]Ernest Q. Campbell, "Adolescent Socialization," ed. David A. Goslin, *Handbook of Socialization Theory and Research* (Chicago: Rand McNally and Company, 1969), p. 846.

[6]Christopher Jencks, *Inequality, A Reassessment of the Effect of Family and Schooling in America* (New York: Basic Books, Inc., 1972), p. 4.

[7]Ibid, p. 219.

research leads him to support the idea that the "outputs" of schools "depend largely upon a single input, namely the characteristics of the entering children. Everything else—the school budget, its policies, the characteristics of the teachers—is either secondary or completely irrelevant."[8] Such a conclusion does place tremendous responsibility upon the families in their respective social settings.

The criticisms of schools concerning their relative failures to provide equal opportunities for children will undoubtedly continue for decades to come. In the spring of 1976, James Coleman again discussed educational equality for children by contrasting the views of John Rawls and Robert Nozick.[9] Rawls' theory of justice holds that inequalities are justified if they benefit the least advantaged segments of a society. Nozick pointed out that most inequalities were not brought into being by some perverse authority but emerge from innate or acquired individual differences in skills, capacities, and other resources. In Nozick's view, justice demands neither equality nor an inequality designed to aid the least advantaged, but, instead, the full entitlement of each individual to whatever he or she has justly acquired.

Both positions represent extremes or polarities, but Coleman sees them as useful in delineating the dilemmas of families and schools in providing a formal education for children. Rawls' perspective would wipe out all "accidents of birth" by giving some children more opportunity than others and so achieving equal opportunity for each child. In essence, children would be removed from family influences and raised as responsibilities of the state. Nozick, at the opposite end, would imply that public education should be abandoned and that each child would receive the full untaxed benefits his or her family could provide. As Coleman does note, these positions are theoretical and are not supported in reality. Families do exist to contribute to inequalities and schools do exist to redistribute benefits so that children can eventually improve their status in life. Families can and do move to new residences and so place their children in schools that represent their views. On the other hand, financial support for schools has increasingly been given over to authorities not necessarily from local districts but from larger districts or jurisdictions under both state and federal funding. These central authorities require equality of opportunity for all children and have the power to withdraw support if their wishes are not carried out. Herein lies an impasse that troubles parents, children, and governments alike.

[8]Ibid, p. 256.
[9]Reprinted with permission of James S. Coleman from *The Public Interest*, No. 43, (Spring 1976), 121–28. Copyright © 1976 by National Affairs, Inc.

Segregation, Desegregation, and the Busing of Children

The impasse with which Coleman is concerned is probably best observed in the issue of "forced busing" or the court-mandated directive to achieve racial balance by transporting children considerable distances from their neighborhoods into school districts that are essentially segregated in terms of race or social class. We do not need to dwell upon the historical factors that led to busing as a governmental policy because they are fairly well known. The movement of southern blacks into the huge urban concentrations of the northern cities and the rapid growth of white "satellite" suburbs is well documented elsewhere. There remain "pockets," "islands," or "enclaves" that consist of socially homogeneous people quite distinct from their urban neighbors. Their children, most likely, attend a local school whose students are quite similar in terms of race, religion, creed, or social class. *De facto* segregation based on residence undoubtedly explains why local school populations are so overwhelmingly similar. *De jure* segregation, however, is quite another matter, and it is de jure segregation that no longer enjoys national or federal support. Where once the "separate, but equal" policy was upheld in the courts, the exposure of separation of children and unequal educational facilities, staff, or programs in reality has brought about new policies more in line with American ideals of respect for all citizens. One of these policies calls for a daily redistribution of children through "forced busing" to schools that are many miles away from the children's homes.

From the very beginning to the present, busing has been an emotional issue. The opening of schools in the fall of each year brings with it countless incidents of protests, marches, demonstrations, violence, and the calling out of police or soldiers to provide security for threatened lives. On the other hand, what is usually not publicized in the mass media are the numerous communities that peaceably, harmoniously, and thoughtfully went about the business of desegregating their public schools. Often the children are quite willing to study with their assigned classmates, but their opposition, fear, or outright hostility toward being with children from other races or social classes is grounded in the rigid views of their elders.

While the rationale for mandatory busing is usually held to be to help achieve educational equality of opportunity, the less discussed rationale involves the view that children of all races or social classes are *educational resources* in themselves. Children may learn from each other, and social heterogeneity may be a more stimulating and challenging environment than social homogeneity. Under segregated local schools, physical distance prevents learning about "others." By busing, by "bringing Mohammed to the mountain," so to speak, because the mountain cannot go to Mohammed, children of different types and backgrounds meet, mix, and come to know each other not as abstractions but as real persons with feelings, aspirations, hopes, talents, and human shortcomings.

In all this, we need to be aware of the counterarguments as well. There are the huge costs of fuel, buses, drivers, and maintenance as well as the wasted time spent in traveling weary miles to and from school grounds. There is no guarantee that moving children about achieves educational quality in their new schools. There can be continued isolation within the new schools for numerous reasons. There can be losses for those children who are required to move away from stimulating, worthwhile educational programs already in operation merely because higher authorities have deemed it necessary to achieve racial or social class "balances."

Few would claim that forced busing is the total answer to educational problems of the young. What seems to be evident is the growing concern of parents and educators alike that all children should be able to experience a high-grade, *quality* educational program.

There seems to be a tremendous array of educational innovations, alternatives to traditional forms, or enrichment programs from which to choose. One effort that has captured the attention of many educators and concerned persons is the Summerhill model of a child-centered, child-dominated "free school."[10] Such schools demonstrate an abiding faith that children are far more judicious and capable than adult-authoritative schools have previously held. Children can and will learn but not necessarily through coercion and dependency upon adult leadership.

Quality education may yet come about, some say, if schools would only abandon the step-by-step progression through the grades by children of the same age. Rather, children would move through various levels of understanding and achievement at their own pace instead of being "locked in" with all others. Individualized education would replace what amounts to the herding of large numbers of children through educational "chutes." While much seems to have been accomplished in this area, the more pragmatic procedure of moving large numbers of children through the "lock-step" methods remains.

Still another suggestion, carried out in relatively few cases, is the proposal of "schools without walls." In this procedure, the children's communities or nearby environs become the focii of attention. Rather

---

[10]See A. S. Neill, "Freedom Works," in Paul Adams, et al., *Children's Rights, Toward the Liberation of the Child* (New York: Praeger Publishers, 1971), pp. 127–52.

than being contained in so many classroom boxes, children are brought out into the world for which they are allegedly being prepared. They would gain firsthand experience in their community or area. Instead of going on one, two, or a few field trips per year, they would be continually examining the public and private facilities, programs, activities, patterns, and peoples around them. Schools would be places of sorting out, ordering, examining, questioning, comparing, briefing, discussing, and organizing data gained by the children. The schools would no longer be places of rote memorization or the scenes of struggles with abstract, distant, nonapplicable information.

Not all education can be attained within the confines of a local, ill-equipped, understaffed, underfinanced, hard-pressed, and hard-working school system. What is proposed is "the campus school" or "the magnet school" that would attract eager youngsters who want to learn more about the world and its multifaceted phenomena. The magnet schools would be large, well-staffed, well-equipped, multifunctional locales on an accessible campus for those children who wish to enlarge their grasp of specific fields of interest. Youngsters would not have to wait until college for a chance to participate in learning some subject or specialty in depth.

While the magnet or campus school concept may still be a possibility in the future, more schools are developing a number of "educational tracks" tailored to specific kinds of students and to achieve specific kinds of goals. Teacher specialists are added to staffs to bring an expertise that would be missing in the teacher with more general knowledge. Along with the teacher specialists there are possibilities for team-teaching and for teacher-aides or paraprofessionals who would ease the burdens placed upon the shoulders of a single teacher confronted with some twenty, thirty, or forty children throughout a school day.

There is nothing new in automated, programmed instructional modules, but "machine-teaching" is not quite established in the elementary schools of America as an everyday procedure. There is nothing new in suggesting that some schools should stress a program in music while others focus upon technical programs or some form of athletics. There are no limits to the educational imagination, but the primary objective is to work toward quality education for all children, one that would build upon the curiosity, verve, and exhuberance of young children.

The Domination of the Classroom Teacher

Schools are allegedly child-oriented, but they are most certainly not child-dominated at the elementary levels. Children are viewed more as empty vessels into which a proper portion of education is poured and measured. The dominant figure in the picture is the class-room teacher into whose domain children have strayed. One might think of school classrooms as the scenes for reruns of the fable of Jack who climbed a beanstalk only to find himself in a rather dangerous country of giants. Little persons, children, must learn how to conduct themselves lest they arouse the wrath of the sleeping giant.

Prichard and Buxton observed the different role-sets that are available to teachers. Although they had in mind more concern for secondary school teachers, their A, B, C, and D types of role-sets have some application to elementary classroom teachers as well.[11] The A type, they note, are "no nonsense" personalities who see the classroom as a place in which to convey formal knowledge. They are businesslike in the matter of promptness, efficiency, and working "by the book." The B type, on the other hand, is less interested in the subject matter and more interested in the students or learners themselves. Children are seen as persons with very human needs and, accordingly, assignments and schedules may be tossed aside in favor of humanizing, socializing, encouraging expression. The C type stresses creativity and innovation. The artistic talents, the originality, and the nonconformity of young-sters are C type concerns. Finally, Prichard and Buxton suggest a D type of teacher who believes in evaluation of educational growth and development. Accordingly, the D type teacher keeps detailed records, strives to improve examinations and grades, and pushes his or her stu-dents "to do their best." These A, B, C, and D types represent "the purists" who select out their particular objectives and then proceed to achieve them. Other types of teachers are more "hybrids" who com-bine the objectives and tactics of their colleagues who are purists.

The delineation of these types of teachers does not mean that somehow they are lacking or inadequate when it comes to being "a good teacher." Rather, these purists or hybrids do contribute to the education of certain types of students. Some students apparently do need the "tough" teacher who requires them to absorb and utilize knowledge to the utmost of their abilities. Some students do not need to master fundamentals or special materials as much as they need sup-port, encouragement, understanding, and appreciation. Such students need more time to grasp what is required of them or the nature of the directions to which they may turn. Still other students may be inspired by the C type teacher who points the way toward self-assertion and self-direction rather than social conformity. The D type works toward

[11]Keith W. Prichard and Thomas H. Buxton, *Concepts and Theories in Sociology of Education* (Lincoln, Nebraska: Professional Educators Publication, Inc., 1973), pp. 119–23.

fair, accurate, and thoroughly honest evaluation of student strengths or weaknesses which is far better than the unfair, subjective favoritism with which some teachers judge their students.

The problem, of course, lies in the fortuitous matching of certain types of students with certain types of teachers. In numerous cases, the chance mismatches can be discouraging and even tragic because academic records can shadow an academic career. The opening of public records for inspection by the concerned parties does help counter some of the more cruel or incorrect assessments of teachers, but not every parent or student exercises his or her privileges in this regard.

Perhaps the matter of serendipitous combinations of teachers and students can be understood as reflecting the nature of social interaction itself. Throughout life, individuals will meet and deal with all sorts of personality types. Schools provide early settings for encountering these numerous types and learning how one procedure or another succeeds or fails given the mix of personalities. There is risk in every human exchange, and to shrink from the challenge of learning how one must confront these encounters is to miss one of the more valuable lessons in life.

Control, Containment, and Conflict

The entrance of children into formal schools is a momentous event. They face a new situation, vastly different from any they have ever experienced. The persons all around them are comparative strangers, and each child must find his or her way safely among them. The norms regulating behavior are now verbalized and made more definite. Rules, routines, and regularity govern what will or will not occur. Personal needs and interests do not necessarily have precedence except to the individual child. Concessions to whims and fancies, tolerance of moods and wishes, allowances for inadequacies and ineptitude may or may not be granted.

Twenty to forty children are "confined" within an enclosure called a classroom. Robert Weber has compared them with "prisons" and found the two practically identical.[12] Students are "sentenced" to custodial care for so many years and, upon demonstration of willingness to accept constraints and to adopt "good behavior," they will eventually be "released" to society.

---

[12]Robert E. Weber, "Separate but Equal" (from a paper "Discipline in the Schools,"), *Saturday Review of Education* (March 1973), p. 62. See also, David Melton, *Burn the Schools Save the Children* (New York: Thomas Y. Crowell Company, 1975), p. 21.

Reimer takes a similar stand when he points to the fourfold functions of schools: "custodial care, social-role selection, indoctrination, and education as usually defined in terms of the development of skills and knowledge."[13] In the custodial care function, restraints are implied. In the social-role selection process, schools help "place" students in privileged or less privileged statuses. In the indoctrination function, propaganda is promoted that supports prevailing views and neglects counterperspectives. In the educational function, provided the first three functions are effective, students acquire abilities to understand and use information. In a democracy, at least, it is the first three functions that attract the ire of school critics.

Even more colorfully, Goffman associates schools as "asylums" for those in need of care.[14] Waller, too, endorsed the conflict model of teachers and students when he wrote: "Authority is on the side of the teacher. The teacher nearly always wins. In fact, he must win or he cannot remain a teacher. Children after all, are usually docile, and they certainly are defenseless against the machinery with which the adult world is able to enforce its decisions."[15]

It is the reference to "machinery" that needs more explanation. In sociological terms, we would now call the machinery *a bureaucracy,* an elaborate, complicated, but ordered social structure composed of authority, subauthority, and underlings to serve some social purpose. Teachers in the classroom, then, are part of a bureaucratic structure and not a power unto themselves. They must act in circumscribed manners in accord with school, district, and board rules and regulations. Teachers are part of "a pecking order," and they are bound to uphold certain specifications or suffer the consequences of dismissal. Children, in this context, are turned over to a bureaucratic structure in the name of the public, their families, and, hopefully, for their own benefits. There are limits to the authority of classroom teachers and in the contemporary world of "accountability," they must touch children's lives with great care. Many teachers would rather satisfy the expectations of their superiors than question their employers or administrators about the fixed curriculum they are supposed to teach. In any event, teachers look to their administrators, their own authority figures, as well as to the children in the classroom. As Banks notes, teachers, too, are subservient

---

[13]Everett Reimer, *School Is Dead, Alternatives in Education* (Garden City, New York: Doubleday & Company, Inc., 1971), p. 33.

[14]Erving Goffman, *Asylums* (Chicago: Aldine Publishing Company, 1967).

[15]Willard Waller, *The Sociology of Teaching* (New York: John Wiley & Sons, Inc., Copyright, 1932, Russell and Russell Inc.) See also, Wilbur B. Brookover and Edsel L. Erickson, *Society, Schools, and Learning* (Boston: Allyn and Bacon, Inc., 1969), p. 82.

and hence not totally in control or responsible for classroom situations or conditions.[16]

SCHOOLS AS POSITIVE FORCES IN SOCIETY

Richard Pratte provides us with some useful distinctions concerning what he calls the Public School Movement or PSM_i and PSM_{si}.[17] These distinctions can help us understand the dilemmas of educators who are trying valiantly to carry out an educational mandate to deal effectively, constructively, happily with children while at the same time trying to be responsive to the criticisms being leveled at them.

Pratte first defines PSM_i as the public school movement *ideology* or the organization of ideas, philosophies, or purposes that brings public schools into being. These ideologies stem from political objectives and economic priorities. They have to do with decisions governing the appropriate relationships between individuals and their groups. They have to do with finding some stability in the midst of social change. They have to do with divisive class, race, religious, ethnic, or creedal systems. Most important of all, there is not a single, all-embracing PSM_i that satisfies all segments of the population. Instead, certain publics endorse certain ideologies and people, individually or in some coalition, move ahead to provide public schools for their children.

The PSM_{si} stands for the public school movement as *social institution,* and it is this that has been the target of rhetoric and serious criticism similar to what we have just discussed. This is the formal organization moving through successive revisions of preindustrial, industrial, and postindustrial American society. This is the elaborate system supported through federal, state, and local taxation to which we send our children. It is to this that Pratte refers when he summarizes the criticisms of schools as:

> ... the center of an attack mounted by parents, minority groups, students, behavioral scientists, book reviewers, politicians, professors of education, academics, and many others. The PSM_{si} is an abject failure. It has become an instrument of oppression: intellectually, politically, economically, and spiritually. Its curricula are irrelevant, its teachers stupid and mindless, and its administrators

[16]Olive Banks, *The Sociology of Education* (London: B. T. Batsford, Ltd., 1971), pp. 161–82.
[17]Copyright © 1973 by David McKay Company, Inc. From the book *The Public School Movement* by Richard Pratte, published by David McKay Company, Inc. Reprinted by permission of the publisher, pp. 23–27.

self-serving or inept. True learning and healthy growth are sabotaged in most American schools today, these critics argue, because of an atmosphere inimical to learning; one in which the emphasis is on the teacher teaching rather than the students learning. The whole process of schooling is frozen into rigid lockstep through the grades, chopped up mechanically into blocks of time and different subjects, dominated by a curriculum fixed in advance and imposed from above. There is no real regard for the students as individuals, people with real concerns of their own and inherent drives to learn, understand, and create.[18]

The Multi-functions of Schools

The PSM_{si} can be no better than its PSM_i and, as we have noted, there is no universal agreement that one ideology is better than another. Yet, in a practical sense, schools have been organized and indeed are entrenched in the midst of society to continue the socialization of the young and, if current trends continue, to be prepared to offer a lifetime of socialization for students of all ages from kindergarten through graduate schools.

Just what are the public schools doing despite the criticisms leveled against them? Anderson suggests at least five universal functions of formal education.[19] They are:

1. Vocational preparation, not so much in terms of training for specific occupations as in identifying and equipping individuals to be able to absorb special skills and necessary knowledge.
2. Enlarging children's perspective of their own cultures far beyond that which they could have absorbed with reliance upon their immediate families and friends.
3. Encouraging individuality by exploring different groups and human models and their life styles; by discovering those behavior modes and ideas that suggest where individual students may have great potential or aptitudes of service to himself or herself as well as to others.
4. Selection and molding of leadership and followership among all participants in society.
5. Perpetuation and improvement of the educational system itself so that, in the end, new understanding and new affective responses can be made. As Anderson expresses it, "Schools in an advancing society are continually making the competence of previous cohorts of pupils obsolete."[20]

[18]Ibid, p. 126.
[19]C. A. Anderson, "The Multi-Functionality of Formal Education," ed. D. F. Swift, *Basic Readings in the Sociology of Education* (London: Routledge & Kegan Paul, 1970), pp. 223–47.
[20]Ibid, pp. 223–25.

These functions do not constitute an exhaustive, comprehensive listing of all the functions performed by schools, but they are broad and varied enough to suggest that schools are indeed meaningful in children's lives and in the collective life of all generations. To be sure, few are satisfied that schools have perfected their abilities to function as they are supposed to do, but with multiple objectives before them, schools do begin the long years of formal education with young children with considerable professional skill, verve, and dedication. Schools are probably not as ineffective as their most severe critics would have the public believe. Nor are they as faultless as their defenders would promote them. Rather, the truth lies somewhere in between. Imperfect systems are to be expected from imperfect ideologies. What we would expect, of course, would be the ferreting out of those errors that hard experience tells us can no longer be tolerated.

SUMMARY

We have examined the charge that schools miseducate rather than educate children. In the main, we found that the public schools take on an awesome responsibility when children are under compulsion to leave their families for many hours of the day, for weeks, months, and years on end, and that in carrying out their mandate, schools do make a difference in the lives of children. Whether that difference is "good" or "bad" depends heavily upon ideology, perspective, and value sets. Schools perform many functions for millions of children and that they might falter in some way is more reflective of their social milieu than many would care to acknowledge.

What are the specific charges laid at the door of the educational enterprise? The chief charges pertain to the inequality of educational opportunity afforded the nation's children, the conscious or unconscious segregation of children, the presence of an adult-dominated system that has far too much control, containment, and conflict built into it, and a disregard for individual differences.

While not trying to affirm or deny these allegations, we did try to present some of the sociological concerns underlying them. The inequalities that were said to be the product of school systems were more the products of the families, communities, and larger political-economic units from which children came. The effort to level out these differences in terms of equality of educational opportunity is a monumental task that depends heavily upon accepting one philosophical view over another. There seems to be no real consensus about helping out the least socially advantaged children.

Efforts to desegregate the public schools in terms of racial balances or social classes have met with resistance of some school districts and with reluctant acceptance by others. Forced busing of children has aroused deep-seated emotions that will not be stilled simply by the mandates of our legal system. What is interesting is the realization that children are educational resources in their own right and that, after all, the concern is to somehow achieve high quality educational programs for children. Individualized instruction, schools without walls, magnet or campus schools, teacher specialists, teaching modules, automated teaching, and a variety of educational tracks are some of the more recent innovations.

When it came to discussing the intimidating figure of the classroom teacher, we found there were several role-sets that teachers can and do take and that certain types of teachers were quite effective with certain types of students. Further, we explained some of the necessity for control and constraint and the participation of the classroom teacher in an educational bureaucracy.

The Public School Movement or PSM has two distinct aspects. One is the public school movement as an ideology, PSM_i, in Pratte's terms, and the other is the public school movement as a social institution, PSM_{si}. Most of the criticism has been directed at the public school movement as a social institution and in many ways contains legitimate complaints. On the other hand, the ideology behind the public school movement has not crystalized into an overriding organization of ideas or perspectives. Instead, a culturally pluralistic society seems to pull its schools in numerous directions at once, and the schools attempt their multi-functions in order to satisfy as many of the constituent elements in society as possible. That schools have performed numerous tasks with considerable success needs also to be acknowledged. Schools have not perfected their services, but in the end, they must be commended for what they have accomplished and supported for what they can become in behalf of children.

9

Politicalization of children

While sociological study of children tends to stress the salient effects of families and schools, there seems to be less inclination to deal with the prominence of the political-economic climate in which families and schools operate. This chapter will focus upon the polity or the system that allocates power while the ensuing chapter will look more closely at the economy or the system that produces, distributes, and consumes goods and services. These chapters seek to examine how power and economic systems make themselves felt in the homes and schools of the land and so, in the end, work their way into the life of children.

Two strategies lend themselves to a study of the relationships between children and the political structures. The first would try to lay bare just how the polity socializes youngsters in anticipation of their future political support. The second would take the form of child advocacy or children's rights in the sense of children acting upon the polity rather than the more familiar role of being acted upon.

THE KEY CONCEPTS: POWER AND AUTONOMY

Power

Power, for our purposes, is defined as the ability to make others behave in some approved way. In American society, power is vested in the hands of representatives of all the people, elected or appointed to their respective offices. In the 1960s and well into the 1970s, there was a strong dissident movement (particularly vocal and militant among college students and also notable in the "hippie" movement that advocated "dropping out of society") that unequivocably proclaimed that politicians served their own or special interests to the neglect of the welfare of their constituents or that of the general public.[1] It was a time of great social discontent, and generations once called "silent" or "apathetic" made headlines with their organized protests against current political policies. While never quite representing the majority of youngsters, the dissidents cultivated the arts of eliciting sympathy and support for various causes including draft resistance, antiwar, and student rights. Confrontation with established authorities was commonplace and often had tragic consequences as in the case of the May 4, 1970 confrontation between the Ohio National Guard and students at Kent State University.[2]

The central issue, of course, was power. The struggle for supremacy among different perspectives was, after all, at the heart of the social unrest. Which perspective may yet prevail in the 1980s and 1990s is anyone's guess, but the conceptualization of young people as subservient to political authority in American society was sorely shaken in the most recent past. School authorities trained in the field of educating the young found themselves in the unfamiliar and uncomfortable arena of political polarization.

Autonomy

The headline-capturing events of the 1960s and 1970s that included political assassinations, civil rights marches, student riots, sit-ins, demonstrations, and the unprecedented removal from office of a vice-

---

[1] See for example, Joe David Brown, ed., *The Hippies* (New York: Time, Incorporated, 1967); Arthur and Lila Weinberg, *Some Dissenting Voices, The Story of Six American Dissenters* (New York: The World Publishing Company, 1970). Walt Anderson, ed., *The Age of Protest* (Pacific Palisades, California: Goodyear Publishing Company, Inc., 1969).

[2] See for example, James A. Michener, *Kent State, What Happened and Why* (New York: Random House, 1971); Stuart Taylor, Richard Shuntich, Patrick McGovern, and Robert Genthner, *Violence at Kent State, May 1 to 4, 1970* (New York: College Notes & Texts, Inc., 1971).

president and a president of the United States would seem to be far removed from our concerns with the socialization of children. However, there are ramifications to these events that rather directly point to the way American children are reared. One of these relationships has to do with autonomy.

In American society children are encouraged to move from their highly dependent state toward independence or autonomy, the ability to handle one's own affairs with responsibility. The process is gradual for most children, and it is generally taken for granted that they will ultimately determine their own course in life without asking parents, teachers, or other authorities what they should achieve or how they should go about their tasks. It is in this process, then, that the earliest lessons of politicalization begin and take shape. In one sense, children must first learn to gain control over themselves before they can begin to exert influence over others.

Autonomy and power are thus linked. First, there must emerge a power over self. Then there may emerge the exercise of power over other lives. As we pointed out in chapter seven in our distinctions between *negative* freedom and *positive* freedom, children receive in their families both the easing of restraints and the assumption of disciplines that will enable them to develop their capacities, interests, and talents. There is never a time when persons may be as free as they please although advocates of negative freedom, no prohibitions, defend this belief. On the other hand, the needs and rights of others never completely supersede the needs and rights of individuals. Balancing the two extremes is no easy task, but it is a task that cannot be deferred or ignored. Written large on the political screen, adult citizens contend with each other to steer the American society in some favored direction, but their childhoods began the effort many years back.

POLITICALIZATION

Representative of the growing literature on the politicalization of children is the publication by the United States Office of Education entitled *The Development of Basic Attitudes and Values Toward Government and Citizenship during the Elementary School Years* by Robert Hess and Judith Torney.[3] In 1967, the publication reappeared in

[3]Robert D. Hess and Judith V. Torney, *The Development of Basic Attitudes Toward Government and Citizenship during the Elementary School Years*, pt. I, Report to the U. S. Office of Education on Cooperative Project No. 1078, 1965.

bookform as *The Development of Political Attitudes in Children*.[4] Hess and Torney studied more than seventeen thousand elementary school children in eight cities in four major regions of the United States, the Northeast, South, Midwest, and Far West. Their most prominent finding was that the political attitudes of elementary school children changed very rapidly as they progressed through the various grades.[5] From naiveté, the children moved toward greater sophistication and a more realistic understanding of the political system and its various processes.

Models of Political Socialization

Hess and Torney postulate four distinct models which children use in acquiring, modifying, and establishing their political attitudes.[6] These are the accumulation model, the interpersonal transfer model, the identification model, and the cognitive-developmental model. Each is useful in understanding how children acquire specific relationships with political structures and processes.

THE ACCUMULATION MODEL. In this model, there is an assumption that children come to understand what is required of them politically as they gain more knowledge, information, and exposure to different attitudes and activities. The different abilities of children to learn new materials and their emotional orientations are considered inconsequential in this model. Children simply absorb what is presented to them by their teachers without question and without distortion.

THE INTERPERSONAL TRANSFER MODEL. This model draws upon children's previous experience with authority figures such as fathers, mothers, or teachers. The president of the United States may be seen as a father figure who looks after the affairs of the nation much as a father looks after his family. The rules and regulations with which children become familiar in school settings are enlarged upon as laws regulating persons in the larger society. In this interpersonal transfer model, the affective feelings and relationships with familiar persons and objects such as teachers and the flag, are reassigned to more distant and unfamiliar persons or topics such as senators, congressmen, or court systems.

IDENTIFICATION MODEL. The emphasis in this model is upon children's imitation of the behavior of "significant others," those who do not

[4]Robert D. Hess and Judith V. Torney, *The Development of Political Attitudes in Children* (New York: Aldine Publishing Company, 1967).
[5]Ibid, p. 14 (Anchor Books Edition, 1968).
[6]Ibid, pp. 22–26 (Anchor Books Edition, 1968).

directly try to persuade children to follow their example but who unconsciously suggest what they consider to be appropriate political behavior such as affiliation and support of a particular political party.

COGNITIVE-DEVELOPMENTAL MODEL. Finally, the cognitive-developmental model considers the abilities of different children to grasp political concepts depending upon their cognitive development. The complex and the abstract escape the recognition and understanding of a very young child. An older child, however, can more readily understand abstract ideas and thus can comprehend relatively complex political concepts such as the making of statutes.

Obviously, no child uses a single model to become politically socialized. Rather, children utilize all four models in part. As Hess and Torney observe, the accumulation model does not explain why children form early attachments to the nation or to governmental figures, but it does suggest that schools do provide children with a fund of knowledge about the government from which they may later draw. The identification model is more useful in explaining party affiliation and preference for certain candidates. The interpersonal transfer model helps understand the early approaches of children to political organization and to anticipated political results. Lastly, the cognitive-developmental model helps to explain how children gradually acquire the ability to comprehend the more complex and abstract ideas of political processes.[7]

The Development
of Political Involvement in Children

In Hess and Torney's view, there are four steps in the entrance of children into the political arena. First, there is *identification of political objects* such as local, state, or federal governments, the United States Senate, the Supreme Court, the United States House of Representatives, or the president of the United States. Secondly, children begin to *conceptualize* what is expected of citizens and their representatives. Thirdly, children develop an emotional or *subjective involvement* with political matters or candidates. Finally, children enter into some form of *overt activity* in which they learn how they may affect political decisions. This activity can involve discussion of issues, wearing identifying political symbols such as buttons favoring a particular candidate, or working with others to organize community support for certain policies or officeholders.[8]

[7]Ibid, pp. 25–26.
[8]Ibid, pp. 18–19.

There is some question as to the precise sequence of these steps in Hess and Torney's minds, but they do point out how even adults might mix these steps. For example, an adult may actively support a candidate or an issue without really knowing what the candidate stands for or what the issue is all about. [9]

Findings of the Hess-Torney Study

In attitudinal terms, children take a positive, appreciative, strong, accepting view of political affairs as far as Hess and Torney can determine. They believe unequivocally that their country is the ideal country in which to live and hence far superior to any other nation. They consider government to be powerful, competent, efficient, trustworthy, and dedicated to protecting and helping children. The president is seen as the major figure in political life, and all others work to carry out the President's wishes. An understanding of the office of the Presidency as something apart from the personal qualities of the individual occupying the office requires additional years of socialization. Police also are political figures of prime importance to children. They uphold and enforce the laws of the land which are, of course, just and proper. The suggestion that police may be subject to errors or that the laws they promote may be unfair or unevenly administered would be unthinkable to children.

Other matters elude them for some time. For example, Hess and Torney found that children knew very little about pressure or lobby groups. They do not quite understand partisan politics or the differences, if any, between major parties. They have faith in the power of the ballot box and believe, once a vote has been taken, that all parties should cease and desist from any further conflict or disagreement with the prevailing view. The ideal portrait of political strength and unity does come across to them. The real political maneuverings including spoils systems, corruption, and compromises are unknown, confusing, or are held to be exceptional deviations from normal political activities.

Mediated by age, sex, intelligence, and social class, political socialization of children occurs, according to Hess and Torney, mainly in the schools. Families play major parts in determining party loyalties or identification, much like religious preferences, but by learning how to comply with school regulations or requirements, children are well along the road toward political socialization at more sophisticated levels before they leave the elementary schools.[10]

[9]Ibid, p. 19.
[10]See "Summary and Conclusions," Chap. 10 in Robert D. Hess and Judith V. Torney, *The Development of Political Attitudes in Children* (New York: Anchor Books, Doubleday & Company, Inc., 1968), pp. 241–57.

Other Politicalization
Factors, A Macrosociological View

It is not sufficient, however, to deal exclusively with families and schools when considering the political socialization of children. There are larger or macrosociological concerns that merit attention also. There are several concerns that cannot escape children's attention because they are rather directly involved. We are thinking, for example, of the passage or rejection of school bonds that affect whether or not schools remain open and are able to provide a wide variety of programs or services. We are thinking, further, about teacher unionization and strikes. We are thinking of token school governments in which students may express some of their convictions about sshool policies. We are thinking about leadership-followership lessons in which children learn give-and-take on the playgrounds or decisions concerning who shall represent them publicly. There are many other examples that could be brought up, but these suffice to support our contention that children gain increasing understanding of power that limits autonomy as they grow older.

Aside from religious and racial issues already discussed, it is well within the experience of thousands and millions of children to find their schools closed for lack of public support on bond issues. The mounting costs of education that take more and more of the tax dollar have brought about some resistance by home owners. Numerous schools have had to curtail their plans or cut back on varied and expanding programs as voters have rejected added tax burdens.

Teachers, too, who have generally held themselves to be educational professionals, have adopted what has been called "the industrial model" or "the workers versus the management" pattern. Instead of being in the classroom or attending to the task of educating children, teachers have militantly taken signs and "struck" their schools for better salaries, released time, a voice in board decisions, or better all-around working conditions. This is not to decry such activities, but merely to observe that children, too, learn something of power politics by such actions on the part of teachers who have tried to impart to children the lessons of being "good citizens."

The adoption of school codes of conduct or the planning and carrying out of schoolwide programs and projects by the students themselves are also early educating experiences in politicalization. The arts of cooperation and organized campaigns are learned in this context along with, at times, the experience of defeat or rejection of various suggestions or policies. The informal politicalization of children does not come as particularly startling information to many, but these and many more cases of political give-and-take, favoritism, and the power of persuasive leadership need greater recognition by adult scholars who tend to stress the formal efforts of schools to help children understand and participate in political processes.

Lastly, and unfortunately, we would be remiss if we did not mention that war or peace drastically affect the politicalization of children. In times of war or threats of war, children are intimately affected. Military drafts, enlistment campaigns, and the temporary or permanent absence of family members caused by war disrupt the lives of children who do not quite understand what is going on in the world. While wars have been fairly distant or removed from the immediate experiences of most American youngsters, this has not been true in other countries where war or threats of war are daily events for children caught up in the crossfires of adult discord. Etched on the memory are two widely circulated photographs of children caught up in the blind assaults upon innocent people in the midst of war. One was from an old newsreel of a bombing attack on a major Chinese city during the early Japanese penetration into China in the mid-forties. It showed a Chinese baby crying on a shattered railroad station platform, dust-covered, frightened, and abandoned. The other was of a Vietnamese girl fleeing down a country road, clothing torn from her body to ease the pain of the napalm-bombing burns she had just sustained. These glimpses of the impacts of war upon children are held by most observers to be relatively mild when compared with the unphotographed casualties and tragedies associated with children's suffering during wartime.

CHILDREN'S RIGHTS[11]

There are at least two theoretical positions from which to consider the rights of children. One holds that children must be protected and controlled because they are children. This is to say that they are vulnerable and not responsible for their actions because there is much that they do not know, understand, or can enforce. The other perspective advocates the removal of controls, restraints, and adult domination because in adult zeal to help children there has been serious damage done to their needs, attitudes, self-images, growth, abilities, concerns, and futures. We can examine with profit both of these contrasting perspectives and strategies to learn where we have been, where we are

[11]A fascinating book issued many years ago suggests the early connection between war and politics and mental-social health starting in childhood: C. S. Bluemel, *War, Politics and Insanity* (Denver, Colorado: World Press, Inc., 1950). See particularly, Paul Adams, et al., *Children's Rights, Toward the Liberation of the Child* (New York: Praeger Publishers, 1971).

now, and where we might be in the future in terms of the rights of children.

An incident reported in the *New York Times* in 1976 under the heading "Lost Garden" suggests something of the dilemma of holding one view or another about children's rights.[12] In brief, inner city children had taken considerable pride and pains to create a garden out of an old abandoned lot near their homes. The garden had been carefully fenced off from intruders and constituted a bright spot in an otherwise drab neighborhood. A fire apparently broke out in a nearby building and firemen called to the scene promptly broke down the garden's fences, trampled the growth underfoot, and carried their hoses directly to the fire. Perhaps it was necessary to do so and perhaps it was not, but the pride and product of the community's children and their right to enjoy what they had worked so hard to develop was given short shrift. There is need to ask in what situations are the rights of all persons to be brushed aside and, on the other hand, in what ways should the rights of children be unassailable?

A Brief History of Children's Rights

A legacy of the civil rights struggles and the War on Poverty which witnessed the establishment of Head Start Programs and an Anti-Hunger Crusade in the 1960s, children's rights, too, have been regarded as proper topics of social change. While the rights of children have historical roots dating back to antiquity, we can profitably start with the early twentieth century to note the dismay of children's advocates over the widespread neglect of children's rights.

In 1896, for instance, Kate Douglas Wiggin directed public attention to children's rights by noting, "A child has a right to a place of his own, to surroundings which have some relationship to his size, his desires, and his capabilities ... the child has a right to more justice in his discipline than we are generally wise and patient enough to give him." And, finally, she wrote, "There is no standard; the child is the creature of circumstance."[13]

Contrast Wiggin's summation with that of Rochelle Beck writing in a summary of the White House Conferences on Children held every ten years since 1909: "In the sweep of seven decades, the image conveyed is one of children, smaller than anyone else, lighter in physical

---

[12] *New York Times*, January 9, 1976, "Lost Garden."
[13] Kate Douglas Wiggin, *Children's Rights, A Book of Nursery Logic* (New York: Houghton-Mifflin, 1896). We are indebted to Professor Clara Jackson, Library Science, Kent State University, for this citation and for her helpful discussion of the rights of children.

weight and political clout, easily picked up and blown wherever the winds of economic, political, and social movements were heading."[14] The difference appears to be miniscule and reminds one of the dean at an educational conference who concluded that rarely do people make "giant steps forward" but more likely "inch forward" with supreme effort.

Moving to the international arena, the Universal Declaration of Human Rights was proclaimed by the General Assembly of the United Nations in December, 1948. It tended to refer to adults rather than children, but in its broad outlook, the declaration did encompass the rights of children as well. Some thirty articles were specified, and we can single out only a few for comment.

Article 1 declared that "All human beings are born free and equal in dignity and rights." There is a question in the minds of some whether or not the article truly regards children as "human beings," but the use of the adjective "all" would suggest that children were not to be left out of the definitions and the conferring of rights.

Article 19 stated that "everyone has the right to freedom of opinion and expression; this right includes freedom to hold opinions without interference and to seek, receive, and impart information and ideas through any media and regardless of frontiers." Here again we can surmise that children are to voice their ideas without fear of suppression.

Children *were* specified in Article 25 and in Article 26. In the former, children were held to be ". . . entitled to special care and assistance." In the latter, children were to have the right to a "free" and "compulsory" education at the elementary levels. Parents, however, were declared to " . . . have a prior right to choose the kind of education that shall be given to their children." The specification of a "free" education clearly meant one that was without direct charge to the children's parents or guardians. A *compulsory* basic education, however, is difficult to square with *rights*.

In 1959, however, doubts were erased about the inclusion of children and their rights by the United Nations Declaration on the Rights of Children.[15] Some ten rights were specified:

1. All children have rights.
2. They have the right to special protection in their homes.
3. They have the right to name and nationality.
4. They have the right to social security.

[14]Rochelle Beck, "The White House Conferences on Children: An Historical Perspective," *Harvard Educational Review*, 43, No. 4 (November 1973), 668.
[15]United Nations General Assembly Resolution 1368 (XIV), November 20, 1959, *Official Records of the General Assembly*, 14th Session, Sup. No. 16, (1960), 19.

5. Children with physical, mental or social handicaps have the right to special treatment.
6. They have the right to full and harmonious development of personality.
7. They have the right to education, free and compulsory, up to, at least, elementary grades.
8. Children should be the first to receive protection and relief.
9. Children should be protected against all forms of neglect, cruelty or exploitation.
10. Children should be protected against racial, religious or any form of discrimination.

Wilkerson suggested in 1973 that new rights for children will probably continue to be enunciated as legal and social agencies make changes in the light of new information.[16] These include the right of every child to maximum education and assistance in developing capacities in an individualized and child-centered educational system, the right of children to seek creative modes of expression and identity, and the establishment of a national, state, and local child advocacy system.

There would seem to be no limit on the rights of children so that, in effect, whatever rights can be granted adults can be granted children. John Holt argues cogently along these lines in his polemic *Escape from Childhood*.[17] Holt specified some eleven rights of children:

1. The right to equal treatment at the hands of the law—*i.e.*, the right, in any situation, to be treated no worse than an adult would be.
2. The right to vote, and take part in political affairs.
3. The right to be legally responsible for one's life and acts.
4. The right to work, for money.
5. The right to privacy.
6. The right to financial independence and responsibility—*i.e.*, the right to own, buy, and sell property, to borrow money, establish credit, sign contracts, etc.
7. The right to direct and manage one's own education.
8. The right to travel, to live away from home, to choose or make one's own home.
9. The right to receive from the state whatever minimum income it may guarantee adult citizens.
10. The right to make and enter into, on the basis of mutual consent, quasi-familial relationships outside one's immediate family—*i.e.*, the right to seek and choose guardians other than one's own parents and to be legally dependent on them.
11. The right to do, in general, what any adult may legally do.[18]

[16]Albert E. Wilkerson, ed., *The Rights of Children, Emergent Concepts in Law and Society* (Philadelphia: Temple University Press, 1973), p. x.
[17]From *Escape from Childhood* by John Holt. Copyright (c) 1974 by John Holt. Reprinted by permission of the publishers, E. P. Dutton.
[18]Ibid, pp. 18–19.

In sociological terms, Holt seeks the elimination of social distinctions made between the status and roles of children and the status and roles of adults, at least within our own society. Holt's views on children's rights may represent "the wave of the future" because he does argue thoughtfully for his rather extreme position. In discussing the counterarguments concerning the right to vote, for instance, he anticipates the observation that children would be ignorant, misinformed, and deluded when it came to casting their ballots. Holt points to people who believe the earth is flat or hollow, that the world was created in seven days, that females came from the rib of a man, or that Asia was made of dominoes; yet these people may vote their will in various elections.[19] It is rather surprising that he did not include those who believe in the myths of racial superiority or inferiority in his list as well. Holt does a commendable job of defending his proposals against the anticipated reactions, and although we do not fully endorse Holt's ideas, his extreme position does suggest a direction in which American society may well drift in the future. If it does comes to pass, it would be a world without precedence.

Social-Philosophical Issues in Children's Rights

We noted at the outset that there were two conflicting theoretical positions from which to consider children's rights: one was to exert control and domination over children on behalf of their own best interests and the other was to remove these controls and constraints so that children could determine for themselves their own destinies. There is obviously more support for the first of these contentions than there is for the second.

The "best interests of children" are generally held to be the prerogative of parents. The state with all its legal apparatus can and will step in or intervene, again "in the best interests" of children under the doctrine of *parens patriae*, if the parents are unwilling or unable to enforce community-held norms with their children. Courts, agencies, attorneys or guardians would act *in loco parentis*, in place of the parents, to seek the well-being of children.[20] That is where the matter of children's rights seems to rest at present. If parents and families render full and sufficient concern for children according to the state of our knowledge, there is supposedly no problem or issue to resolve. As we have noted in our discussions and examination of parenthood and fam-

[19]Ibid, p. 168.
[20]See for a useful source, Hillary Rodham, "Children Under the Law," *Harvard Educational Review*, 43, No. 4 (November 1973), pp. 487–514.

ily life, however, all is not satisfactory, and more and more children are brought under the protection of the courts by the defaults of their parents and families. Our legal system, however, is uncertain, uninformed, ill-equipped, or woefully inadequate in providing surrogate parents and families for children. The move to enlarge the freedom from controls upon children in the form of children's rights is a logical consequence of the present legal tangles that have ensued.

Maurice Cranston, an English political philosopher, has produced a number of provocative essays that can possibly help us find the way out of the impasse we seem to be in concerning children's rights.[21]

It is all well and good for the rights of children to be identified by experts or by well-informed lay persons, but the enunciation of these rights does not in itself assure that they will be upheld for all children. The White House Conferences on Children, for example, no matter how skillful in assessing the rights of children, could not bring these rights into being.

Cranston discusses some of these problems in *The Mask of Politics*.[22] He notes, for example, the complaints of Rousseau who holds that actors are sheer counterfeiters who have developed an art of assuming a different personality. Neither the words nor the behavior of the actor are his or her own. Rousseau, however, had only praise for orators, persons who speak their own minds with conviction and sincerity. Cranston faults Rousseau on both counts. The actor is not in error to perform as he or she does in some convincing manner. Neither is the politician who must conduct his or her affairs with an eye on the constituency he or she represents. The "mask" of the politician refers to his or her *public* life and does not necessarily reveal the *private* life of the political leader. Both the actor and the politician are doing their job as best they can. Cranston observed, "A politician has good reason to be nervous of words, and to want to soften all those sharp edges, in case they cut him."[23] We would have to say the same thing about authors for what we put down on paper for readers to consider are "frozen words" which may or may not have a chilling effect upon their creators.

In the end, Cranston brilliantly observes that the doctrine of a value-free social science, in Max Weber's elegant German, *wertfrei*, may be popular but unrealistic. The divorce of information from interpretation is sterile and unproductive; mountains of information must be examined, sifted, understood, and communicated before intelligent ac-

---

[21]See for example, Maurice Cranston, *What Are Human Rights?* (New York: Basic Books, Inc., 1962); Maurice Cranston, *The Mask of Politics* (London: Allen Lane, 1973); Maurice Cranston, *Freedom* (New York: Basic Books, Inc., 1967).
[22]Cranston, *Mask of Politics*.
[23]Ibid, p. 14.

tion can occur. In terms of children's rights, values do play a part, and political moves to state them clearly do not necessarily mean they will be implemented or acted upon. They wait upon social consensus, and in our pluralistic society such a social agreement does not come swiftly.

In *What Are Human Rights?*, Cranston distinguishes between *positive* rights and *moral* rights.[24] Positive rights are those recognized in the actual written laws. They are enforceable and backed by the courts and judges. Moral rights, on the other hand, are not necessarily enforceable and are not necessarily supported by the legal system. One must justify one's own claims while those opposed seek to justify their counterclaims. Further, Cranston seeks to test whether or not a human right is a *universal moral right*, something applicable to all persons, including children. The two tests Cranston would apply are those of *practicability* and *paramount importance*.[25] If the rights cannot be accomplished in a practical sense and if they do not stand very high in the hierarchy of human values or priorities, then their declaration, such as the United Nations' listing of children's rights, is only a beacon of light by which to steer in troubled seas but which may or may not help keep confused societies away from the dangerous rocks and reefs of reality.

SUMMARY[26]

The politicalization of children has been discussed from two perspectives. In the first, the relationships between children and political structures were considered. In the second, the rights of children were examined.

Power, the ability to control the behavior of others, and autonomy, the ability to handle one's own affairs with responsibility, were found to be central to problems involved in the politicalization of children. Power, certainly, has remained out of the hands of children by virtue of the controls placed upon them by their parents, families, schools, or larger society through elected or appointed officials. Autonomy is held to be the objective of those who socialize children, but this, too, is elusive and difficult to implement.

[24]Cranston, *What Are Human Rights?*, p. 8
[25]Ibid, pp. 36–38.
[26]Useful materials may be found in Byron G. Massialas, Chap. 2, "The Political Socialization of Children and Youth," *Education and the Political System* (Reading, Massachusetts: Addison-Wesley Publishing Company, 1969), pp. 18–41, and in Special Issues of the *Harvard Educational Review*, *The Rights of Children*, Pt. I, 43, No. 4 (November 1973), and Pt. II, 44, No. 1 (February 1974).

The Hess and Torney study was used to represent the numerous studies of deliberate efforts to prepare children for their future roles as citizens in a political state. Their key finding was that children may learn by different models—through accumulation of knowledge, through interpersonal transfer with authority figures, through identification with significant others, or through growing in ability to handle complex, abstract matters. However, in the end, their changing views of the political structure and processes are rapid and more realistic over time.

Macrosociologically, other political concerns call for attention. These include children's observations and reactions to the ways their parents and other adults support school authorities, the power moves of their teachers and school boards, the tokenism of student governments, the establishment of school codes, the give-and-take of leadership and followership among their peers, and, of course, the violence of wars among adults.

As to their rights, we found the doctrine of adults operating "in the best interests of children" far more prevalent than a policy of granting more and more autonomy to children. Children are controlled by adults "for their own good" according to the "best interests" theory. The granting of all adult rights, privileges, and responsibilities to children is the extreme position of, for example, John Holt. But there is also a middle ground in which children might possibly be granted far more rights than they currently enjoy. These are suggested in such lists as those issued by the United Nations in 1948 and in 1959.

We found, also, that while dedicated and talented persons have become child advocates with their insistence on children's rights, there has really been very little change in some seventy or eighty years. Children of the future may, indeed, have their rights recognized and enforced by law, but as conditions exist at the moment, the movement for children's rights proceeds at a snail's pace.

10

10

*The economy
and
childhood*

Identification with the world of work is the hallmark of the adult. It would appear, then, that the economy, the system that provides for the production, distribution, and consumption of goods and services, would be far removed from the world of children. However, as we shall see in this chapter, there are numerous ties or relationships between the economy and childhood. We have selected certain relationships of economic significance that deal with the broad fields of *play, games,* and *work.*

DISTINCTIONS BETWEEN PLAY, GAMES, AND WORK

Play refers to mental and physical activity for expressive purposes, for sheer enjoyment, amusement, or even abandonment. Erikson has designated play as one of the eight stages of life: infancy, early childhood, play age, school age, adolescence, young adulthood, adulthood, and old age.[1] We need not limit play exclusively to childhood, because, as we now know, playfulness accompanies every stage of life well into old age. Play, however, tends to be a prominent feature of being a child and consequently is highly associated with childhood. Eventually, it has been said, persons put aside childish things and become adults. Playing does not obviously qualify as "a childish thing" because it does not cease throughout life. It only takes on different shapes or forms. As some are fond of observing, "Men and boys differ only in the size and cost of their toys."

The Intrinsic Worth of Play

What is worth stressing is that play is sustained for its own sake, its own intrinsic worth. In choosing between means and ends, it is the means that is paramount in play. In this we tend to concur with both Wohl[2] and Miller[3] who emphasize that playing is a process and is less concerned with goal-achievement. Whether a child builds a sand castle along the beach, pushes a stick through the sand of a sandbox, slides down a slide, or explores the shapes of flowers, the joy is in the doing because the process will be repeated over and over again. The sandcastle will be abandoned to the waves and winds. The sand contours will be erased. The slide will be forgotten in the playground, and flowers will soon wilt and pass from sight. What will be remembered with pleasure is the molding of the sand into place, the patterning of the sand, the rush of the wind as one landed safely from the slide, or the beauty of the petals one once held so close.

Play may be solitary or it may be carried out with numbers of other players, but in its broadest forms it is self-assigned and minimally regulated.

Games, Organized Play

Games are particular forms of play, namely, they are organized play that call for some symbiotic combination of both competition and cooperation carried out according to fixed or predetermined rules. Games may be either solitary or performed in company with others, but they more often involve groups of players operating under a system of norms.

[1]See Erik H. Erikson, *Childhood and Society* (New York: W. W. Norton & Company, Inc., 1963).

[2]Andrzej Wohl, "The Social Conditioning of Play in Motion," *International Review of Sport Sociology,* 9, No. 1 (1974), 63–81.

[3]Stephen Miller, "Ends, Means, and Galumphing, Some Leitmotifs of Play," *American Anthropologist,* 75, No. 1 (February 1973), 87–98.

The Extrinsic Worth of Work

Work, on the other hand, is utilitarian and is done to achieve practical ends or goals. It is an activity that serves other purposes that directly or indirectly sustain life itself.

Whereas play focuses upon giving participants pleasure, work may or may not be pleasure-oriented. Fortunate is the man or woman who can engage in work and find it enjoyable in and of itself. However, for most workers, work may be difficult, routine, drab, exhausting, tedious, and even hazardous. We have in mind those engaged in manual labor, those who are semiskilled in the fields of manufacturing or mining, those service workers who carry out policies set down by large corporations, those confined in place because their jobs are repetitive and unchallenging, and even those professionals who reach a certain level of productivity but who conduct their work unenthusiastically.

In a sense, one has to "recover" from work in sharp contrast with play in which one is renewed, or "re-created," the root meaning of "recreation," in vigor or zest for living. Weekends, holidays, or vacations represent some of the institutionalized times in technological society when workers can play and renew their strength and vitality of their eventual return to the work place. The coffee break or rest break are shorter responses to the need for cessation of work so that rest and recuperation can occur. Shortening the work week and the tendency toward earlier retirement are other indications of the need to "get away" from work whenever possible.[4]

Much work is accomplished out of necessity; one has to earn one's living somehow. Some work out of habit while others work out of social expectations that they are to perform some useful tasks as adults. There are those, of course, who are "workaholics," those "addicted" to work; for them, playing and pleasure-seeking are anathemas. These are the persons who refuse to even consider retirement and seek "to die with their boots on."

We are dealing, of course, in generalizations, admitting always to exceptions. We have described play as expressive, pleasure-oriented, and of intrinsic worth. We have described work as utilitarian, not necessarily pleasurable, and of extrinsic worth. Play, of course, can be exhausting, boring, and uninspired. Work, of course, can be highly

---

[4]See Woodrow W. Hunter, *Preparation for Retirement* (Ann Arbor, Michigan: Institute of Gerontology, The University of Michigan-Wayne State University, 1973); Alan Sheldon, Peter J. M. McEwan, and Carol Pierson Ryser, *Retirement, Patterns and Predictions* (Rockville, Maryland: National Institute of Mental Health, 1975); Richard A. Kalish, *Late Adulthood: Perspectives on Human Development* (Monterey, California: Brooks/Cole Publishing Company, 1975); Studs Terkel, *Working, People Talk About What They Do All Day and How They Feel About What They Do* (New York: Pantheon Books, A Division of Random House, 1974).

rewarding, exhilarating, and satisfying. But, as we also noted, these latter qualities of play or work are so different from the experiences of many people that they are considered exceptional or noteworthy.

Interconnections between Play and Work

In childhood, children are introduced to the work world of adults through their play and games. In the imaginative, make-believe, fantasy play of childhood, we witness the beginnings of anticipatory socialization for occupations, vocations, or careers.

The division of labor that has proliferated into untold numbers of specializations is seen at a distance in childhood. Undoubtedly, children grow in the ability to understand the tremendous variety of jobs or work conducted daily by adults. They may witness some of this variety, or they may be asked something about what they would like "to be" when they "grow up." More likely, they note the sexual division of labor in which "mother's work" becomes distinguishable from "father's work." The traditional doll play of girls in imitation of their mothers and the more rigorous "roughhouse" play of boys with tools, trucks, or guns in imitation of their fathers comes quickly to mind.

What is missing in this fantasy playing are the less appealing, less attractive, harsher aspects of working. The day-to-day cleaning, shopping, budgeting, cooking, or health planning responsibilities of mothers are observable but often escape the attention of little girls. The significance of sex-role typing awaits in adolescence or young adulthood, but for small children imitation of their mothers is fun-oriented. The same applies to the imitation of fathers although "the missing father syndrome" in which fathers conduct their work away from their children in some distant place makes all that goes into work or a career less comprehensible. The many years of preparation for work, the failures in achieving appropriate work, the unappreciative superiors or peers, the dissatisfied customer or client, the penalties of working in various careers are neither experienced nor understood in terms of anxiety, frustration, sacrifice, or anguish.

In examining toys, pets, games, and play activities, we can determine for ourselves to what extent the adult world of work affects childhood.

TOYS

Toys or the playthings of childhood are commonly diminutive versions of objects associated with the work of adults. Whether one looks at dolls, trucks, puppets, airplanes, guns, uniforms, musical instruments, household appliances, tools, railroad trains, or elaborate plastic models of work places or equipment, one can readily see that work-orientation appears quite early in the playthings of children.

Further, toys are carefully age-graded so that "appropriate" toys are placed before children to aid them in such basic tasks as coordination of sensory-muscle-brain systems that will later be employed in sophisticated adult work. From preschool blocks, mobiles, rings, or colored balls, to the older children's electronic, chemical, or mechanical gadgetry, toys mirror the world of work and, in most instances, prepare children for this world.

It is also important to note that the adult world is consciously aware of the market in children's toys. Multimillions are invested annually in the production, distribution, and sale of toys that usually reaches its zenith in the Christmas season. To be able to market a popular, best-selling toy product is the dream of quite a few sober-minded entrepreneurs.

Dangerous Toys

Commercially profitable playthings are designed to aid the play activities of children, but unfortunately there are instances when the profit motive has been more salient than the well-being of children. Toys alleged to bring pleasure have instead brought pain. Some of the more familiar examples are sharp-edged metallic trucks, glass or plastic items that can shatter, dolls with pins that can puncture, and skateboards that can lead to serious falls and broken bones. Lead poisoning from toxic paints on toys that are mouthed or chewed by smaller children or toys with parts that can be detached and swallowed are other cases in point.

Over the years, the toy industry has learned something of policing its own products and has set higher standards in order to protect its tiny consumers. Parents or toy purchasers, too, need to learn something about the potential harm that lurks behind the use of a given toy. "Child proofing" a toy is necessarily a part of adult responsibilities because youngsters seem to have a remarkable ability to quickly disassemble it or damage themselves, others, or the toy in their exploratory play.

Improvised versus Commercial Toys

While the toys produced by the toy industry are highly attractive, inventive, and capable of entertaining, educating, or absorbing the time and attention of children, children improvise toys as well. This ingenuity and ability to make something useful out of very little is admirable in adults but is particularly notable in the case of children.

Pots and pans, for example, can become homes, castles, luggage, hiding places, musical instruments, noisemakers, or caves depending upon children's whims or fancies. This type of imaginative play is further evidence of the role of fantasy in the child's mind. This imaginative ability, however, is encouraged and enhanced as children are made increasingly aware of the adult activities around them. Again, these activities are usually economic in nature.

The Popular Toy-of-the-Day

Just as fads or fashions sweep across the nation and consume the time, energy, and funds of numerous people, so do popular toys or "gimmicks."[5] The various playthings that have captured collective attention include Silly Putty, yo-yos, Hula Hoops, trampolines, miniature golf, Barbie dolls, Sesame Street characters, Disneyland characters, and Davy Crockett hats. These items, for all intents and purposes, tend to "date" or mark a certain period of time because they appear and disappear so quickly. Some, however, stand the test of time and become part of the toy repertoire from which parents and children choose. Other items are reintroduced to successive generations of children and so become quite profitable over many years. The return of new editions of the Mickey Mouse Club and the Howdy Doody television shows are examples of this periodic stimulation of the potential market.

Advertising for the Children's Market

Vance Packard once popularized advertisers as *The Hidden Persuaders.*[6] He included in his analysis a revealing section on what he called "The Psycho-Seduction of Children."[7] His data, while suffering from preselection to support his thesis, document the elaborate campaigns waged by industry and business to sell children's playthings. The Davy Crockett craze, for example, based on a popular Disney television series, produced some three hundred different Davy Crockett items that earned some $300 million![8]

We are not ferreting out dark plots to cheat American consumers.[9] We are, however, stressing the massive character of marketing products, a normal feature of a mass, profit-oriented, self-promoting society.

[5]Paul Sann, *Fads, Follies, and Delusions of the American People* (New York: Bonanza Books, A Division of Crown Publishers, Inc., 1967).

[6]Vance Packard, *The Hidden Persuaders* (New York: David McKay Company, Inc., 1957).

[7]Ibid, pp. 157–66.

[8]Ibid, p. 164.

[9]See for an outstanding example, Elijah Jordan, *Business Be Damned* (New York: Henry Schuman, Inc., 1952).

As in all cases, consumer education, consumer awareness, and consumer consciousness would go a long way in preventing unsatisfying purchases, but there is also need for some form of consumer advocacy and consumer protection. Qualifying almost as a sociological principle is the expectation that a well-organized minority can control a poorly-organized majority. Filling the void for consumers has been the development of consumer advocacy groups in recent years.

But the business of coaxing consumers to buy products or services is well out in front. Kenneth Roman and Jane Maas, for instance, have provided professional advertisers with the expertise of some twenty-five years of experience on-the-job.[10] Roman and Maas observe that the toy industry has been operating under the guidelines of the National Association of Broadcasters for some ten years and that new regulations, yet to come, will be formulated to avoid charges of exploitation of children under ten who are less able than older persons to distinguish between fantasy and reality.[11] They call for effective, socially responsible advertising and note seven rules to follow:

1. Children emulate other children, particularly older children and particularly boys.
2. The three different children's markets are one-to-five-year-old preschoolers who depend upon parental decisions; the six-to-nine-year-olds who favor fads and watch television very attentively; and the ten-to-thirteen-year-olds who look to teenagers for appropriate tastes or preferences.
3. The product must meet the promises of the commercial.
4. Repetition of commercials is acceptable to children.
5. Build loyalty to products through a personality such as "Barbie."
6. Include humor in children's advertising as children are fun-oriented.
7. Reassure parents that the product is safe and free from any ill-effects for children.[12]

Robert Snow's recent study of the way children look at television programs suggests that children probably should be given more credit for distinguishing between fantasy and reality.[13] It is Snow's finding that children do approach television presentations as part of their play orientations, but they are quite clear about *real* violence and *make-believe* violence.

[10]Kenneth Roman and Jane Maas, *How to Advertise* (New York: St. Martin's Press, Inc., 1976).
[11]Ibid, p. 140.
[12]Ibid, pp. 141–42.
[13]Robert P. Snow, "How Children Interpret TV Violence in Play Context," *Journalism Quarterly*, 59, No. 1 (Spring 1974), 13–21.

The majority of the investigators and interpreters of the data are more convinced, however, that mass media, particularly television, are linked with violent behavior that erupts sooner or later in children. Otto Larsen, for example, brought together pertinent scholarship in his informative book, *Violence and the Mass Media.*[14] A report to the Surgeon General entitled *Television and Growing Up: The Impact of Televised Violence*[15] also suggests that television may be the leading offender in its antisocial effects upon children. The report does observe that there are predisposing conditions that foster the undesirable results such as circumstances within families or the larger society. Further, consistent and conclusive data was held to be unavailable.[16] Nevertheless, continued reports appear in the press that the play of children is affected by exposure to mass media. The Horace Mann School for Nursery Years, ages three to six, reported from New York that peaceful block-building sessions were interrupted by cries of "Earthquake" after seeing a film by that name, and the block constructions were promptly destroyed.[17] Children at the school would chorus together, "I'm Batman. I'm Superman. I'm a monster!" or "Pow, wow, chop, chop" and follow this announcement with a series of karate chops or wrestling holds.[18]

In all this, we can only observe that a violent world begets violence, and with so much violence presented as daily news or dramatized on the stage, films, or television, it will predictably intrude upon the playful, fun-oriented, expressive behavior of young children. Indeed, not to find it there would be beyond expectation.

The Role of Pets, the Living Toys

The appeal of live animals has not escaped the attention of those who make their living from the play orientations of children. The fantasy worlds of Walt Disney, for example, have made household words out of Mickey and Minnie Mouse, Donald Duck, Pluto, and Bambi. Porky Pig, Woody the Woodpecker, Brer Rabbit, and the zany Roadrunner are also familiar cartoon characters. The animal character is not only given human qualities but can perform impossible deeds such as walking on air or surviving a free fall from an airplane. The real-life adventures of animals that Disney filmed have become respected clas-

[14]Otto Larsen, ed., *Violence and the Mass Media* (New York: Harper & Row, Publishers, 1968).
[15]*Television and Growing Up: The Impact of Televised Violence, Report to the Surgeon General* (Washington, D.C.: United States Public Health Service, 1972).
[16]Ibid, pp. 182–83.
[17]*Akron Beacon Journal,* Monday, June 9, 1975, p. A–10.
[18]Ibid, p. A–10.

sics. Other highly attractive products have been the "Wild Kingdom" program with Marlin Perkins, "Survival," and "The World of Animals." Jacques Cousteau has built a fine reputation from his film records of fish, mammals, and sea birds. No matter how presented, living creatures are meaningful participants in the lives of children.

James H. S. Bossard was, perhaps, one of the early students of childhood who sensed the importance of living animals in the socialization of children. He often spoke of the single article that provoked the greatest response among all his numerous, scholarly publications, "The Mental Hygiene of Owning a Dog."[19] A dozen years later, Nelson Foote acknowledged how frequently sociologists overlook the most common household pet, the family dog.[20] More recently, in 1972, Boris Levinson produced a booklength exposition of the psychological and social functions that pet ownership makes possible.[21] Earlier, Levinson enlarged upon the theme of mental health in his *Pet-Oriented Child Psychotherapy.*[22]

Levinson suggests that children have need for some "soft, cuddly, yielding, and always present" agent[23] and that this need is best supplied through the presence of a living pet animal. Further, pets become participants in the make-believe stories of children, serve as companions, provide training in the assumption of responsibilities, make steadfast friends, become love objects, and teach lessons in life and in death, such as in sexual education, the expenditure of money, or coping with the demise of a beloved pet.[24]

Not everyone waxes enthusiastic over providing pets for children. Read Bain of Miami (Ohio) University once brought howls of outrage from his fellow sociologists when he presented a tongue-in-cheek paper provocatively titled "The Sociopathy of the Dog Complex."[25] In his paper, he had deliberately and assiduously gathered as many of the negative aspects of dog ownership as he could. The "sociopathology" to which he pointed were examples of how dog ownership harmed persons, both young and old, rather than provided their human caretakers with pleasing results. Bain noted the absurd costs of dog care that could

[19]James H. S. Bossard, "The Mental Hygiene of Owning a Dog," *Mental Hygiene* (July 1944), pp. 408–13.

[20]Nelson Foote, "A Neglected Member of the Family," *Marriage and Family Living,* 18, No. 3 (August 1956), 213–18.

[21]Boris M. Levinson, *Pets and Human Development* (Springfield, Illinois: Charles C. Thomas, Publisher, 1972).

[22]Boris M. Levinson, *Pet-Oriented Child Psychotherapy* (Springfield, Illinois: Charles C. Thomas, Publisher, 1969).

[23]Levinson, *Pets and Human Development,* p. 40.

[24]Ibid, pp. 43–53.

[25]Read Bain, "The Sociopathy of the Dog Complex," A paper presented at the Ohio Valley Sociological Society Meetings, and in private possession of Marvin R. Koller.

be used for human needs, the carrying of disease to humans, the dog-bite cases, the damage to personal and public property, the soiling of lawns, gardens, and shrubs to the dismay and discomfort of neighbors, and the lessons in neglect and lack of responsibility that children can learn when they and their parents treat their dog's needs casually and even cruelly. Some 15 to 20 million cats and dogs are turned into city pounds or shelters annually; some 75 percent of these came from owners who found pet ownership inconvenient.[26] Of these "sheltered" animals, some 90 percent are destroyed.[27]

Children may truly care for their pets and so learn useful lessons in life. On the other hand, there are those children, while few in number, who have treated stray animals with considerable cruelty. Reports of dogs strangled with piano wire and kittens whose eyes have been shot out by gangs of boys are local items that have recently reached the author's desk. Much of this sort of treatment is rarely publicized because of its vicious nature. In sum, pets provide *opportunities* for children to acquire cues to maturity, but much depends upon the use or abuse to which these opportunities are subject.

GAMES[28]

As we have noted, games are particular forms of play, the organized formalization of play through rules and through limitations governing the behavior of each player. This, in and of itself, provides considerable growth for children in understanding and dealing with themselves and with others.[29] Games provide experiences in winning and in losing. They provide opportunities for decision-making, sharing, team-experiences, leadership-followership, preparations, and concentration of attention over periods of time. The sum total of the playing of games is often called the learning of "good sportsmanship."

Games Involving Minimal Numbers

Solitary play of little children soon gives way to group play with a few other children or players. These playmates may be siblings, relatives, or neighboring children. Later, with the child's entry into formal schools, playmates may and often do include school friends. The enlarg-

---

[26]Data from Northeast Ohio Dog Services, Inc., Tallmadge, Ohio.
[27]Ibid.
[28]Eldon Snyder and Elmer Spreitzer, "State of the Field—Sociology of Sport, An Overview," *The Sociological Quarterly*, 15, No. 4 (Autumn 1974), 467–68.
[29]Rafael Helanko, "Classification of Children's Outdoor Games," *International Review of Sport Sociology*, 9, No. 2 (1974), 103–6.

ing play-circle calls for some form of mutual agreement to play together in organized activities of one kind or another.

Jumping rope, hopscotch, doll play, seesaw, jigsaw puzzles, drawing, card playing, or block building are some of the simpler types of games that are enjoyable because a small number of players are involved. More sophisticated games such as checkers, Monopoly, Scrabble, or chess are pleasing because of the operations of chance and the anticipation of countermoves by others.

These games, however, do far more than teach cooperation with others. Players are transformed into opponents, rivals, or competititors, and play takes on the attributes of a struggle, a seeking of objectives for personal glory or gain. In the process, some players are necessarily "out," "defeated," or "set back." As those who have described the Olympic Games express it, some experience "the triumphs of victory" while others experience "the agonies of defeat."

There is nothing new in all this for veteran players or grown-ups who know that players "win some and lose some" only to resume new games yet to come. For children, however, the early frustrations and failures can become traumatic and troubling experiences that are stored for future reference in future encounters.

Prepackaged Sports For Child Players

Games take on new significance when team play is introduced both in and out of schools. Representing one's grade or school may mean disappointment for one's friends and associates, and this added burden increases the pressure to perform well. Playing with the Little Leagues, Pee Wee Football, or Children's Hockey demands uniforms, practice sessions, and serious attention to immediate situations in order to achieve championship status. Much depends upon coaching staffs, the reasons for participating, and the understanding of parents. Now and then partisanship and tempers flair up on the part of adults, more frequently, from all reports, than on the part of young players.

In this team context, it is worth mentioning the economics of *observation* of sports in contrast with *participation* in sports. Huge crowds gathered to watch favorite teams engaged in football, baseball, basketball, soccer, or hockey are commercially significant. The investments in arenas, stadiums, ball parks, rinks, or fields are tremendous and do not even begin to touch equipment, administrative staff, maintenance men and women, security needs, advertising, ticket distribution, sales promotions, and the like. The contracted salaries and incomes of professional players are huge and, while limited to relatively few years of play, are impressive.[30] Rather early in life, youngsters find models in these sports figures and set themselves goals along these same lines. Relatively few will achieve fame and fortune in sports, but many begin in childhood to work toward these goals.

Watching or observing sports provides vicarious thrills. Some have negatively viewed the phenomenon as "spectatoritis," the vocal critics who sit on the sidelines and offer adivce but who cannot and do not enter into the team play itself. For children, at least, interest and value are contingent upon participation. This they gain by engaging in team sports at a fairly early age. The "training" they receive is transferable to "the games of life." At least this is the rationale that is offered in support of children becoming active in sporting events.

Sex-role typing manifests itself in sports activities as well as in other areas previously discussed. For many years, the games of boys were distinguishable from the games of girls. Boys played rougher, body-contact sports whereas girls tended to play more sedate games such as croquet, tennis, or archery. Girls might cheer from the sidelines, but they were to play exclusively with girls and under "girls' rules." The mixing of boys and girls on team sports has been a more recent phenomenon of the 1970s. Increasingly, one hears of boy and girl baseball players on the same teams. Basketball and volleyball involve mixed teams of boys and girls. The Soapbox Derby held annually in Akron, Ohio not only welcomes girls as well as boys but has already produced a number of girl champions in the gravity-race competitions.

Whether the trend will continue in amateur and school-oriented sports remains to be seen. In the Olympic Games, the pinnacle of amateur sport participation, the separation of men and women is quite evident. Indeed, "sex tests" have become routine in Olympic competition to guard against "unfair" competition between men and women representing their respective nations. In professional sports, sex separation is well entrenched and will probably not be changed in the 1980s or 1990s.

Other Group-Oriented Leisure Activities

There are a great many other group-oriented leisure activities that merit attention if we are to understand the relationships between play and work as they apply to childhood and children. These would include musical training, drama, travel,[31] and pursuit of specialized interests such as swimming and hiking.

[30]Howard L. Nixon, "The Commercial and Organizational Development of Modern Sport," *International Review of Sport Sociology,* 9, No. 2 (1974), 107–35.
[31]Paul C. Rosenblatt and Martha G. Russell, "The Social Psychology of Potential Problems in Family Vacation Travel," *The Family Coordinator,* 24, No. 2 (April 1975), 209–15.

For the most part, whether one is dealing with music, drama, travel, and other specialized interests as an avocation or as a vocation, there seems to be general agreement that these interests are rooted in early childhood experiences. All of them call for considerable investments in time, money, and energy and cannot be pursued for very long without them. For particular fields of endeavor, early childhood is held to be the best time to lay the necessary foundations upon which all else depends. To enter some fields, young adulthood may not be the most favored time of the life cycle to do so. We are referring, of course, to generalized aptitudes and abilities whose early discovery in childhood sets persons in directions from which they do not depart as they mature. Such a perspective places considerable responsibility upon parents and other adults to provide a wide range of interests and activities from which to make avocational or vocational choices. What constitutes play and what constitutes work over a lifetime can be traced back to the formative years of childhood.

WORK

Much of what we have discussed in terms of play, games, and work has been concentrated upon children themselves. But, if we are to fill out more comprehensively the connections between childhood and the economy, it would be helpful to consider the work of adults as it affects childhood and children.

Working Mothers

Mothers have always worked, but their participation in the work force *outside* of their homes and *away* from their families has increased in the last several decades. Of interest to us are the effects, positive or adverse, if any, upon their children. Fortunately, speculation or hypotheses about this matter have been tested empirically and do shed light on the relationship.[32]

Popular belief has held that the employment of mothers is essentially detrimental to their children. The children are alleged to be more susceptible to antisocial behavior, more likely to be nervous, anxiety-ridden, and disturbed, more likely to do poorly in school, and as adolescents, rebel against authority in a series of delinquent acts.

In the main, the differences that have been found to exist between the children of working and nonworking mothers have been due to

[32]Probably the best single source is F. Ivan Nye and Lois W. Hoffman, eds., *The Employed Mother in America* (Chicago: Rand McNally and Company, 1963).

chance factors rather than to causative factors. Statistically interpreted, this means that repeated studies do not support the thesis that children of working mothers will necessarily have troubles because of this condition. Rather, repeated studies reveal that some children of working mothers do have ensuing problems while other children of working mothers do not. Of course, research will continue and what will be found in the future with refined methods and measurements may alter the present state of knowledge.

Certain controls placed on the conditions of working mothers such as social class, the ages and sex of the children, the attitudes held by mothers toward their outside employment, and whether or not they are working full or part time, have been shown to have measurable effects upon the children. Nye found that middle-class children were more likely to become delinquent in adolescence whereas Glueck and Glueck found no such results among children of lower-class working mothers.[33] Part-time employment of mothers seems to be a better procedure than full-time employment as far as children are concerned.[34] Those who work by choice and are not motivated by economic necessity present a different role model to their children than mothers who have no choice and must work to economically support their families. Although younger children require more care and guidance from surrogates if their mothers work outside the home and younger families usually have a greater economic need to establish themselves than older families, in the main, the ages of the children seem to be of no major consequence if their mothers work.

Girls whose mothers work seem to have more self-confidence concerning their ambitions and less support for the notion that there is a difference between women's work and men's work. Boys, on the other hand, seem to be adversely affected by developing more dependency, less aggression, and low achievement.[35]

The attitudes of mothers toward their outside work are important variables to take into account. When mothers enjoy their work, they seem able to maintain a close, mutually satisfying relationship with their children. When, however, their approach to their work is one of dissatisfaction, their bitterness carries over to their relationship with their children and increases the burdens upon children to perform household tasks to which the mothers could not attend.[36]

[33]Ibid, pp. 133–41.
[34]Ibid, pp. 142–64.
[35]Ibid., pp. 67–81.
[36]Ibid., pp. 142–64, and Constantina Safilios-Rothschild, "The Influence of the Wife's Degree of Work Commitment Upon Some Aspects of Family Organization and Dynamics," *Journal of Marriage and Family,* 32 (November 1970), 681–91.

If the known trends continue, the likelihood is that the ranks of working mothers will increase. The traditional role of mothers who work only inside their homes with their children will remain a viable alternative, but a less popular one if current trends persist.

There is another overriding circumstance that could sharply alter what seems to have been happening in the area of working mothers. The assumption that the economy will continue to expand, providing more jobs, occupations, and careers, may be without foundation. Indeed, work opportunities may be sharply reduced as machines and automation develop apace. Men have felt the reductions in the work force that new technologies have brought about. Women, with their newfound freedom to work outside the home, may find that a saturation point will be reached. In that event, the leisure world long associated with childhood will become far more significant for adults.

Working Fathers

Working fathers are nothing new or remarkable. Of importance, however, are the effects of unemployment or underemployment upon children. These effects have to do with the changing role models of men as the chief economic providers for their families. The exodus of mothers from the home seems to suggest the growing return of fathers to their children. The traditional view was that fathers were too preoccupied with their work to deal directly with their children. Father-absenteeism during working hours, while often decried by mothers and children, was also understood. But with shortened working hours, more holidays, vacations with pay, earlier retirements, or the lack of full employment for millions of men, the chances increase for more contact between men and their children. Again, as with working mothers, the overall economy will determine the ultimate relationships that can develop between fathers and their children.

SUMMARY

By concentrating upon play, games, and work, we have examined the numerous ways in which the economy affects childhood and children in American society. Play is intrinsically pursued for purposes of self-expression, enjoyment, and amusement. Games are organized play that operate under fixed and predetermined rules that set limits upon the behavior of the various players. Work is utilitarian or instrumental because it sustains life itself.

Play has been the province of childhood, but in the midst of imaginative, fantasy play, there is anticipatory socialization for future work or vocations. From childhood, work is seen at a distance, but their play and the apparatus used in play, toys, reflect much of the adult world of work.

The toy industry is "big business" in and of itself. There has been concern in recent years that profit making has been of greater interest than the production and sale of safe and worthwhile toys for youngsters. Television, too, has come under attack with its promotion of violence as entertainment. In both instances, self-imposed industrial codes have been utilized to control potential harm of children. There is a children's market that advertisers try to exploit, but in this, too, there is growing recognition of social responsibilities toward the consumer.

Pets or, as we have expressed it, the living toys, are of special interest in this context. The positive, constructive expectations are that children's associations with animals are beneficial. On the other hand, we tried to modify any Pollyannish portrayal of pets by noting the detriments of pet ownership and association as well. Pets provide opportunities for maturity, but much depends upon the use or abuse of these opportunities.

In our discussion of games, we balanced the socialization to be gained with the potential difficulties. The arts of cooperation, harmony, and knowing how to work under rules and regulations were weighed along with the issues of failure, competition, organized sporting programs, participation versus observation, and sexism.

Further, we maintained that other group-oriented leisure activities or interests took on special significance because many of them are acquired during early childhood. Their early acquisition in the formative years of childhood is almost a necessity and can help set directions that apply to both work and play in maturity.

Lastly, we looked briefly at working mothers and fathers as they affected their children. We found the interesting phenomenon of mothers working away from their children in increasing numbers and fathers having increased opportunities to be with their children. The economy, however, will set the ultimate conditions as to the work and play of adults and their offspring.

FOUR

Social psychology
of
childhood

11

Children's self-concepts

At the outset, in chapter one, childhood was introduced as a multidimensional status. Although we have stressed the sociological approaches to childhood, we have not abandoned the other approaches discussed in the initial chapter. In turning to children's self-concepts, we begin to focus upon the *social-psychological* aspects of childhood.

Psychology, we noted, concentrates upon the individual, the unique being or creature who, while sharing and experiencing similar processes or events, stands apart from all others mainly by reason of the special combination of observable and less-observable traits subsumed by the term, *personality*.

Sociology, by contrast, devotes major attention to *the human group* with all its variant structures, interactional, and intraactional processes, and its diverse impacts or significance.

The criticism concerning this factorial analysis is that synthesis is thereby neglected. In the professional zeal and expertise of specialization, it is said, it is possible to lose sight of the *gestalt*, the total picture in which each minute factor or variable works in combination with all other factors or variables. In this reasoning, the psychologically-oriented underestimate or undervalue the human group or groups while the sociologically-oriented, such as ourselves, underestimate or undervalue the individuals who compose human groups and provide their real impetus.

The interstitial specialization of psychologists and sociologists who are concerned about both individuals and group phenomena is the field known as *social psychology.* Noteworthy is the fact that *psychology* is the noun and *social* is the modifying adjective, a product of usage over many years by academics. Legitimately, one might call the specialization *psychological sociology,* but such a labeling has not been commonly used. We bow to custom and identify Part Four as selected aspects of the *social psychology of childhood.*

Social psychology, then, deals with the study of *individuals in group situations.* It is a specialization that is particularly suited to illuminate childhood because it provides significant insights concerning the introduction of young children into human society. It takes into account not only the *exterior* environment in which children live, but also the *interior* environments that guide and direct children's behavior.

For a thorough treatment of the theories and research literature in social psychology, concerned readers should explore more comprehensive sources.[1] Our purpose is to discuss selected components of social psychology that bear upon the shaping of childhood in specific ways. The *self-concept* is the first of these. Chapters that follow direct attention to reference-group theory, significant others, and symbolic interaction.

DEVELOPMENT OF SELF-CONCEPT

The Selfless Neonate

Newborn infants do not begin with a self-concept that, like their bodies, is small and undeveloped. Rather, they are selfless or unaware of who they are, why they live, what their potentials may be, what is distinctive about them, and how they are related to those about them.

---

[1]A good beginning can be made by consulting for example, David A. Goslin, ed. *Handbook of Socialization Theory and Research* (Chicago: Rand McNally, 1969). Another useful source is Martin L. Hoffman and Lois Wladis Hoffman, eds., *Review of Child Development Research*, Vols. One and Two (New York: Russell Sage Foundation, 1964 and 1965).

Certainly a consciousness or awareness has begun because infants act and react to the combined effects of their inner needs and the changes in their external environment. This consciousness or awareness, however, is organismic-centered or primarily based upon imbalances or physiologic discomforts that require attention and the restoration of greater body comfort. Their inner needs and impulses, which are imperative, unrestrained, and unsocialized, cry out for attention. Other individuals are unknown and self is unknown. The development of a sense of others and a sense of self requires interaction with a complex network of social systems and unique experiences with identifiable persons. It obviously waits upon a finer tuning or sensing of organisms that can finally bring the self-concept into being.

Social life, by its very nature, requires limitations, restraints, or controls upon the organic imperatives of human infants. Indeed, identifying them as "human" refers only to their *potentials* or possibilities as the newest members of *homo sapiens.* Infants become human as they acquire increasing abilities to appreciate and use the symbols and embellishments brought into being by those who preceded them.

One such restraint or control over organismic imperatives applies to the toilet training given to infants. As Lawrence Frank expressed it: "The infant at birth has a well developed capacity for eliminating both urine and feces, having rehearsed these functions, at least for urination, before birth. When the pressures within the bladder and rectum build up through accumulation of their contents, the sphincters automatically release and allow the contents to be discharged. Infants are expected to learn to withhold urine and feces until they can deposit these in the designated vessel or place, often at a specified time. The intent of this 'toilet training' is to curb and regularize spontaneous elimination so that the infant will not soil himself (herself) but will learn to be continent as a preparation for becoming progressively more sanitary and capable of living in the public world with only occasional and approved times and places for such elimination. As in feeding, these demands for self-regulation of elimination may be viewed as another intervention of the outside world, intended to bring this physiological functioning under external regulation and control."[2]

The continued "failures" or "accidents" that occur for little children over many years become the source of shame, guilt, and ridicule when discussed openly in the presence of comprehending youngsters. Sooner or later, preferably sooner, children must learn control over their body functions and so develop a positive self-image in company

[2]Lawrence K. Frank, *On the Importance of Infancy* (New York: Random House, 1966), p. 144.

with others. Incontinence among the very elderly can and does occur, giving rise to the claim that some elders "return to childhood" in their advanced years. The incontinent elders probably require even more sensitive handling than immature infants because these older persons certainly have well-established self-concepts at this stage in their life. Sudnow carried this "social infancy" even further when he discussed the preparations made for hospital patients who have died.[3] At this final stage, the person becomes an object to be handled because inner-feeling states are lacking, and significant others no longer seek to be present.

The Self-Concept, A Social Product

The newborn begin with selflessness, unaware that they even exist, but soon enough, a self-awareness, a self-consciousness is established and develops over time. Just how does this process operate? For answers, turn to inventive theorists who explain their ideas by means of a variety of constructs and mechanisms.

CHARLES HORTON COOLEY'S LOOKING-GLASS SELF. Cooley's *Human Nature and Social Order*, published in 1902, established the major sociological perspective on the origin and development of the self-concept.[4] In a three-step interactional pattern, Cooley explained the how and why of self-conception. First, there is an image of how one appears to others; secondly, the individual's perception of how he or she makes a judgment of how that appearance is received by others; and thirdly, the individual achieves a self-feeling based upon that imagined judgment of his or her appearance.

A few observations based on Cooley's "looking-glass self" that postulates self-concept as a mirroring or reflection of one's self through the reactions of others are in order.

For one, Cooley places great store in *the imaginative.* He stresses that an accurate, correct, or undistorted image of an individual may or may not be received by others. An exaggerated or highly distorted perspective has the same effect as a more precise and accurate perception of the individual. In either case, imagination continues to operate within the individual because that individual can only guess the judgments of his or her appearance in the mental processes of others.

For another, Cooley urges persons to pay major attention to *ideas,* because these ideas, right or wrong, provide the rationale for social

[3]David Sudnow, *Passing On, The Social Organization of Dying* (Englewood Cliffs, N. J.: Prentice-Hall, Inc., 1967), p. 77.
[4]Charles Horton Cooley, *Human Nature and the Social Order* (New York: Schocken, 1964, published originally by Scribner's Sons in 1902).

action or behavior. Thus, whatever the truth may be, fantasy, half-truths, and misperceptions can be treated as both input and output in the processing.

Lastly, *other persons* are actors or participants in one's life whether the individual appreciates them or not. The individual child does not live in a social vacuum, but is always in the company of others on a real or fantasized basis. In this view, Cooley places himself squarely in the ranks of sociologists who make social interaction the root of their concerns.

GEORGE HERBERT MEAD'S "I" AND "ME". George Herbert Mead's *Mind, Self and Society*, published in 1934, presented his seminal explanations of the development of the self-concept.[5] His distinction between *I* and *me* is standard fare in social psychological and sociological discourse. With Cooley, Mead agreed that the self is not in existence at birth, but emerges through social experiences, social processes, and social interactive processes. Unlike Cooley, however, Mead took the position that the community or "generalized others" with whom individuals deal do not completely dominate the development of self-concepts. In this, Mead anticipated Wrong's classic article that cautioned sociologists about their "oversocialization" conceptualizations.[6]

The *I*, in Mead's view, is that portion of the self that remains unpredictably aloof, removed, insulated, or apart from the attitudes of others. The *me* is the conventional part of self that accepts the attitudes of others and guides the individual to behave predictably according to the expectations of others. The *me* conforms to the wishes of others so that the individual child will "fit into" society. The *I* part of the self remains unconvinced that others should have such influence. This inner sanctum or inner conversation provides the uniqueness of the individual, according to Mead. The *me* of a child accepts the criticisms of parents, teachers, and friends. The *I* of a child comforts and assures the individual that he or she is a far better or different individual than others believe.

Mead's distinctions help explain why conformists can also be individualists, different from those about them despite common experiences or treatment. Further, Mead's separation of *I* and *me* allows for changes within the self that can alter social situations just as children experience change as the external conditions of their lives change. If social expectations are rigidly enforced, the *me* of children becomes

[5]Anselm Strauss, ed., *George Herbert Mead On Social Psychology* (Chicago: The University of Chicago Press, 1964).
[6]Dennis H. Wrong, "The Oversocialized Conception of Man in Modern Sociology," *American Sociological Review*, 26 (April 1961), 183–93.

dominant, and the *I* of children is stifled by strong measures such as rejection and withdrawal of love or support. If, however, norms are more adaptable or flexible, then the *me* of children can be more relaxed because the *I* can be expressed with greater confidence, without fear of ridicule, rejection, or reprisal. The reciprocal interplay between self and society remains in Mead's analysis.

SIGMUND FREUD'S ID, EGO, AND SUPEREGO. The duality of self in Mead's terms is conceptualized more elaborately by Sigmund Freud's triadic elements of the id, the ego, and the superego. The id is the unconscious, animalistic, primitive, basic component of self in Freudian terms. The ego develops out of the energies of the id and generally seeks to control or restrain the excesses of which the id is capable, particularly in the areas of aggression and sexuality. Ego-awareness on the part of the individual develops in childhood, according to Freud, as basic drives are brought under restraint or control. Finally, and unconsciously, the superego comes into being as an individual makes the ideas, values, and expectations of his or her social milieu a part of his or her own personal qualities. At the conscious level, the superego corresponds to the conscience, the inner voice that talks with the individual and counsels the individual "to do the right thing at the right time and circumstance."

What Freud has labeled *id*, Mead has identified as the unsocialized, insulated *I* and Cooley has described as *original nature*. What Freud called *superego*, Mead identified as the socialized *me*. Freud's contribution portrayed the third element, *ego*, as the mediator between id and superego so that neither could dominate the individual; the ego thus directs the individual into appropriate actions. Freudian analysis stressed early childhood as central in the life of the individual because these inner mechanisms determined the fundamental personality of the person. It has taken decades to modify this contention by recognizing that socialization is a lifelong process and that the self-concept undergoes changes in adolescence, young adulthood, middle age, and old age. We who work in the field of childhood are indebted to Freudian emphasis upon the earliest years of a lifetime, but we would be in error if we insisted that socialization stops at ages five, six, or twelve.

ERVING GOFFMAN AND MULTIPLE SELVES. The developing and ever-changing self-concept has an expressive advocate in Erving Goffman and his essays.[7] Goffman represents one theorist out of many who have

[7]Erving Goffman, *The Presentation of Self in Everyday Life* (Garden City, New York: Anchor Books, Doubleday & Company, Inc., 1959).

developed symbolic interactional theory along dramaturgical lines. Most people recall Shakespeare's "All the world's a stage and the men and women all players." Goffman admittedly uses theatrical terminology as a device to explain the variety of selves each individual plays. These multiple selves are brought forward or "frontstage" depending upon changed situations. A child will use one "routine" or action with playmates and another with parents or teachers. The child acts differently as a brother or sister than when he or she is "performing" as a grandchild in front of grandparents. One must listen for "cues," know when to use certain equipment or "props," and when to make certain "entrances" and "exits."

In brief, Goffman suggests the fluid, dynamic, *situational* nature of interplay between persons and their relationships with other "actors" and "actresses" that calls for a whole repertoire of "selves" rather than a single, monolithic self suitable for all occasions. The "masks" children use in their early years are only part of their "equipment" to which they add as they grow more sophisticated. To intimate friends and trusted associates, the individual may go "backstage" and reveal another self in privacy and assurance. To "audiences" who are "frontstage," a public "performance" is in order and is carefully "rehearsed" to convey certain impressions.

These are useful conceptualizations employed by Goffman to explain the self-concept. They do not contradict sociological concepts such as status, role, or social distance. Rather, they effectively reach persons who do not communicate or think in sociological terms, making them aware of the varied and complex nature of self-conceptualization.

REPRISE, THE SELF-CONCEPT, A SOCIAL PRODUCT. Whether one favors the analyses of Cooley, Mead, Freud, or Goffman, there is fundamental agreement that self-concept is learned, acquired, or gained and refined through group participation and social interaction. Cooley takes the middle position that the individual secures a reflection of himself or herself through others and subjectively determines self-awareness. Mead and Freud tend to focus on those portions of self-conceptualization that resist manipulation, control, or input from others. Freud, more than Mead, could be interpreted as contending that there is a hostile, aggressive, antisocial element in individual personality. Goffman draws attention to the situational nature of self so that the same individual may act out many "selves" depending upon circumstances. Finally, in the usage of constructs or concepts to explain self-development, caution must be exercised to avoid the error of *reification,* to make real that which is essentially not real but is instead a contrived device to help

persons understand an important abstract idea. For example, Mead's
I and *me* are hypothetical but useful tools in understanding the self-
concept.

CONFLICTING SELVES

If Goffman and other theorists are describing the real socialization
of children in terms of the development of self-concepts, and there does
not seem to be contradictory information that indicates otherwise,
there is the possibility of internal conflict within the introspective processes of the very young.

For one thing, children do not develop one, simple self-concept
that serves in any and all situations. As Goffman and others have noted,
there are multiple selves that are adapted to different situations. For
another, the assumption that a self-concept is always consistent and
serves the best interests of the child can be challenged or is unwar-
ranted. For still another source of inner turmoil, distress, and confusion,
self-concepts can be seriously undermined and disrupted. The troubles,
tribulations, and traumas of childhood can be said to have their beginnings in the damage done to children's self-images.

Children of Divorced or Separated Parents

Some 60 percent of divorces in the United States involve minor
children and with the annual number of divorces rising to the record
heights of about a million, there is a clear and present threat to the
stable family environments of children. Parents who could, together,
produce and rear children find that their relationships as husbands and
wives do not involve the same type of cooperation and satisfaction. The
option to break apart is theirs, and obviously, more and more men and
women are taking that option. There is no quarrel with those who seek
to correct their errors in spouse selection or with those who have ex-
hausted the possibilities of coming together again as a mutually-bonded
and pleasing dyad. Indeed, the breakup of mothers and fathers has been
found in some cases to be the beginning of the first years of personal
relief from tensions that children may enjoy.

Recognition of positive effects of divorce and separation, however,
does not mean that there are no negative effects upon children. It is
these negative effects, particularly the damage done to self-concepts,
that concern us. Children whose self-images reflected their relationships with two parents find they must revise their self-assessments to
include two separate self-concepts with one parent-up-close and an-

other parent estranged or at-a-distance. The dissolution of a marital relationship is felt within the feeling-states of the children who came from that union. The hurt and confusion within children of divorced and alienated parents has also been documented. We are not arguing for or against breakup of marital relationships. We are arguing that the breakup of homes does bring about necessary changes in self-conceptualization among children and that some of these adjustments are painful and have long-range unhappy consequences.

Self-Concepts of Children
In and Out of Their Homes

Conflicting self-images that cause children to be "at war with themselves" can also be traced to the differential treatment they encounter inside and outside their homes. If they have a warm, secure, happy homelife, children may define themselves as flexible, compatible, and capable beings. But outside their homes, comparative strangers may treat them as inconsequential, incapable, self-centered beings. The contrast can be as shocking as moving from a warm and comforting shower to a cold and numbing shower. The reverse can be just as shocking. Outside their homes, children can be encouraged, emboldened, or empowered by nonfamily persons such as teachers, neighbors, or friends to explore their potential abilities. Inside their homes, however, children can and do run into discouragement, denials, and a defeatism that inform children that they lack the essential qualities for reaching desired goals and so should not even begin to try.

The Bruised Self[8]

Kaoru Yamamoto has called attention to the idea of the "bruised self." Yamamoto seeks to alert those who work with small children to be aware of the psychic wounds that manifest themselves as predictable outcomes of psychic battles. He provides a suggestive listing of these "bruised selves" or symptoms of psychic stress, as follows[9] :

Accident proneness	Feeding problems
Attention-getting behavior	Fears, phobias
Bad dreams	Hair-pulling, eyebrow-plucking
Bed-wetting	Health or physical
Cleanliness compulsion	preoccupations
Cruelty	

[8]Robert and Evelyn Kirkhart, "The Bruised Self; Mending in Early Years," from *The Child and His Image* by Kaoru Yamamoto, ed. © 1972 by Houghton Mifflin Co. pp. 121–77.
[9]Ibid. Reprinted by permission of the publisher, p. 138.

Daydreaming, fantasizing	Hyperactivity
Depression, apathy	Joylessness
Defiance, sullenness	Lying
Excessive emotionality	Nailbiting
Nervousness	Shyness
Muscular spasms (tics)	Sleep disturbances
Obesity (nonglandular)	Social withdrawal
Obsessive interests	Soiling (bowel)
Passive resistance	Stealing, delinquency
Perfectionism	Stuttering
Poor peer relations	Superiority complex
Psychosexual disturbances	Temper tantrums
Psychosomatic problems	Tenseness
School phobia	Thumbsucking
Self-abasement	Underachievement
Sexual disturbances	Worry
(exhibitionism, peeping)	

Anticipating objections to this list because these behaviors are fairly common, Yamamoto noted, "Most children will manifest some of these symptoms at special times when things have temporarily gone poorly for them. The sign that a child is really in trouble is when several symptoms begin to occur together and they become time-spanning and situation-spanning, that is, when the symptom crops up again and again over an extended period and in several contexts."[10] It is the persistence and pervasiveness of these symptoms that cry out for attention, and Yamamoto suggests that they are an "acting out" of the conflicting self-concepts within the psyches of children. They are "hurts" that need therapeutic measures just as much as a bruised knee needs cleansing and medication in order to heal properly.

SELF-CONCEPT AND MOTIVATION

Self-concepts that originate in childhood and are modified by increasing experiences in adolescence and later adulthood take on considerable significance in terms of motivation. Depending upon one's self-concept, there is either a willingness to exert effort to reach socially approved goals or a reluctance or inability to find one's self in society. Self-concepts can be either energizing or debilitating when situations call for investments of one's self in order to reach certain objectives. An example of the negative influence is the overly shy child who sees himself or herself as inadequate or incapable in relation to other per-

[10]Ibid, p. 183.

sons' qualities. Such a condition requires patience and help from others to provide the motivation to move forward.

The usual response to children known to have developed self-concepts that defeat them before they can even begin to perform effectively is one of sympathy and the offering of help. The mechanisms that have led to a type of social paralysis because of alleged self-unworthiness can perhaps be unjammed and set in another direction. The introspective action of the child led to a self-concept that may or may not be a correct appraisal of his or her real aptitudes and abilities. In such instances, sympathetic therapy on the part of professionals and laypeople may provide a better grasp of who an individual child is and what potentials that child possesses.

When, however, the sources that gave rise to a nonmotivating self-concept lie outside the child and originate in the conditions imposed by an established social order, there is grudging reluctance to make amends. Indeed, there is inaction when social responsibilities are diffused and the origins of self-defeatism and doubt are the social systems under which everyone lives. Social changes in a mass society wait upon glacierlike shifts in public perceptions or are contingent upon more dramatic, drastic events that require public realignments.

Self-Concepts of Minority Children

In chapters four, five, and six, we dealt with the "sensitive areas" or unresolved issues of sex, religion, and race in the lives of children. One of the serious effects of societal treatment of sex, religion, and race is the damage done to the personalities of minority children with special reference to their self-concepts, self-esteem, and subsequent motivations. When a female child, a black child, or a Jewish child is confronted with rejection, isolation, and general disapproval based upon long-established majority norms rather than upon any particular act or behavior of the child, self-concepts are fostered that lead to lack of motivation. These include self-hatred, self-derogation, and self-deprecation. The same applies to certain ethnic children, such as American Indian children, or to lower-class children who encounter deep-seated hostility far beyond their control or comprehension.[11]

At a much later phase of the life cycle, those who enter retirement or simply grow older experience the syndrome of social segregation or

[11]See for example, T. P. Carter, "The Negative Self-Concept of Mexican-American Students," *School and Society*, 96, (1968) 217–19; see also, James C. Hansen and Peter E. Maynard, *Youth: Self-Concept and Behavior* (Columbus, Ohio: Charles E. Merrill Publishing Company, 1973).

social isolation that engenders self-devaluation and lack of motivation similar to that which minority children develop.[12] In this sense, individuals long associated with social majorities may, for the first time in their lives, get a participant-observer, inside view of what it feels like to be judged inadequate. The youth-orientation of American society provides the seedbed for self-hatred and apathy that occurs so frequently among the elderly. This need not occur, of course, if countermeasures are taken. With accumulated resources and growing social support, older persons have achieved a more positive view of their potentials and so are motivated to active participation in society once again. For children, however, advocacy, support, and acceptance waits upon "grown-ups" to change the social scenery and so encourage motivation.

Self-Insulation

The sociological studies of Walter Reckless and his associates provide another clue as to the motivational or impelling force of self-concepts.[13] Reckless and his students suggest that *self-insulation* explains why some children do not get into trouble with the law despite the fact that many youngsters who live in the same neighborhoods are frequently delinquent. Figuratively, "good boys" and "good girls" in a high-delinquency area have wrapped themselves in an impermeable blanket that protects them from the antisocial or criminal-prone climate in which they live. The "good boys" and "good girls" see themselves as living well within the laws of the land and, consequently, quite capable of further growth, hope, and accomplishments of a satisfying nature. Such youngsters circumvent the pitfalls that entrap so many others around them because their self-concepts lead them into quite different paths of preparation and achievement. Clinard, a specialist in deviant behavior, observed that those who become delinquent can be "turned around" or "successfully treated" when they "see themselves" differently and so conduct themselves in a nondelinquent manner.[14] It is the self-concept that must be altered in these instances before a difference in behavior can be manifested.

[12]See Richard A. Kalish, *Late Adulthood: Perspectives on Human Development* (Monterey, California: Brooks/Cole Publishing Company, A Division of Wadsworth Publishing Company, Inc., 1975), "Aging, Self, and Personality," pp. 47–69.
[13]Walter C. Reckless, Simon Dinitz, and Ellen Murray, "Self Concept as an Insulator Against Delinquency," *American Sociological Review*, 21 (December 1956), 744–46. See also Simon Dinitz, Frank R. Scarpitti, and Walter C. Reckless, "Delinquency Vulnerability: A Cross Group and Longitudinal Analysis," *American Sociological Review*, 27, No. 4 (August 1962), 515–17.
[14]Marshall B. Clinard, *Sociology of Deviant Behavior*, 3rd ed. (New York: Holt, Rinehart and Winston, Inc., 1968), p. 65.

The Self-Awareness Trap[15]

The power of the self-concept has been well publicized so that numerous programs have been designed to deal with specific problems among the young such as runaways, emotional disorders, or sexuality. Edwin Schur does not quarrel with those programs of rehabilitation in which participants reassess their self-concepts or "get in touch with themselves." Allegedly, once an individual knows his or her "self," the person knows how to match self-interests with social interests or needs and so finds fulfillment. Schur, however does caution that emphasis upon self-awareness can become an inner retreat that fails to change social conditions that brought about self-defeatism in the first place.

Schur's point is a familiar one because it is a criticism that has been leveled for many years at such dissimilar fields as, for example, religion and social work. The argument is that in the search for inner peace and tranquility, there is little or no concern for external, societal conditions. The status quo is merely accepted, and social protest and change do not occur. Marx's famous charge that religion is "the opiate of the people" carries this connotation. As to social work, the clients served by professional social workers are constantly being generated by causative factors within the social system. Social workers, in effect, treat those who have suffered in some way, but their professional services do not alter the major structures and functions of human society which lie beyond their expertise and control. Their professional services are limited to appropriate amelioration within the personality of the clients, and the ranks of those processed or helped are swiftly filled again in a neverending sequence because fundamental social changes do not occur.

As sociologists who seek to understand childhood, we have no special ax to grind in behalf of self-awareness or in behalf of social change. We are aware, however, of the reciprocal nature of social circumstances and self-concepts and so suggest that they are not mutually exclusive entities that can be adequately dealt with when considered singly.

SUMMARY

With this chapter, we begin to examine some social-psychological dimensions of childhood. Social psychology is a specialization that ex-

[15]Edwin Schur, *The Awareness Trap, Self-Absorption Instead of Social Change* (New York: Quadrangle/New York Times Book Co., 1976). See also, Howard B. Kaplan, *Self-Attitudes and Deviant Behavior* (Pacific Palisades, California: Goodyear Publishing Company, Inc., 1975).

tracts from both sociology and psychology those tools of analysis and synthesis that explain the nature of individuals in group situations. In this chapter, we concentrate upon what many social psychologists would call the most critical element in human personalities, the self-concept or self-attitude.

First, we established that newborn infants do not begin their lives with a ready-made, innate self-conceptualization. Instead, neonates are selfless or unaware of who they are, why they live, or what distinguishes them from all others. They are, we noted, organismic-centered or oriented toward seeking a reduction of body imbalances or physical discomforts. Taking control of one's body, such as in toilet training, is the initial step toward self-conceptualization.

The genesis of the self-concept occurs in the interactions of a given child with others, usually persons already socialized in some particular manner. Theorists such as Cooley, Mead, Freud, and Goffman offer similar but somewhat different explanations of how persons arrive at a self-conception. Cooley sees the self-concept as the subjective reflection of interpretations by others of what the person believes he or she has presented to others. Mead distinguishes between the self as known, the *me,* and the self as knower, the *I.* Freud has suggested the self is a triadic composite of id, ego, and superego with the ego serving as moderator between the unconscious, animalistic, primitive id and the internalized, socially-derived ideas, values, and expectations of the superego. Goffman uses dramaturgical models to stress multiple "selves" within a given individual that emerge under situational conditions. These analyses are essentially heuristic devices and, provided they are not reified, can be used to help understand how children begin the lifetime process of self-awareness.

The possibility of conflicting "selves" or changes in looking at one's self elicits traumas or bewilderment, particularly among children still forming their self-concepts. Children of divorced or separated parents and children who experience quite different conditions in and out of their families are cases in point. Yamamoto's work calls attention to "the bruised self" or the damage done to self-concepts among children that is acted out in observable behavior. These symptoms should signal a call for attention by those who work or deal with children.

Finally, we stressed the relationship between self-concept and motivation. Minority children who experience social rejection provide an example of the self-devaluation and self-defeatism that can occur. On the other hand, through self-insulation, children can escape the hazards that harm so many others who share their milieu. As Schur cautions, however, self-awareness can be so totally consuming that it turns the person inward to the neglect of external conditions requiring social changes.

12

Children's health

Like air and water, so fundamental, pervasive, and life-supporting, health is often taken for granted. Only in the absence of health do many persons become alarmed or painfully aware of the discomfort and losses they sustain by their inability to function as in the past. But this is a negative approach. It attempts to tell us what health is by telling us what it is not. The absence of disease, injury, or disability does not provide us with positive clues to good health. What is needed is a recognition of health as a comprehensive state of well-being that provides the motivation and means by which individuals can function happily and constructively to meet their personal needs and those of society or those about them. It is basic to childhood, the launching stage of life, and to all successive stages of life.

Health, A Tripartite Unity

We are indebted to the World Health Organization of the United Nations who defined health as "a state of complete physical, mental, and social well-being, not merely the absence of disease or infirmity."[1] In this definition, we see the interconnections between three distinct

[1]World Health Organization Constitution, United Nations, 1947.

elements that produce healthy children. First, there is the *physical,* a body that is anatomically intact and functioning biochemically and physiologically in a wholesome, effective way. Next, there is the *mental-emotional* life, the inner environment of conscious and unconscious thinking and feeling-states that can dominate individual actions or behavior. And, finally, there is the *social* component of health that has to do with the ability to live pleasantly and harmoniously with others.

These three components form a close knit interdependence that constitutes the state of health of the host-individual. Perhaps the first concern of expectant mothers and fathers is that their child arrive in this world physically complete. Being "well-born" provides the foundation upon which all else depends. Assuming all is "in place," the child can begin the life journey secure and comforted by the careful administrations of adults who provide essential emotional and intellectual support. This idyllic picture of a healthy child is completed by the growing recognition that there are many other individuals in the world and that the child takes his or her place among them.

Unfortunately, however, many children do not experience this progressive development. At any step or in the interconnections between physical, mental-emotional, and social conditions, they are vulnerable. Health eludes them because, in one or more aspects of health, the positive results are thwarted or weakened. While our concern is "the whole child" and not the emphasis of one component of health over another, we do not pose as health experts who can offer complete guidance toward healthy childhood. It is within the pooling of knowledge or the team-efforts of specialists that there is some confidence that healthy childhood can be guarded and sustained.

As students of sociology, what can we contribute to efforts to achieve, maintain, and renew healthy childhood? Our answer, of course, depends upon the extent to which *social responsibilities* in the context of person-to-person, person-to-group, group-to-group interactions and relationships are recognized.

Perhaps the oldest academic debate concerning health has been between those who look to *heredity* and those who look to *environment.* On the one hand, the *innate* qualities, present at birth, awaiting development according to genetic codes, were held to be the prime factors in health. On the other hand, the *acquired* qualities, those gained after birth and continuing for a lifetime, were held to be paramount. The debate was laid to rest, allegedly, by redefining the question from one of heredity versus environment to heredity and environment. This recognizes the reciprocal relationships between heredity and environment and the importance of both in the health histories of childhood.

In the field of public or community health, the action proposals embodied in *eugenic* or *euthenic* programs continue to mirror the old heredity versus environment model. *Eugenics* are those proposals that seek to improve the inherited characteristics of children. *Positive eugenic* programs suggest that mating of men and women whose genetic combinations would produce healthy children, sturdy and resistant to disease or malfunctions. *Negative eugenic* programs suggest the prevention of matings of men and women who could possibly produce malformed, feeble, or unhealthy children.

Positive eugenic programs are particularly suspect because there is widespread opposition to such social control or social domination of personal decisions. Negative eugenic programs are opposed for the same reasons, but they seem to have won more acceptance when persons, such as lawmakers, are convinced that the risks of producing unhealthy children are too great. Laws regulating who may or may not marry each other are cases in point. Prohibitions against licensing marriages between brothers and sisters, mothers and sons, or fathers and daughters are even more specific illustrations of negative eugenics.

Euthenics is concerned with the best possible rearing of children through improvements in the social conditions of childhood. Undoubtedly, those working in the sociology of health can be said to be more identified with euthenic efforts than they are with eugenic efforts. Their studies of family, school, hospital, or community settings suggest some of their concerns.

Again, the specter of social control or limitations on personal freedoms is raised in opposition to euthenic programs. As long as persons remain unconvinced that certain social conditions produce unhealthy children and adults, social resistance to change continues. In a society pledged to personal freedoms, such resistance is understandable and even commendable. The task of the sociological research in public health is to produce positive evidence of the efficacy of social interventions. The social responsibility of determining public policies, of course, belongs to all citizens.

The Psychosomatic Connection

Health has been dichotomized as originating in *organic* or *inorganic* sources. Medical practitioners who are consulted when health fails or is threatened usually begin their diagnoses with a search for organic factors. Structural damage within the body or functional difficulties of physical systems become their primary targets because their basic training moves them in the direction of being body-oriented or somatic specialists. It is only when organic explorations do not yield explanations for discomfort or illness that inorganic sources are suspected and investigated.

There was a time in medical history when inorganic explanations for ill-health were rejected, but that time is long past. Clinical psychologists, psychoanalysts, and psychiatrists for instance, are integral, respected, and valued participants in the healing arts and welcomed for their considerable insights and contributions to health. These contributions and insights have to do with the intimate connection between the *soma* or body and the *psyche* or particular mental-emotional state of an individual. The anguish felt by a student taking an important examination, for instance, is not experienced by a calm, prepared fellow student, one seat away, who is taking the identical test and is under the same pressure to perform in the best possible manner. The difference between the two responses to stress can be attributed to their mental-emotional sets rather than necessarily to the state of their phyisical health.

Lee Salk, a specialist in pediatric psychology, suggests that human infants lack the resources to cope assertively with any kind of stress.[2] Awake, children can signal the presence of stress by crying; asleep, children can blot out unpleasantness through this form of withdrawal. Later on, in adulthood, these primitive, unsophisticated procedures are elaborated in behavior that cries out for attention or represents withdrawal from stressful realities such as alcoholism, drug abuse, fantasy, and suicide. As Salk expresses it, "Babies *always* cry for a reason."[3] That reason lies in the psychosomatic connection that needs recognition and appropriate attention lest the discomfort grow unbearable and cause the individual to become socially paralyzed and unable to interact with others.

What is needed, of course, is training in dealing with stress or in coping with conditions that are stressful. Some parents are aware of such socialization and gradually lead their children to deal with their physical-mental-emotional circumstances. Other parents, however, impatiently demand that children quickly take on adult attributes without the necessary experiences, support, understanding, and ability to make the transition from childhood to adulthood. These parents become the abusive parents as we shall see.

[2]Lee Salk, "Growing Up Mentally Fit," *Stress*, XXV, No. 1 of *Blue Print for Health* (Chicago, Illinois: Blue Cross Association, 1974), p. 20.
[3]Ibid.

Social Health

The one dimension that was lacking in the health of children was attention to *social* factors. It is well and good to produce healthy bodies and to school individuals in dealing with their mental-emotional states. It is not sufficient, however, to concentrate such attention on individual children. The next lesson in life is to acquire social habits that take other individuals into account. The prejudices of sexism, racism, elitism, ethnic rejection, or religious bias are counterproductive in healthy lives as we have attempted to elucidate in this text. Egomania, ethnocentrism, or age-biases are further examples of poor social health and, again, we have elaborated upon their significance in prior chapters. Lawrence K. Frank suggested many years ago that instead of attempting to heal individuals whose health has failed them, attention must be given to the societal environment that has been the catalyst in helping to bring about such ill health. In Frank's terms, it is "society who is the patient."[4]

We have discussed the dimension of social health in the past tense. Fortunately, over the years since Frank's warnings about providing the best possible societal life for children and adults, there has been progressive awareness and interest in developing such a world. We would be remiss if we did not recognize the numerous agencies and efforts being made to bring about social conditions that enable persons to flourish and enjoy healthy lives. At the same time, however, most will readily admit that a truly healthy society has not become a reality. It eludes us because all of us are "less than perfect beings" and so create and maintain "less than perfect social systems." The result is that children continue to cry, to suffer, and to reach maturity with social blemishes and scars that affirm their trials and tribulations. The less fortunate do not even survive their childhood.

ABUSED CHILDREN

A notorious case of child abuse involves a little girl who was literally "walked to death" by her abusive parents. While still an infant, the little girl was badly battered by her mother and father. She was taken away from the parents by court orders and her parents were given imprisonment. In time, however, and despite public outcry, the courts returned the child to her natural parents. The old routines were resumed, and the little girl was again the target of extreme punish-

[4]Lawrence Kelso Frank, *Society As the Patient* (New Brunswick, N.J., Rutgers University Press, 1948).

ments. She was told that because she was so "bad," she would have to walk, without rest, a certain route in her home. The parents apparently took turns to keep her on the move and without nourishment, until she collapsed and died. The details came to light when her death was reported to the authorities.

A single case of child abuse is shocking enough, but literally thousands of such cases are known to occur in the United States each year. Because these cases are known to be "under-reported" for fear of retaliation by courts or social agencies, only estimations of their frequency are available. The estimations vary from a conservative figure of ten thousand annually to over seventy-five thousand.[5] Of these numbers, hundreds die, are paralyzed or deformed for life, or spend their lives scarred, physically and mentally-emotionally. Children have been beaten with sticks or belts, burned with lighted cigarettes, had their hands held over flames on the stove, been scalded in boiling water, suffocated, thrown down stairs, had their heads banged against the wall or floor, been sexually abused, tortured and starved, or given large dosages of drugs.

There are some clues as to which types of children are likely candidates for such abuse.[6] They are the innocent victims of parental or adult wrath, not because they have behaved in some outrageous manner, but because they are living reminders of the errors or defects of the adults who brought them into the world. They are, for example, children born out of wedlock who were "legitimatized" by a "forced" or begrudging marriage; children who were "extra children," unwanted or economic burdens, whose parents had accepted the few earlier children, but who rejected those later children who were "accidentally" conceived; the children who were deficient in schoolwork and so brought shame and remorse to their families; or children who reminded parents of hated relatives such as their own parents or uncles and aunts.

The abusing parents themselves reveal the poor personal, mental-emotional, or social health that is associated, in their cases, with violence against their own children. The abusing parents are usually found to be emotionally unstable, mentally deficient, in conflict with each other, and often under the influence of alcohol when they become unduly hostile to their offspring. Of particular importance is to note that parents who abused their children were often abused themselves when they were very young. The intergenerational-socialization pattern is

[5]Jerome E. Leavitt, ed., *The Battered Child, Selected Readings* (Morristown, New Jersey: General Learning Press, 1974).
[6]Ibid, p. 216.

evident in these specific instances. Lastly, the abusing parents are frequently found to be under grave stress themselves or to conduct their family affairs in discord or disharmony that provokes them into aggressive acts against their own children. It is not unusual to learn of numerous instances reported in the newspapers of suicides in which their children were first slaughtered before parents took their own lives.

Child abuse, while associated with economic distress, is not necessarily confined to the lower socioeconomic classes. It is found in all classes although with declining frequency as socioeconomic conditions improve.[7] For example, in a nationwide study of some six thousand cases of abused children in 1967, close to 38 percent of the families were earning less than $3,500 a year; about 52 percent were earning less than $4,500; and approximately 4 percent were earning $10,000 or more.

The detection of child abuse and appropriate treatment of both the abused children and their abusers are, of course, the remaining steps in dealing with the battered child syndrome. Detection of child abuse is not a simple matter of observation because damaged or brutalized children often may not display the results of child abuse for considerable lengths of time. Clothing may hide body bruises; children may not openly complain to strangers; explanations may be offered that satisfy casual observations of physical disabilities; or children may be kept out of sight for prolonged periods of time. Further, many do not care to become involved or fear retaliation if they report child abuse to police or child-care agencies. There is protection from legal action, however, for those willing to do whatever is in their power to locate and treat child abuse cases. In Ohio, for example, the Child Abuse and Neglect Law requires physicians, nurses, dentists, school authorities, and other professionals who deal with children to report cases of child abuse or suspected cases of child abuse and grants them immunity from any civil or criminal liability that might occur or be imposed as a result of such action.[8]

The abusing parents or adults also require attention. Many of the underlying sources of child abuse are amenable to treatment or prevention, and child abusers can be given therapeutic consideration. Utilizing the model probably best known through the Alcoholics Anonymous organization, those who have experienced the rage, anger, or frustrations brought about by social and personal pressures that overwhelm them and that led to their child abuse get together for mutual support and understanding. The first step toward their social health has already

[7]Ibid, p. 217.

[8]Child Abuse/Neglect Prevention Kit (Columbus, Ohio: Ohio Department of Public Welfare, Children's Protective Services).

been taken in the recognition on their part that they need help; the second step is begun when they voluntarily seek counseling to correct their behavior. Under such groups as Parents Anonymous, child abusers ventilate their feeling-states and discuss rationally what can be done to deal effectively with their situations. Through the rapport gained by knowing they are in company with understanding, sympathetic, and supportive persons, they can take positive steps to bring themselves back to responsible parenthood.

Group therapy does get results, but unfortunately such help is not readily available to those who may need it the most. Large cities are the most likely locales for such groups, but in smaller towns and villages or in rural areas with scattered or widely dispersed populations, the accessibility of supportive groups and therapeutic expertise constitutes a problem in itself. The *delivery* of health services far too often lags behind the health services known to be effective.[9]

MENTAL-EMOTIONAL HEALTH

In addition to the fundamental maintenance of a physically healthy child or the prevention of physical damage to children as in cases of child abuse, there remains the huge area of mental-emotional health. Just as physical health in its positive and negative nature is closely associated with social conditions, so is mental-emotional health.

Positive Mental Health

Raymond Mangus suggested what is meant by "good" mental health in his early studies of Ohio school children.[10] Mangus suggested that good mental-emotional health consisted of such elements as:

1. Growing control over one's own actions
2. Reasonable aggression when necessary, but free from a need to dominate others
3. Reasonable compliance to the wishes of others, but without compliance simply to escape criticism
4. Ability to spend time alone for purposes of self-improvement, but not from fear of contacts with others

[9]See Milton I. Roemer and William Shoneck, "Health Maintenance Organization Performance: The Recent Evidence," *The Milbank Memorial Fund Quarterly,* 51, No. 3 (Summer 1973), 271–317.
[10]A. R. Mangus, *Personality Adjustment of School Children,* A report on studies conducted jointly with the division of Mental Hygiene, Ohio State Department of Public Welfare, The Ohio State University, and The Ohio Agricultural Experiment Station, Columbus, Ohio, July, 1948.

5. A strong sense of personal security, but without smug complacency
6. No lack of emotional conflicts, but mastery of effective techniques to resolve conflicts constructively
7. Self-respect and self-confidence without egotistical arrogance
8. High levels of maturity in terms of others, inner emotions, thought processes, and moral codes

Some twenty years after Mangus' suggested list of positive mental health manifestations, the National Association for Mental Health offered the following guidelines to good mental health[11]:

1. Feeling comfortable about one's self
   a. Not overwhelmed by fears, anger, love, jealousy, guilt, or worry
   b. Can accept disappointments
   c. Have a tolerant, easygoing attitude about one's self
   d. Neither underestimate nor overestimate abilities
   e. Accept shortcomings
   f. Possess self-respect
   g. Can deal with most situations
   h. Derive satisfaction from simple, everyday pleasures
2. Feeling right about others
   a. Give love to others and consider the interests of others
   b. Form longlasting, satisfying personal relationships with others
   c. Like and trust others
   d. Respect individual and social differences in people
   e. Are not aggressive to others, but do not allow over-control from others
   f. Feel a sense of belonging or identification with groups
   g. Have a sense of responsibility to others
3. Able to meet life's demands
   a. Do something about problems as they occur
   b. Accept responsibility for one's actions
   c. Shape the environment when possible or adjust to conditions beyond one's control
   d. Plan the future, but without fear of the future
   e. Welcome new experiences and ideas
   f. Use natural abilities
   g. Set realistic goals
   h. Can think for one's self, self-reliance
   i. Perform to the best of one's abilities, deriving satisfaction from doing the best possible.

As John La Place comments, these qualities are idealistic, and most children and adults will fall short of them at various times.[12] In this sense, most individuals tend to be both healthy and unhealthy through-

[11] *Mental Health Is 1, 2, 3* (Washington, D.C.: National Association For Mental Health, 1968).
[12] John LaPlace, *Health* (Englewood Cliffs, N.J.: Prentice-Hall, Inc., 1972), p. 47.

out their lives. The goal, of course, would be to be as healthy as possible and to take proper measures to regain health should it fail at times. It is the sustained, prolonged, negative manifestations of ill health that call for attention and not necessarily the brief episodes of human inadequacy that befall each individual.

Negative Mental Health

Childhood mental illness is made up of a bewildering array of symptoms that sorely trouble children, their caretakers, and those with whom the troubled children associate. Mental ill health consists of complicated, deep-seated patternings that require the services of trained professionals. These services, mainly diagnostic and therapeutic, are often successful, but there remain a substantial number of cases that can be treated only with moderate success. In these instances, behavioral and personality disorders among children can be modified, kept under control, or made tolerable, but are not completely eliminated. Nevertheless, the knowledge that can be brought to bear upon problems is considerable and merits public confidence.

Bruno Bettelheim once observed during a seminar on childhood at Kent State University in the late 1960s, that if a seven year old boy with personality problems was brought to him for attention and therapy, he would require at least another seven years to have any degree of success with him and, even then, could only hope to modify the difficulty. Bettelheim, of course, was recognizing the years of input that brought about the child's difficulties and was seeking a balance of equal time to achieve some level of therapeutic success. Those persons who recognize that children in their care are laboring under certain mental ill health burdens will be performing the initial steps in restoring the mental-emotional health of these youngsters. Such persons, however, should not expect immediate or overnight changes. Neither should they expect the excising of experiences that children have endured. The healing process should be expected to leave some psychological "scars," but they are a small price to pay for some measure of recovery to good mental-emotional health. Because children are involved, the prognosis, the chances for success if proper therapy is applied, should be favorable. Far too often, professional attention is delayed until adulthood, and by that stage of life, mental-emotional problems are well rooted and not as easy to treat.

As we have already noted, ill health may be due to organic causes. We will reserve chapter fifteen to discuss some of the problems of retarded children or those with learning disabilities that stem from brain damage. Those mental-emotional disorders that are inorganic in origins are more our concern in this chapter.

The severity of mental disorders are codified at three levels. Behavioral and personality disorders are held to be the least severe; neurotic disorders are more severe; and psychotic disorders, the most severe or serious.[13] Benjamin Wolman sees mental disorders as a continuum of deterioration. Like rocks falling down, some roll to one level; some roll a bit farther; and some roll all the way down.[14] Examples of behavioral disorders would be destructiveness, overaggressiveness, or cruelty. These, it will be noted, are directed outward or against the environment of the child. Examples of personality difficulties would be hyperactivity, temper tantrums, or sleeping problems. These are directed inwards or are self-aggressive. Neurotic disorders are strongly associated with inabilities to handle anxieties and are observed as fears of meeting new people or new situations, inability to handle even small failures, or constant fidgeting with hands and leg motions. Psychotic conditions in children are manifested in autistic children who are extremely withdrawn or self-insulated or in symbiotic children who seem to be developing normally, but who begin a regression to more infantile levels of behavior or develop a relentless dependence upon a mother or mother-figure.

SOCIAL HEALTH

On a one-to-one basis, we leave the identification and treatment of mental-emotional disorders in children in the capable hands of specialists, calling only upon lay persons to become sufficiently sensitive to inadequate mental-emotional health in children to bring them under competent professional attention and care. For our part, we would stress the salience of social health and note that, in company with others, children acquire qualities that provide them with the assets of physical as well as mental-emotional health. Shortcomings in social health, in harmonious and constructive relationships with others, lead in the opposite direction and foster inabilities and inadequacies in living with other persons. In these conditions, both physical and mental-emotional health sustain considerable damage.

[13]See Haim G. Ginott and Ernest Harms, "Mental Disorders in Childhood," *Handbook of Clinical Psychology,* Benjamin B. Wolman, ed. (New York: McGraw-Hill Book Company, 1965), pp. 1094–1118.
[14]Benjamin Wolman, "Mental Health and Mental Disorders," in *Handbook of Clinical Psychology* (New York: McGraw-Hill Book Company, 1965), p. 1135.

Significant Others

In childhood, individuals begin the long journey through life with increasing contacts with persons already advanced in their own socialization processes. The widening world of human contacts includes those who are close and intimate as well as those seen vaguely and at a distance. Out of the many sustained or fleeting contacts, children begin to distinguish those who are significant and those who are, relatively speaking, inconsequential in their lives. While there is something to be said about every human being as potentially offering meaningful relationships, we are pointing to those few individuals who are notably significant in shaping the lives of children. These are the *significant others* in children's lives who so impress youngsters that an indelible mark is left upon them and, in a very real sense, guide and direct their life careers and life styles. In many instances, the personality attributes of significant others "wash off," are transferred, or adapted within the personality structures and processes of individual children. The significant others are the status and role models that suggest what decisions should be made as children gain increasing autonomy.

One device that has proven useful to students of sociology of childhood has been the voluntary assignment of a project in ex post facto analysis in which individual students report on their own childhood and what has become of the "little boy" or "little girl" they once were.[15] Employing the concept of social distance, we suggest the use of five concentric circles in locating and describing significant others, as shown in Figure 12–1.

The innermost circle is reserved for the individual ego and his or her family of origin. The second circle provides social space for persons who are in the maternal or paternal kinship of ego. The third circle represents the arena in which close friends and associates operate. The fourth circle marks the positions of functionaries, teachers, doctors, social workers, and the like, who in the course of their work have contacted the child and treated him or her in special ways. The fifth or outside circle provides for distant personalities, those the child may know through fiction or in real life through mass media.

Using small squares and circles to symbolize males and females respectively, significant others are placed by each student in their appropriate circles. For those who seek to suggest a three-point scale evaluation of these significant others, students are instructed to place a "V" (Villain) or an "H" (Hero) inside their symbolic square or circle.

[15]For fuller discussion see Figure 14–1, "Class Study Assignment in Sociology of Childhood," Marvin R. Koller, *Families, A Multigenerational Approach* (New York: McGraw-Hill, Inc., 1974), pp. 290–91.

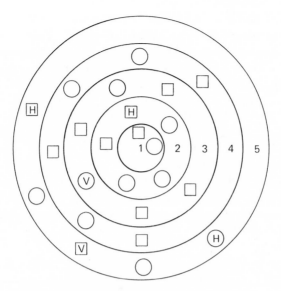

FIGURE 12-1 *Significant Others in Childhood*

Those left unmarked are held to be evaluated neither negatively nor positively. They may possess both negative and positive qualities or be simply "significant" in the life of the evaluator, but not in a strictly negative or positive sense. The visual diagram lends itself to various counts, tabulations, or comparisons. Some persons are highly selective and place only a few persons, or none, in the various concentric circles. Others may place an amazing number of "significant others" in their diagrams, tend to favor one sex over another, or concentrate their selections within certain circles.

Finally, each student is asked to explain why a given person was selected as a "significant other" through a brief statement or narrative. The effort is a record that has heretofore been covert in a given person's mind but is now crystallized for others to see and share, with the permission of the individual involved. Persons thought long forgotten are recalled and judged in an adult perspective rather than when first encountered as a child. Many students cherish their reports and retain them for reference at some future date or circumstance such as sharing them with their own children or their most intimate friends. The only caution we would suggest is to point out to students that such a project is voluntary and should be used in such a manner that it brings no harm or pain to those who may be involved.

This caution is necessary because the rights of human subjects must be very carefully guarded. Opening up old wounds or unhappy events in childhood can trigger behavior and moods that go far beyond the abilities of many to control them. Further, our experience with hundreds of students has taught us that those who are significant others in the lives of children, now grown to young adulthood or maturity, who come to know the contents and evaluations placed in such an analysis are also deeply touched or affected. In most cases there are no serious problems, but for those with rather unique circumstances, there must be tact and careful assessment in making explicit that which was previously stored away in the innermost recesses of one's memories. We vividly recall, for instance, the case of a young woman whose mother discovered the contents of her daughter's significant-other diagram and report and their ensuing all-night crying and confessional spree. In their case, fortunately, the ventilation of long-suppressed feelings and ideas improved their mother-daughter relationship from that point forward.

Symbionts

When significant others can be used as therapeutic agents to restore or sustain children's social health, the special term of *symbionts* seems to be useful. The term was suggested by Bernard G. Guerney, Jr. in his *Psychotherapeutic Agents.*[16] As Guerney explained, symbionts are those persons with whom one can form mutually beneficial relationships. The professional resources to serve physical, mental, emotional, and social health needs have performed yeoman services, but they appear to be inadequate when it comes to reaching certain segments of the population. For example, services flow in the direction of those who can pay for services and those who have the socioeconomic background to best utilize them. For others, however, such as the poor, the less educated, and the residents of widely dispersed communities, professional help and care are less accessible. The good friend, the considerate neighbor, or the cheerful working associate are symbionts who can do wonders in maintaining and developing the positive health of individuals. For children who have just begun to lay down the foundations of their lives, symbionts go a long way in establishing their physical, mental, emotional, and social good health.

When one goes through the exercise of naming, identifying, and expressing how significant others have shaped one's life, it may be useful to note that these individuals are significant and can serve as symbionts because they have been willing to take the time and energy

[16]Bernard G. Guerney, Jr., ed., *Psychotherapeutic Agents, New Roles for Non-professionals, Parents, and Teachers* (New York: Holt, Rinehart and Winston, Inc., 1969), p. 247.

to give something of themselves to other persons. Perhaps children may also learn that they, too, can become significant and can act as symbionts as they reach out to others in helpful ways.

SUMMARY

Health is a tripartite unity of physical, mental, and social well-being. Childhood is a particularly important period in which the foundations for good health are laid down. Unfortunately, in all three elements of positive health, children do not uniformly experience those progressive developments necessary to their maturation and socialization.

Eugenic programs have attempted to provide the best possible genetic combinations; euthenic programs have attempted to provide the best possible social experiences for children. With heredity and environment working in tandem and in mutually helpful ways, children are well launched toward the best possible health.

The connection between the physical body and the mental-emotional state of an individual, the psychosomatic connection, deserves special attention. Coping with stress calls for anticipatory socialization that parents or parent surrogates can provide children. Perhaps the entire social system or society can be said to be "sick." As Lawrence Frank expressed it, "society is the patient" rather than individuals who may suffer poor health because they are required to survive within it.

We see the less-than-perfect social systems and the less-than-perfect societal members in action when we consider instances of abused children. We observe these systems and individuals again when we examine the nature of mental-emotional health in children and in adults. Finally, we can see their handiwork in the kind of social health that ensues from significant others and from symbionts.

13

Symbolic interaction in childhood

Perhaps one of the most general observations we can make concerning ourselves is that we are *social* creatures. It is a quality that we share with many other species including those that school in the seas, flock together in the skies, and form far-ranging herds in their own earthbound ecological niche. Our "sociability" may take the form of violence against our own kind or exploitation of other animal or plant communities. In the main, however, the quieter, unobtrusive, prosaic manifestation of our togetherness is what Petr Kropotkin identified many years ago as *mutual aid*.[1] Its value, of course, lies in the survival of the species and redounds to the benefit of otherwise vulnerable individuals.

Central to this overriding sociability, mutual aid, and survival is the ability to communicate, to interchange, or, as sociologists prefer, to

[1]Petr Kropotkin, *Mutual Aid, A Factor of Evolution* (Boston, Massachusetts: Extending Horizons Books, Reprint of 1914 Edition).

interact. Again, these qualities or abilities are not the exclusive properties of our species. Through signs, sounds, or body postures even the bees communicate the location of a source of food at some distance from their home hives. What our species has accomplished, however, is the development and elaboration of complex forms of communication, chief of which is language. While the communication systems of other species continue to be studied and some intelligent animals have been taught something of our language systems, our species seems to stand alone in the field of *symbolic* interaction.[2]

LANGUAGE ACQUISITION

It is this symbolic interaction that makes up a large part of childhood socialization. In a real sense, parents and parent surrogates take speechless, illiterate, uncomprehending infants and transform them into speaking, literate, and sophisticated persons able to acquire the contents of their respective cultures and societies, to communicate their own ideas, and to make contributions of their own to enrich other lives. It is a miraculous feat, but one that passes as a normal expectation or a matter-of-fact event. Its accomplishment provides an ability to join with previously socialized individuals in their day-to-day activities.

Oral Symbols

For those who study "foreign tongues," mainly in adolescence, young adulthood, or adulthood, there are tremendous difficulties to be overcome. It is true that some language students possess the facility to learn quickly and easily. Far greater numbers, however, find language acquisition an almost insurmountable barrier and gain minimal ability to communicate in such languages. We are pointing to, of course, second languages, those acquired or attempted only after learning, as a child, a first language. What we are calling "miraculous" is this ability of normal children everywhere to sort out the sounds of adults "buzzing" all about them and to establish communication with them in their native tongue.

While there is no universal agreement that language acquisition

[2]See for example, W. N. Kellogg and Luella Kellogg, *The Ape and the Child* (New York: McGraw-Hill, 1933); Catherine Hays, *The Ape in Our House* (New York: Harper, 1951); R. Allen and Beatrice T. Gardner, "Teaching Sign Language to a Chimpanzee," *Science,* 165(August 1969); Anne James Premack and David Premack, "Teaching Language to an Ape," *Scientific American* (October 1972).

occurs in some certain, step-by-step manner, there seem to be about five broad stages that children go through in order to communicate in a first language. These are:

1. a babbling stage

2. a holophrastic stage

3. a two-word stage

4. a telegraph stage

5. an adult language stage[3]

The babbling stage consists of experimentally producing all sorts of oral sounds. These have no particular linguistic significance other than being a "tuning-up" stage in which infants try out the possibilities of their vocal apparatus. This random, hit-or-miss vocalization will undoubtedly correspond to sounds found in oral symbols. Those sounds that are missing or rarely used in the specific languages being learned, are discarded, controlled, or forgotten as experience dictates.

The holophrastic or one-word sentence stage is reached by children at some point after the first year. In this stage, children have attached *meaning* to a single set of sounds. The sounds may not be precise, but they are close enough for adults to understand and to take appropriate action. A typical example would be, in English, the familiar "Mama" or "Dada" sounds. Less typical was the sound "moo" that one of our children used to communicate a wish to drink milk.

Fromkin and Rodman provide examples of the two-word stage in such "sentences" as "it ball," "more wet," and "allgone sock."[4]

It would seem that three, four, or five-word stages should follow the two-word stage, but such does not necessarily occur. Instead, children begin stringing words together in rather clipped, edited, key-word style. This is the form used in telegraphic messages in which connecting words such as "to," "it," or "the" are eliminated to save time, space, and expense. Fromkin and Rodman provide the examples of "Andrew want that," "Cathy build house," and "no sit there."[5]

The final stage is the adult stage in which children may not possess the fine points of grammar characteristic of their "first language," but

[3]Victoria Fromkin and Robert Rodman, *An Introduction to Language* (New York: Holt, Rinehart and Winston, Inc., 1974), pp. 317–18.
[4]Ibid, p. 318.
[5]Ibid, p. 318.

they are able to hold detailed, prolonged conversations with adults. If mistakes occur in communication, they are held to be charming or "cute" and are long remembered among close associates. Most speakers of native languages are not necessarily completely familiar with the grammatical rules of their languages, nor do they know every word or phrase that conveys meaning in their tongues, but they can nevertheless communicate with each other in oral symbols within a larger community of similar speakers. Adults, as well as children, would have to spend many years in language acquisition to become true masters of their own original language.

What is important to keep in mind is that these vocal symbols are sufficient communication tools to be able to conduct normal human activities. They are, as Sturtevant noted, systems of "arbitrary vocal symbols by which members of a social group cooperate and interact."[6] The key word in this definition is "arbitrary." The oral symbols used display a confusing array of sounds and unique ways to combine them, but we continue to marvel at the relative ease with which children go about understanding and using them. Centuries of chance usage have produced the languages of people, and these heritages are acquired by normal children throughout the world. This oral link allows them to learn all that speakers of their language can convey.

Written Symbols

Language exists in all known societies of humankind. Because it is essentially oral in nature, the writing down of symbols for others to sound out later and to store for future reference may or may not occur in human societies. Indeed, anthropologists have long preferred to draw a distinct line between those societies that are "preliterate" and those that are "literate." The older term that has been dropped from scientific usage is "primitive." To describe the oral languages of isolated, preindustrial, "folk" people as primitive is to overlook the complexities and shades of meaning found in every language.

Just as literacy constitutes a step beyond that of language acquisition, so children come to the reading and writing stages later on in their lives. Again, the progression from illiteracy to literacy is nothing short of amazing.

Paul McKee, seeking to explain to future teachers of reading in elementary schools what confronts their future students, ingeniously

[6]Edgar H. Sturtevant, *An Introduction to Linguistic Science* (New Haven, Connecticut: Yale University Press, 1947), p. 2.

substituted a series of arbitrary geometrical designs for those of the English alphabet symbols.[7] The substitutions were as follows:

Possession of the keys to the substituted symbols helps, of course, but trying to use these symbols to convey ideas provides those who grapple with their usage some of the difficulties facing youngsters when they are initiated into reading. It is a lesson worth remembering because adults tend to forget childhood experiences in which they grappled with unfamiliar and baffling substitutions for their own vocal speech. The shape or form of the letters must be memorized labori-

A B C D E F G H I J K L M

＋ ∏ ✕ ⊔ ⊗ △ ⋔ ⊏ ∪ ∩ ⊐ ∨ ⑨

N O P Q R S T U V W X YZ

♂ ╪ ＝ ‖ ⌐ ⊥ ∧ ⊸ ⊶ ⊷ － ⊇ |

Under McKee's system, a sentence such as, "Look, son, I just found a stray puppy," would look like this:

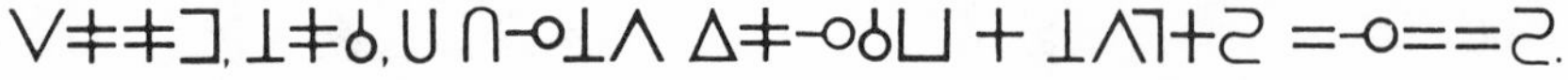

∨╪╪⊐, ⊥╪♂, ∪ ∩⊸○⊥∧ △╪⊸○♂⊔ ＋ ⊥∧⌐╪⊇ ＝⊸○＝＝⊇.

FIGURE 13–1 *English Alphabet Symbols*

Source: Paul McKee, *The Teaching of Reading in the Elementary School.*

ously, silently sounded, and then brought together in some approved grammatical fashion to convey abstract thoughts. This facility is precisely the means by which the letters printed on this page, strange black-line squiggles to the non-reader and uninitiated, permits thoughts of the writers to be shared with untold thousands.

The perfect alphabet, according to Sturtevant, would have one symbol, and only one, for each phoneme of speech sound.[8] He observes that "a number of European alphabets come near enough to it so that children, once they learn to write, need not waste any appreciable further time learning to spell."[9] Nevertheless, there are silent letters or combinations of letters that represent a number of different sounds when placed in a certain context. These seemingly indiscriminate and

[7]Paul McKee, *The Teaching of Reading in the Elementary School* (Boston: Houghton Mifflin Company, 1948), p. 24.

[8]Sturtevant, *Introduction to Linguistic Science*, p. 24.

[9]Ibid, p. 24.

arbitrary alterations, of course, are based upon conventions that have accumulated over the centuries of language development. In a sense, they appear to the learner to have no rhyme or reason and continue to plague children for many years. Indeed, adults long familiar with words and their sounds are well advised to keep a good dictionary handy to check upon their spelling according to the conventions.

The combination of the letters "ough" provides an excellent example. In the word *bough*, the "ough" symbols are sounded as "ow." In the word *though*, the "ough" combination is assigned the sound of "o." The addition of a new symbol, "r," to make the word *through*, alters the combination of "ough" to sound like "oo." The word *rough*, however, standing alone, is assigned the sound "uff," and the learner can by this time be totally confused. If the word is *cough*, the "ough" is pronounced as "awff." Finally, in the word *hiccough*, the "ough" has the sound of "up." The six different sounds of "ough" provide no defensible logic, but children who learn English must nevertheless master their usage through trial and error.

Symbols as Abstractions from Reality

Symbols, after all, represent something other than the symbols themselves. In and of themselves, they are unimportant, but for what they represent, they are fundamental to acquiring human knowledge. They are abstractions from reality and hence provide some sense of reality without having firsthand, direct experience. If it were otherwise, every child or learner would have to have a real set of experiences in order to comprehend realities. Lacking symbols, every generation would have to experience the realities of life and would not be able to store and pass along what they know reality to be.

Take the word *war*, for example. To many children in various parts of the globe that are battlegrounds for warring factions, in the recent past in such places as the Middle East, Southeast Asia, or in certain African countries, war is a familiar experience. In Northern Ireland, probably generations of children are indelibly marked with the internecine conflict that has marred their nation for so long. For such children, war conjures up pain, sorrow, and deep anxieties. For other children, however, those who have only experienced war vicariously in movies, television programs, books, magazines, newspapers, or parades, the symbol is also understood, although not in precisely the same way that children caught up in actual wars understand it.

William Graham Sumner in his classic *Folkways* wrote along similar lines. Sumner dealt succinctly with the arbitrary, symbolic, and confusing nature of language acquisition for children when he wrote:

How can a child understand the combinations of sound and sense when it must know language in order to learn them? It must learn to speak without knowing previously how to speak, without any previous suspicion that the words of its mother mean more than the buzzing of a fly.

Every vocable was to us (children) an arbitrary and conventional sign; arbitrary because any one of a thousand other vocables could have been just as easily learned by us and associated with the same idea; conventional, because the one we acquired had its sole ground and sanction in the consenting use of the community of which we formed a part. We do not, as children, make our language for ourselves. We get it by tradition, all complete. We think in sentences. As our language forms sentences, that is, as our mother-tongue thinks, so we learn to think.[10]

Language, A Means of Communicating or a Barrier to Communication

Language acquisition, we have insisted, is a means of communication between persons who have experienced similar socialization. Normally, language is acquired through sound-symbols and, for literate peoples, through written symbols with variant referents, real or abstract. However, despite its objectives, language can also become a barrier to communication.

We have in mind, for example, the rather frustrating and isolating experience of those speaking one language in the midst of people who speak a totally different language. This is the adult experience of travelers, tourists, military personnel, politicians, or businessmen and women who visit or live for extended periods of time in foreign lands. Fluency in more than one language is a highly admired ability and a credit to those who possess it. This ability to communicate with speakers of different languages is highly appreciated and, once again, uses language as it was intended—as a means of communicating.

Not all persons have the ability, time, or desire to learn additional languages, no matter how much it re-establishes language as a communicating device. Instead, a second language, usually the language of a prominent world power, becomes the bridge-language for communication. Such has been the case for French among European nations, and such appears to be the case for English in the present. We might include the common language of mathematics, music, art, science, or computers, but we seek to deal with spoken and written languages in their broader applications in this particular context. Those who learned a

[10]From *Folkways* by William Graham Sumner, 1906. Used by permission of the publisher, Ginn and Company (Xerox Corporation).

new language, in addition to their first language, rarely fail to admire the facility with which very small children have already acquired the language that they laboriously acquired later in life. The ability of children everywhere to gain fluency in their native tongues is mute testimony to the importance of the early years of childhood and the tremendous learning capacities of youngsters.

SEMANTICS, THE MEANING OF WORDS, IDIOMS, OR PHRASES

Communication can be clear and unmistakable, but it can also be fuzzy and garbled. It can be the source of much good humor, or it can be the beginning of misunderstanding and tragedy. Our topic now is the various meanings attached to words, idioms, expressions, or phrases. This is the *semantic differential* that obfuscates communication and one that entraps children easily until they gain more referents for language symbols. It is recognizable among college students trying to understand what is asked of them during examinations or assignments. It is the same problem that this or any text encounters when it addresses an unseen, unknown number of readers. Language taken out of context or understood to mean something other than what was intended makes communication hazardous to say the least.

Humor in Word-Play

Much humor has been found in the fumbling manner with which children try to break through language barriers. From the vantage point of adulthood, these childish errors in communication are amusing and appealing because they often reflect the innocence of children and their inexperience with nuances or finer shades of meaning. These early attempts at communication are often treasured in families and recalled quite fondly. They are concomitants of the language-learning process and are viewed as normal. Later, however, continued failure to grasp meanings is less appreciated and elicits correction, reprimand, and in some instances, outright hostility. Older age-grades are assigned greater responsibilities and can no longer receive the tolerant, conciliatory, supportive help they once received as children.

The French phrase is *double-entendre*, double or multiple meanings attached to the same words or set of words. In English, the appropriate term would probably be ambiguity, multiple intent, or different implications or referents. In maturity, adults deal with the problem by carefully choosing or editing their words. From the vast store of words in their vocabulary, adults have a tremendous advantage of being able to select the most appropriate or apt terms. The limited vocabulary of children increases the chances that their particular choice of words will fall short of their thoughts. The precision with which they speak will be improved in time, but to expect linguistic accuracy among children is to demand too much too soon.

The following examples could be multiplied a hundredfold in the experiences of readers, but we caution readers to understand that our semantic examples are not attempts at deliberate humor, but are rather serious illustrations of linguistic communication problems.

What is "Outside"?

During a session of a first-grade class, one of the children asked permission to get a drink of water from a water fountain located in the school corridor. The teacher, apparently quite perturbed because she felt there would be some interruption in the lesson with the other children, reluctantly granted the request but added the comment, "You will have to stay *outside* until I call for you. I cannot have children going in and out of my room when I am teaching." The term "outside" had only one meaning to the child and that was "out-of-doors" or outside the school building. Because it was a cold, wintry day, the child was dismayed that he would have to stand outside the building after getting his drink. Without protesting, however, because he was accustomed to authoritative instructions within his family, the child quietly left the room, satisfied his thirst, and went promptly outside the building to await the arrival of his teacher. Lacking a coat, he was unable to endure the chilly weather and ran across the school yard to the nearby home of relatives. Shortly thereafter, when the child was missed by the teacher and could not be found, the whole school was alerted, and a frantic search for the lost child was begun.

This incident is not fictitious because this semantic difference occurred to one of the authors in his childhood. The whole affair seems ridiculous in retrospect, but it does illustrate the semantic differential between child and teacher. Had the teacher been specific and said, "Remain *outside* of the classroom, but *inside* the corridor until I call for you," the child would never have taken the action he did. Both teacher and child knew the denotation "outside," but the connotations of "outside" were multiple.

What is a "Cat"?

The word "cat" is frequently cited as one of the earliest terms understood by small children. Yet this simple noun does not merely refer to a small, domesticated, soft-furred, rather independent feline creature that purrs, meows, pads stealthily through a home, or demands attention and petting. It could refer to much larger, carnivorous mammals such as lions, tigers, cougars, jaguars, or leopards. It has been used to describe a woman who makes spiteful remarks about a person without that person's knowledge. Construction workers refer to their caterpillar tractors or earthmovers when they speak of "cats." For some, a "cat" may simply be a person or, if used in the vernacular as "a fat cat," the referent is a wealthy individual. Still another referent for "cat" would be "a secret" when one is speaking about "letting the cat out of the bag." There are other connotations to the symbol, but we leave them to the fertile minds of the readers.

What is a "Cuscus"?

Ralph Hall, former director of the Audio-Visual Center, Kent State University, conducted an interesting experiment that was much in line with the Chinese maxim, "A picture is worth a thousand words." Taking the noun "cuscus" at random, he copied the full description of this small animal from a large, standard, unabridged dictionary. Submitting this description to elementary school children in the vicinity, Hall requested that they draw a picture of a cuscus in one of their art classes. The sketches he obtained followed the description of a cuscus faithfully, but not one drawing was accurate or true to life. The children had simply not seen a cuscus, and no amount of words could quite convey the true referent.

What is a "Post-Office"?

A study of an isolated folk society in the Blue Ridge Mountains of Appalachia yielded the following:

> The children were asked to define a "post-office." The majority of those who tried to define this word said that a post-office was a place with a basket of apples in front of it. Some added further details, such as, "and some men sitting at the door." They had seen the post-office in Oakton Hollow which is the general store. Not one directly associated mail with the definition of post-office because mail rarely comes into Colvin Hollow.[11]

What is a "Formation"?

A father and son taking a walk noticed four airplanes flying overhead. Three of them had formed a "V" in the skies, and the fourth one lagged slightly behind in the pursuit-and-defense training mission in

[11]Mandel Sherman and Thomas R. Henry, *Hollow Folk* (New York: Thomas Y. Crowell Company, 1933), p. 124.

which they were engaged. The father, wishing to call attention to them in greater detail, remarked, "Look, son, there is a formation of planes!" He went on to explain how the planes worked together under combat conditions.

Some time later, the same young boy, eager to prove to his father that he had learned something valuable from his prior explanation, upon seeing two planes flying together, pointed to them and said, "Look father, a two-mation!"[12]

What is an "Equator"?

Punning is based upon words that sound similar but have very different meanings. The following pun is cited here because it illustrates how children try to listen closely to their teachers' instructions but still may be laboring under some misapprehension.

A child, after being asked to tell the class what "equator" meant, proudly replied, "An equator is a menagerie lion running around the earth!"

Idioms, Phrases, or Concepts

Moving to word combinations, a whole new area is opened up that may well confuse neophytes. Idioms, phrases, and concepts take on particular meanings that can be understood only after considerable familiarity with their intent or purpose. Children, particularly, are in the apprentice role when it comes to idioms, expressions, phrases, or concepts, and their errors in comprehension and usage are understandable.

We can cite a few illustrative examples in the following:

BEING POLITE AND COURTEOUS. A foreign student in a major state university came storming into the office of the advisor for foreign students quite indignant and distressed over an incident in the Registrar's Office. The student demanded to know, "Is it or is it not customary in this country, when someone has done something for a person, that it is proper for that person to thank the other person for his or her kindness?" The advisor, puzzled, agreed that this was the courteous thing to do. "Then why," asked the unhappy student, "when I thanked the clerk in the Registrar's Office for helping me register for my classes next quarter, did she tell me, 'Don't mention it!'?"

Children, too, can display this same sort of confusion over being polite and courteous. Why should a child have to say, "Please" and

---

[12]Sturtevant, *Introduction to Linguistic Science*, p. 98.

"Thank you"? Why should a child shake a stranger's hand or kiss a strange woman just because she was introduced as his or her aunt? Why should children "take turns" or "share" their toys? Why should there be some deference or respect shown when a cross, a flag, a Star of David, or a policeman's badge is displayed?

"I'M GOING TO LEAVE YOU." Children depend highly upon their parents for a sense of security. Their absence, no matter how brief, can be very threatening to a child's existence, especially when very young. A case in point was that of a nursery school child who was found crying on the nursery porch steps one summer day. An aide tried to console him but without much success. It took much prying to uncover the real cause of his deep grief. What the aide discovered was that the father of the child had deserted his mother and that when the mother left her son at the nursery school earlier in the day, she mentioned something about "leaving him." It was obvious that his interpretation of the remark was that not only had his father left him behind but now the same pattern would be followed by his mother, and he was all alone in a strange world. The possibility of "leaving" someone temporarily and then coming back did not occur to him, and consequently he felt that his one link to security was effectively shattered.

"STAY IN LINE." While there probably are numerous children who look for exceptions when told to do something or simply forget what they were told, there are those children who will obey quite literally whatever instructions are given them. Such a child was in the class of an elementary school teacher who, thinking in terms of school efficiency, told her pupils that when the bell rang for dismissal at the end of the school day to line up single file and to "stay in line" until they left the front doors of the building. Further, she solemnly told them, they were not to loiter but to return home promptly so their mothers would not worry about them. The obedient child did precisely what he was told, but he did arrive back home, apprehensive, expecting a scolding or spanking, because his trousers were wet. He really had had to use the washroom before he left school that day, but being the sort of child he was, he had "stayed in line" and without a single murmur marched out of school as his teacher had ordered.

GOING TO SCHOOL. There is a certain joy and anticipation on the part of many youngsters about attending school for the first time. However, the novelty effect or the "honeymoon period" soon ends when children begin to realize how long they are expected to attend schools. This happened for one child when he attended the first day of classes in the first grade. He proudly announced to his parents, "Well, that's that. I've been to school. I'm finished now!" When his parents explained that there were many more days to follow before he passed the first grade, he began to wonder about what lay beyond the first grade. "Am I finished then?" he asked. It took quite a while to make it clear that there were quite a few grades yet to go, and even after twelve grades, there would be many more educational levels to reach.

GOING TO BED. In infancy, children generally welcome sleep or bedtime. There comes a time, however, when going to bed is symbolic of their childhood and that staying up late is the special prerogative of older persons. It is not uncommon to find parents reporting how versatile children are at stalling the inevitable pressure to go to bed at some early hour. There is always a good television program they might wish to watch. They want a drink of water or a good-night kiss. They may want a story or they may decide that this is the strategic time to discuss their plans for the next day or week. Or they forgot to brush their teeth or wash their face and hands. Finally, they may ask why their parents don't go to sleep the same time children do. Don't adults need sleep, too?

PAYING FOR ITEMS. Children have observed how their parents and other adults move about in supermarkets and place various foods or goods in their carts. What seems to escape their attention and comprehension for a while is that there are cash registers at the exits, and before persons may leave the store, they must pay the cashiers for whatever is in the carts. Thus, it is well within the experience of many persons to find a small child valiantly "helping" with the shopping by placing the nearest available bit of merchandise in the metal cart. It does not matter what the item may be or what it may cost. It only matters that whatever one places in the cart somehow appears later in one's own home, and this is the crux of the matter for the child. Explanations of a money system, cash or credit, honesty, or profits and losses are concepts that can be understood at a more mature level when dollar and cents symbols take on greater significance. We may well add that there are adolescents and adults who never quite learned the lessons normally given in childhood that one does not take goods or services from others without acknowledgment, payment, or consent.

STREET NUMBERS AND LOCATIONS. When one of the authors was a little boy, his father happened to see him enter what was then called a candy store along one of the major streets of the city. This was the day of the "penny-candy stores" in which one penny would purchase quite a tasty morsel after school, provided one could find a penny. Instead of weighing his words, that is, making certain that his son knew the meaning of his statement, the father asked, "What were you doing on East 123rd Street yesterday afternoon?" The reply was a puzzled denial, "But, Dad, I wasn't on 123rd Street yesterday!" Thinking he had caught his son in a deliberate falsehood, the father scolded him severely for being a liar. It took a great deal of discussion to bring out the fact that the child, at that particular age, did not know the numbering system for city streets and was completely unaware that the candy store in question was, of course, located on a given street numbered as East 123rd. There are probably times when ignorance may be bliss, but in front of a wrathful father, knowledge would have been much more helpful. Orientation to one's home in reference to other locales is a lesson persons learn at different paces. Having been a ranger-naturalist in summer seasons at Yosemite National Park, the writer of this section recalls how the policy was to refer to "lost parents" rather than to "lost children." Rangers would know where a child was, but the parents could not be found temporarily because they had strayed away from their child.

REQUISITES FOR SYMBOLIC LEARNING[13]

At least three qualities seem to be needed if symbols are to be acquired during childhood socialization. These would make the process open to control and to understanding that, at times, are missing for many children. We are referring now to patience, pondering, and pain.

The first quality, patience, is needed because understanding the fullest possible meanings of a symbol requires time for absorption. Ideas that took whole centuries for a society to evolve and develop cannot necessarily be digested immediately upon their introduction to little children. A number of children report that an idea introduced to them when quite young finally "dawned" on them later. The ability to appreciate, savor, or comprehend cultural symbols which are foreign to the limited experience of children requires the passage of time. Those who work with children such as parents or teachers can often only plant the seed of an idea, but the full flowering of that idea may come at a time, place, and circumstance long after the parents or teachers have passed from the scene. The words and the symbolic deeds of those who teach children linger on, almost immortal, to instruct and guide for the life-time of children. Adults often say, "I can hear those words now, just as

---

[13]A most useful reference source is Ithiel de Sola Pool, Wilbur Schramm, *et al.*, eds., *Handbook of Communication* (Chicago: Rand McNally College Publishing Company, 1973).

if it were yesterday." Patience, then, on the part of both teacher and student goes a long way toward drawing out the meanings of cultural symbolism.

The second quality, pondering, is required because thought must be expended or invested before a given abstraction can acquire significance. Whatever the stimulus and whatever the avenues by which symbols are introduced, they must be intellectually savored. They must be considered along with the store of knowledge already acquired and filed for future reference. Like the modern computer, although far more complicated and not yet fully understood, the human brain must call into consciousness repeatedly the ideas stored therein so that they may not lie dormant and useless. Ideas are sharpened or honed by contact with sometimes conflicting ideas before their meanings can become functional.

The final quality, pain, is suggested not because it is necessary to experience it in learning situations, but because learning is not necessarily always a joyous, pleasing, easy examination of interesting phenomena. Learning is frequently a rigorous, tough, demanding operation. Sacrifice, agony, anxiety, and prolonged frustration may not be pleasant feeling-states in gaining insights, but knowledge thus attained is rarely forgotten. Whether it be the meaning of money or the gaining of an education, to have received these without some anguish can make them matter-of-fact rather than deeply appreciated and precious. One does not have to work at making learning difficult, but when learning is, indeed, difficult, the extra effort and energy needed to surmount the problems often leads to appreciation and a tolerance that suits people well.

SUMMARY

Being social creatures, men and women survive through communication, interchange, or symbolic interaction. While other species have elaborate and complex communication systems, our species stands alone in the ability to use symbolic interaction for mutual support. Chief among the symbolic acquisitions is language, and the foundations are laid down in very early childhood.

Oral and, later on, possibly written symbols are among the key gains that bring children out of infancy and well on the road to adulthood, a procedure that is nothing short of miraculous given the diversity of tongues and visual symbols that human beings have created and brought into usage.

Symbols, after all, "stand-in-the-place-of" all sorts of referents. They are abstractions from realities and assume rather arbitrary and contradictory connotations that confuse learners or make their mastery difficult. Instead of being bridges to understanding and intellectual growth, they can and often do become barriers to communication, whether in intragroup communication or in intergroup communication.

The semantic differential obfuscates the meaning of words, idioms, phrases, or concepts. While often humorous, the errors and failures in conveying and understanding meanings or shades of meanings is a serious one for both children and adults.

There seems to be no easy formula to follow in getting a firm grip on symbolic interactions in childhood, but we did suggest that the process calls for patience, pondering, and, at some point in time, discomfort.

FIVE

Problems
in
childhood

14

Deviancy, delinquency, dependency, and deprivation

Probably, from the earliest beginnings of the field of sociology, there have been differing opinions as to the main thrust or purpose of such a discipline. It would appear that what has been called "scientism" has been the central concern of sociologists. Accordingly, the twin processes of research and theory, rigorously pursued, have been the hallmarks of the full-fledged, professional sociologist seeking to understand the nature of human society.

Nevertheless, there has also been a strong tradition among sociologists to deal with social issues or social problems.[1] It is all well and good to find that everything seems to be falling into place, that social expectations are met, that persons and their relationships achieve some harmonious end. But all too often, "things" go awry, norms are not followed meekly, and individuals find themselves "in step with another drum-

---

[1]A useful history of social problems approach may be found in Edwin M. Lemert, *Human Deviance, Social Problems, and Social Control,* 2nd ed. (Englewood Cliffs, N. J.: Prentice-Hall, Inc., 1972), pp. 4–6.

mer." Robert Burns touched upon this theme when he wrote, "The best laid schemes o' mice and men gang aft a-gley; And leave us naught but grief and pain." It is this grief and pain, this personal anguish, and the special suffering that comes to individual men and women that calls for attention. In the context of the socialization of children, we turn to examine those instances, conditions, or circumstances that are identified as deviancy, delinquency, dependency, and deprivation.

The fundamental question involves the extent to which childhood is the source of the problems we have called deviancy, delinquency, dependency, and deprivation. There may well be a foreshadowing of adolescent or adult behavior in childhood, but it may or may not be predictive of adolescent or adult outcomes in terms of deviancy, delinquency, dependency, or deprivation.

DEFINING DEVIANCY,
DELINQUENCY, DEPENDENCY, AND DEPRIVATION

Deviancy[2]

In lay terms, deviancy has been expressed as "getting out of line," "moving away from the straight and narrow," "being abnormal," "being very sick," or simply "being different" from those with whom persons live. Others have said deviancy consists of "being out of control." While these referents are in common usage and convey meaning to many, they are not quite what sociologists have in mind when they identify deviancy. We must quickly add that deviancy has variant semantic referents for sociologists, just as it does for lay persons. There are serious objections to any single all-inclusive definition, an admission that the sociology of deviance is still emerging just as any science is ongoing and constantly in "a state of becoming."

In the most general terms, deviancy is defined by sociologists as behavior that does not follow the norms or social expectations. But from that point on, there are precautions to be taken, qualifications to be noted, and embellishments to be taken into account. For example, this definition of deviancy as a failure to follow group expectations makes most persons appear to be deviant because they belong to some groups

[2]Deviancy literature abounds. See for example, Marshall B. Clinard, *Sociology of Deviant Behavior*, 3rd ed. (New York: Holt, Rinehart and Winston, Inc., 1968); Robert A. Scott and Jack D. Douglas, eds., *Theoretical Perspectives on Deviance* (New York: Basic Books, Inc., 1972); David Matza, *Becoming Deviant* (Englewood Cliffs, N. J.: Prentice-Hall, Inc., 1969); Arnold Birenbaum and Edward Sagarin, *Norms and Human Behavior* (New York: Praeger Publishers, 1976).

but not to all groups. The conforming Roman Catholic is obviously a deviant from some Protestant denominations. The devout Jew is a deviant from a Christian perspective. The agnostic and the atheist are deviant from both Christians and Jews and so on *ad infinitum.* When parents ask, "Where did we go wrong?," there is the implication that they somehow are responsible for the deviancy of their children. From the sociological perspective, of course, the explanation is that both the parents and their children are "guilt-free." Neither parents nor children went "wrong." Children, adolescents, or adults choose from diverse groups, and they then conform to new norms or new expectations. *Deviants* from one set of norms *are also conformers* to another set of norms. Deviants have shifted their loyalties and bonded themselves to new groups.

What has been called the Neo-Chicagoans, a reference to those not associated with the structural-functionalists of the University of Chicago's department of sociology; the West Coast School or the Pacific Seminar, because many of the sociologists relocated to Pacific Coast schools; or the new deviance sociology has been developing almost thirty years. This school of thought holds that deviance is a social product, an artifact of labeling certain behavior as deviant or in violation of current expectations.[3] The shift from operating an automobile at "reasonable speeds," depending upon such factors as highway conditions, weather, or number of other vehicles on the highway, to a maximum of fifty-five miles per hour brought a number of previously "safe" and "legal" drivers into deviancy. These new "unsafe" and "illegal" drivers were in direct violation of a norm imposed by a national effort to conserve fuel. What had been acceptable for many years became "deviancy" by the passage of new highway safety regulations. In addition to conserving fuel, an allegation that has not been supported by accelerated usage of fossil fuel resources, there is the rationale that thousands of lives have been saved by the new speed limits. This bonus is documented and does lend itself to continued support for the new regulations. In this example, we see vindication for the labeling theory of deviancy. But, as we shall also see, there continues to be debate and disagreement when social dimensions are considered.[4]

If sociologists debate among themselves as to what deviancy is, it would come as no surprise to find that they cannot agree as to who, precisely, are deviants. Reflecting their times, sociologists have pro-

[3]Lemert, *Human Deviance,* pp. 16–17.
[4]See for example, Edwin M. Schur, *Labeling Deviant Behavior, Its Sociological Implications* (New York: Harper & Row, Publishers, 1971).

vided such as examples as "the Negro, the career woman, the criminal, the Communist, the physically handicapped, the mentally ill, the homosexual"[5] (1961 vintage); "knaves and cheats, criminals and malingerers, wicked folk, and sinners,"[6] (circa 1966); "the world of hip, drug addicts, jazz musicians, cab drivers, prostitutes, night people, drifters, grifters and skidders: the 'cool world,' "[7] (1968 style); marijuana users and jazz musicians, (Becker in 1963)[8]; drug users, thieves, fanatic soccer fans, suicides, homosexuals and their blackmailers, industrial saboteurs, (a 1971 British perspective)[9]; "cabbies, suicides, drug users, and abortionees," (Henslin in 1972)[10]; and "others have found deviance in alcoholics, nudist campers, protest demonstrators, topless barmaids, motorcycle gangs, jockeys, and hippies," (reported by Sagarin in 1975).[11]

Looking for the common denominator in such a list of deviants, Sagarin suggests that whoever the deviants are and whenever the social climate seems to find them at odds with the rest of their society, they are "disvalued people."[12] With a few other qualifications, Sagarin indicates his support for Edwin Schur's definition of deviance: "Human behavior is deviant to *the extent that* it comes to be viewed as involving a *personally discreditable* departure from a group's normative expectations, *and* it *elicits* interpersonal or collective reactions that serve to 'isolate,' 'treat,' 'correct,' or 'punish' *individuals* engaged in such behavior"[13] (italicized by Schur). Sagarin settles for both "disvalued people and disvalued behavior that provoke hostile reactions" as deviant.[14] We accept Schur's and Sagarin's definitions of deviancy and deviants, keeping in mind, of course, that refinements and other perspectives will undoubtedly be added as specialization continues to develop.

[5]Fred Davis, "Deviance Disavowal: The Management of Strained Interaction by the Visibly Handicapped," *Social Problems,* 9 (1961), 120–32.
[6]Albert K. Cohen, *Deviance and Control* (Englewood Cliffs, N. J.: Prentice-Hall, Inc., 1966).
[7]Alvin W. Gouldner, "The Sociologist as Partisan: Sociology and the Welfare State," *American Sociologist,* 3 (1968), 103–16.
[8]Howard S. Becker *Outsiders, Studies in the Sociology of Deviance* (New York: The Free Press of Glencoe, Macmillan Company, 1963).
[9]Stanley Cohen, ed., *Images of Deviance* (Middlesex, England and Baltimore, Maryland: Penguin Books, 1971).
[10]James M. Henslin, "Studying Deviance in Four Settings: Research Experience with Cabbies, Suicides, Drug Users, and Abortionees," ed. Jack D. Douglas, *Research in Deviance* (New York: Random House, 1972), pp. 35–70.
[11]Edward Sagarin, *Deviants and Deviance, An Introduction to the Study of Disvalued People and Behavior* (New York: Praeger Publishers, 1975), p. 5.
[12]Ibid.
[13]Edwin M. Schur, *Labeling Deviant Behavior, Its Sociological Implications* (New York: Harper & Row, Publishers, 1971), p. 24.
[14]Sagarin, *Deviants and Deviance,* p. 9.

Delinquency

Historically, childhood and children in the eighteenth and nineteenth century in both Europe and America might fit Sagarin's "disvalued" analysis of deviancy. Neglect, abandonment, flogging, imprisonment, hard labor, or indenture were fairly common conditions for many unfortunate children. Reformers and philanthropists called attention to these disvalued children, but their efforts did not result in any comprehensive societal program until the establishment of the first juvenile court in Chicago, Illinois in 1899.[15]

While the juvenile court system spread from state to state as part and parcel of the legal machinery to handle those said to deviate from the statutes and regulations of the jurisdictions, it was designed to go beyond the usual practices of trying alleged lawbreakers. Children or juveniles were to be treated as "being in the care of the courts," similar to the model of concerned parents who seek the "best interests" of the children. They may or may not have been judged "delinquent," but they certainly were not to be treated as potential adult offenders or violators of the laws of the land.[16] In this sense, children were held to be incapable of committing a crime. Some juvenile court systems operate with an age-floor of seven, but usually all those under the age of eighteen come under the care of the juvenile court system.[17]

The labeling theorists of deviancy can certainly find support in the definitions applied to delinquency, for, as Sol Rubin noted, "juvenile delinquency is what the law says it is."[18] These laws vary from state to state, but truancy from school, incorrigibility, or acts of carelessness or mischief that harm themselves, others, or property are examples of behavior that often bring children to the attention of the juvenile court authorities and may well start them on a path toward adult criminality. Delinquency, then, is a specific form of deviancy that is particularly ascribed for children.

Dependency

Dependency can be said to be the normal state of affairs for children. It signifies the need for care, comfort, and control of children with the responsibilities placed squarely upon adults. As indicated in the

[15]See "Origin and Development of Juvenile Courts," in Helen I. Clarke, *Social Legislation*, 2nd ed. (New York: Appleton-Century-Crofts, 1957), pp. 372–77.
[16]See Sol Rubin, "The Legal Character of Juvenile Delinquency," ed. James E. Teele, *Juvenile Delinquency, A Reader* (Itasca, Illinois: F. E. Peacock Publishers, Inc., 1970), pp. 4–10.
[17]Ibid, p. 8.
[18]Ibid, p. 4.

development of the juvenile court system, children are placed in positions of dependency and are to receive special treatment accordingly. Eventually, they are "to grow up" and become independent and responsible adults, but for the first twelve years of childhood and for another six years as adolescents, not quite adults, dependency upon others is a hallmark of their lives.

The dependency of children has two fundamental bases; one is biological and the other is social in origin. The biological foundations of dependency rest upon the prolonged states of physical helplessness that mark infancy and growing childhood. The very young in other animals are, relatively speaking, "on their own" almost from birth. Fish fingerlings or newly hatched turtles face a hostile or threatening world within minutes of their arrival. Cougar kittens receive care for about one year; bear cubs are given protection and sustenance for about two years. Elephant mothers will nurse their young for about two years and spend an additional two years watching over their calves.[19] Among humankind, however, approximately twenty years is devoted to bringing children safely to maturity, a rare quality, indeed, in the animal kingdom.

The social foundation of dependency rests upon the elaborate complexities of coping with social structures and processes. There is so much to learn that even two decades are an insufficient amount of time to acquire some grasp of its nature. Socialization, we have said repeatedly, is begun in childhood and, as we now know, continues for a lifetime and is terminated only with the end of an individual's life. Social dependency in this perspective is an asset that maximizes the chances that children will gain the necessary fundamentals to help them through the five, six, or seven decades that lie ahead of them.

In Bowlby's terms, there are reasons for "attachment" and reasons for "separation" between children and their parents, caretakers, or guardians.[20] It is, perhaps, the nature or degree of the attachments and separations that become the problematic issues. Thus, one might speak of "overattachments" or "underattachments" between children and their parents. For children, autonomy, self-reliance, or a type of inde-

[19]Other possible readings include S. C. Kendeigh, "Parental Care and Its Evolution in Birds," *Illinois Biological Monographs,* 22 (1952), 1–356; J. Bowlby, "The Nature of the Child's Tie to His Mother," *International Journal of Psycho-analysis,* 39 (1958), 1–24; M. Gunther, "Instinct and the Nursing Couple," *The Lancet,* March 19, 1955, pp. 575–78; H. F. Harlow and R. R. Zimmerman, "Affectional Responses in the Infant Monkey," *Science,* 30 (1959), 421–32; R. A. Hinde, "The Early Development of the Parent-Child Relationship," *Discovery* (February 1961), 48–55; John Bowlby, *Attachment and Loss, Attachment,* Vol. I (New York: Basic Books, Inc., 1969); John Bowlby, *Attachment and Loss, Separation, Anxiety and Anger,* Vol. II (New York: Basic Books, Inc., 1973).
[20]Bowlby, *Nature of Child's Tie.*

pendence are beacons that beckon them towards adulthood. For parents, however, there may be the problems of weaning their children to seek autonomy or their own reluctance to let their children go. While some parents find their status and responsibilities onerous, others may well enjoy the dependency of their children and be quite reluctant to reach the state of, in a sense, no longer being "needed."

In all this, we do not wish to convey the erroneous conceptualization of childhood as a state of dependency and adulthood as a state of independence. Rather, we would view dependency and independence as two facets of a greater *interdependency,* an understanding that no single human being operates in a social vacuum. Whether the individual is young or old, there is an exchange or reciprocity that colors human relationships. In childhood, dependency is understood. In adulthood, there is still dependency but with a few more options to decide upon. Who among us is "free" to do as he or she pleases?

Deprivation

For our purposes, deprivation in childhood is confined to the problems that ensue from sociocultural failures to provide the very young with the essential relationships that guide and guard them through the vicissitudes of life. In chapter nine, The Politicalization of Children, we dwelt at length on the "rights" of children. In this chapter, in the context of deprivation, we see these rights eroded away, undermined, or missing from the beginning.

Two examples of deprivation in childhood are the shattered or broken relationships children have with significant others, particularly mothers, fathers, siblings, friends or peers, and, even more pervasive, their participation in society at the lower social class levels. In the first example, there is the burden of finding enduring relationships that may well be beyond the capabilities or opportunities of children. In the second example, there is the victimization of children who suffer from "relative deprivation" when compared with those of middle or upper socioeconomic strata.

The making and breaking of ties between two or more persons can be valuable lessons in the maintenance or repair of social networks, something that is continually happening to most individuals. It becomes problematic or potentially harmful when children are denied any sense of durability and continuity in the midst of the changes that surround them. Losing contact with one's mother or father through death or serious accidents is one thing, but to lose them because they make choices that separate them from their children is even more self-rejecting or demoralizing.

CHILDHOOD AS A SOURCE OF DEVIATION, DELINQUENCY, DEPENDENCY, AND DEPRIVATION

Given the definitions of deviation, delinquency, dependency, and deprivation, we ask again to what extent childhood is a source of these problems.

Childhood Acted Upon

One set of theories that deals with deviation in general and delinquency more specifically stresses the individuals themselves. Something in their makeup, with particular emphasis upon their personalities, is said to be the wellspring of their actions. Specialists in psychiatry, psychoanalysis, psychology, or in social psychology would be prone to adopt these theories. In a sense, some deviancy or delinquency occurs, and the question then becomes, "What kind of person would act this way?" An ex-post-facto procedure is initiated to trace those personal traits that are said to be the motivators of deviancy or antisocial acts.

Granting, as we are prone to do, that childhood lays down the personality organization of individuals, what Kardiner called the basic personality structure, then these theories do explain and predict deviant or delinquent outcomes.

However, there are more dimensions to consider than personality organization in and of itself. Albert Cohen has summarized the various ways to examine deviant behavior in the research strategies suggested in Figure 14-1:[21]

In Figure 14-1 A, samples of the personalities assumed to have a propensity for deviancy would be isolated from those personalities that led to nondeviance. In Figure 14-1 B, the next question is answered by delineating those developmental backgrounds that produced the personalities (or kinds of people) in the first place. Cohen suggests that attitudes and characteristics of parents, early frustrations and deprivations, and social class backgrounds are potential topics for investigation.[22]

It may well be, of course, that those who behave in some deviant manner are not special kinds of people, but that anybody would behave in a deviant way if the appropriate conditions occurred. These situations may be found in, as Cohen suggests, provocation, temptation,

[21]Cohen, *Deviance and Control,* 1966, pp. 42–45. Reprinted by permission of Prentice-Hall, Inc., Englewood Cliffs, New Jersey.
[22]Ibid.

example, extreme stress, or opportunity.[23] This procedure of investigation is outlined in Figure 14–1 C.

Figure 14–1 D presents both the kinds of people involved and the situations in which they find themselves, a model called "conjunctive"

[23]Ibid, p. 44.

A. Kinds of people and frequencies of deviant behavior

Kinds of People	Behavior	
	Deviant	Non-deviant
P_1		
P_2		

B. Developmental background and kinds of people

Developmental Background	Kinds of People	
	P_1	P_2
B_1		
B_2		

C. Kinds of situations and frequencies of deviant behavior

Kinds of Situations	Behavior	
	Deviant	Non-deviant
S_1		
S_2		

D. Conjunction of persons and situations and frequencies of deviant behavior

Kinds of People	Kinds of Situations	
	S_1	S_2
P_1		
P_2		

FIGURE 14-1 *Research Strategies for Theories of Deviant Behavior*

Source: Albert K. Cohen, *Deviance and Control.*

FIGURE 14-1 *(continued)*

E.   Interaction process and deviant outcome.

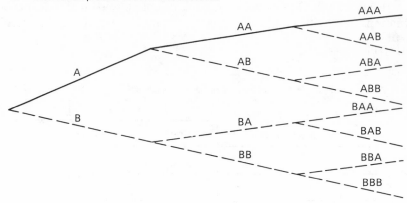

by Cohen.[24] An example of this possibility would be a test of the hypothesis that some people would and some people would not yield to temptation to deviate from legal norms even if they felt strongly that they would not be apprehended or held accountable.

The model depicted in Figure 14–1 E follows a more interactive or sociological processing in which deviant or nondeviant *careers* are followed. At certain critical points, decisions are made that lead individuals into pathways of disvalued or valued actions.

Childhood Left Behind

The "career" model offers a different perspective in terms of deviancy and delinquency and childhood than we have heretofore entertained. It suggests that childhood itself may not be the source of the problem. Instead, it may be during the difficult transition from childhood to adulthood that individuals begin their real careers. We are referring mainly to adolescence, that period of life in which childish ways are supposed to be shed in anticipation of assuming adulthood. It is a critical test of childhood backgrounds, to be sure, but all too often the controls once so securely in place for children are gradually released or modified, and adolescents find in their newfound freedom the opportunities to test their ideas. Deviancy and delinquency can now manifest themselves much more easily than in the protestations of children when asked to conform to normative expectations.

[24]Ibid, p. 44.

There is further support of the thesis that it is in adolescence that rebellious, uncommitted, unconvinced persons may turn to vengeance for their past subordination as children. Their dependencies are diminished but not yet gone, and they can "act out" the fantasies of childhood now left behind. Indeed, there is a type of "declaration of independence" that has occurred, and "a war of rebellion" may or may not be begun. There is the view that the deviance and delinquencies in adolescence are not so much rebellious behaviors as they are cries for recognition or status long denied young men and women. Notice is served that they are no longer children but are quite capable of taking a significant role in adult society.

There are, of course, many other ways to leave childhood behind, rebellion being only one way of doing so. Some of the individual adaptations are suggested in what has been called one of the most frequently cited paradigms in sociological literature, the patterns first offered by Robert Merton.[25] (See Figure 14–2)

Cultural goals refer to those needs and values held up to men and women as desirable objectives. Institutionalized means are provided in the social structures so that persons may have opportunities to achieve cultural goals in keeping with legitimate norms. The sign + indicates an "acceptance"; the sign − indicates "rejection"; and the combined sign ± represents a "rejection of prevailing values and substitution of new values."

By conformity, adolescents may continue within social systems in accord with their childhood acquisitions of what is expected of them and how they may utilize current means to achieve these expectations. By innovation, however, they continue to seek the goals of money, property, or status, but they create "new and disapproved" ways to reach them such as stealing, lying, or cheating. The ritualists "go along" with their peers or superiors but are so devoted, loyal, or bound to their routines that they can and will overlook some of the approved procedures. Perhaps the Watergate conspirators fit the pattern of the ritualists who will go to almost any lengths to maintain their positions within a bureaucratic structure. Retreatism, of course, is the familiar rejection of both goals and the means to achieve them. This mode of adaptation is exemplified by drifters, drop-outs, alcoholics, drug abusers, and what used to be called "the hippies." Finally, there are the rebellious who seek both radical ways to break with the past and the achievement of goals of their own design and purposes. In Becker's view, such persons

[25]Robert K. Merton, *Social Theory and Social Structure*, rev. and enlarged ed. (Glencoe, Illinois: The Free Press, 1957), p. 140.

Modes of Adaptation	Cultural Goals	Institutionalized Means
Conformity	+	+
Innovation	+	−
Ritualism	−	+
Retreatism	−	−
Rebellion	±	±

FIGURE 14-2 *A Typology of Modes of Individual Adaptation*

Source: Robert K. Merton, *Social Theory and Social Structure*, revised and enlarged edition, Glencoe, Illinois: The Free Press, 1957, p. 140.

become the "outsiders" because not only are they participants in "out-groups" rather than "in-groups," but they also turn the whole pattern around and see themselves as participants in a new "in-group" and all others as "outsiders."[26]

In sum, except for continued conformity, childhood is left behind by reasons of innovation, ritualism, retreatism, or rebellion.

Childhood Continued

Prolonged childhood, however, continues the state of dependency upon the resources of others into adolescence and adulthood. This aspect of childhood is retained for an indefinite number of years. The adolescent or adult who cannot become self-reliant, not because there is some character flaw or lack of ambition, drive, or energy, but because conditions are far beyond his or her control or capacities, the helpless cripple, the dependent student who must devote attention to studies rather than to the mundane tasks of finding food, shelter, or clothing, or the disprivileged who cannot find employment or satisfaction of needs because of a lack of demand for their services are cases in point. We may properly include the retired and chronically ill elderly persons who truly fear and despise their dependency.[27]

Deprivation, too, is a concomitant of dependencies. It does not necessarily follow dependency, but it is frequently found in association with dependency. The losses are so severe that from childhood on, recovery or recuperation are well nigh out of reach. Yet, with the

[26]Becker, *Outsiders.*
[27]Richard A. Kalish, *The Dependencies of Old People*, Occasional Papers in Gerontology, No. 6 (Institute of Gerontology, The University of Michigan-Wayne State University, August, 1969).

amazing resilience of human beings, even deprivation is not insurmountable. The shattering of kinship ties experienced by those forced
into concentration-extermination camps in World War II, the enforced
separations of refugees in wartorn Korea, Vietnam, Northern Ireland,
Middle East countries, or certain emerging African nations, and the
breakup of countless homes through death, desertion, dissolution, or
divorce have victimized children and scarred their lives, yet all these
can also recite wondrous tales of coming through such torments with
some measure of recovery or success. Their cases represent the few
who can survive, and much depends upon whether one stresses the
exceptions or the many who continued their suffering to the end of
their days.

Deprivation, too, is intimately connected with the distribution of
life-chances through the social class system. Harrington's *The Other
America, Poverty in the United States*[28] is often credited with bringing
to the public's attention the need to recognize the deprivations brought
about by extreme poverty in the midst of an otherwise comfortable or
even prosperous country. Depending upon definitions of "poverty levels," and these vary from time to time depending upon such factors as
inflation, patterned income, numbers of dependents in a family, and so
on, Harrington determined that some 25 percent of the population
lived at the poverty level in 1963.[29] By 1970, the Bureau of Census
placed the percentage closer to about 13 percent of the total population.[30] Among blacks and other nonwhites, the proportion was about
one-third at the poverty line.[31] The figures and proportions as of September, 1976, indicated that close to 26 million Americans or some 12
percent of the total population in 1975 were at the poverty level, then
defined as $5500 per year for a nonfarm family of four.

Frank Field has suggested that what is needed is a constant reassessment profile so that official figures do not mask the real deprivations
of the people.[32] Among the indices that need monitoring are the number of persons receiving supplementary benefits, the relation between
the earnings of the lowest 10 percent and the mean average earnings,
the number of persons who are dependent on selected means-tested
benefits, the number of persons who have given up claiming any benefits, the number of homeless families and individuals, and housing con-

---

[28]Michael Harrington, *The Other America, Poverty in the United States* (New York:
The Macmillan Company, 1963).
[29]Ibid, Penguin Ed. (1964), p. 185.
[30]*Statistical Abstract of the United States, 1970* (Washington, D.C.: U.S. Department of Commerce, Bureau of Census), p. xviii.
[31]Ibid.
[32]Frank Field, "What Is Poverty?," *New Society*, 33, No. 677 (September 1975),
688–91.

ditions. Field concluded that, in all but the last indicator, there was deterioration rather than improvement between 1970 and 1975.

It is usual to point to the inverse relationship between income and numbers of dependent children. This is to say that the higher the income, the fewer the children, or the lower the income, the greater the numbers of children dependent on these limited resources. Dudley Poston, Jr., however, has found that this relationship is grounded more in involuntary parenthood. When applied to those who control their fertility the relationship does not hold for all subpopulations.[33] Poston calls for more research on the childless, highly educated women of today.

SUMMARY

The processes of socialization are problematic, filled with events and circumstances that do not quite fit social or personal expectations. In this chapter, deviancy, delinquency, dependency, and deprivation were examined. In ensuing chapters, other problems associated with children, such as those who are physically handicapped or those who are "overprivileged," are considered. The list is not exhaustive but suggestive of the many ways in which the rearing of children to maturity can go awry.

Much depends upon the definitions or referents when deviancy, delinquency, dependency, and deprivation are discussed. Deviancy and delinquency are particularly subject to different interpretations because these specializations have received considerable attention from a variety of perspectives. Dependency and deprivation, by contrast, have received less evaluation by sociologists.

Deviancy is generally defined by sociologists as behavior that does not follow norms or social expectations. This generalized definition is criticized because it permits the inclusion of most persons at some point in their lives. People simply belong to different groups with different values and expectations. By conforming to one set of norms, persons are obviously deviant from other sets of norms. Their loyalties and affiliations shift from one group to another in the making and breaking of group bonds.

Deviancy is possible in the negative or positive sense; the negative refers to the failures to meet the norms, and the positive refers to the "overdoing" or going beyond the norms. In the end, the underconform-

[33]Dudley L. Poston, Jr., "Income and Childlessness: Is the Relationship Always Inverse?," *Social Biology*, 21, No. 3 (Fall 1974), 296–307.

ing is what elicits interpersonal or collective reactions to isolate, treat, correct, or punish the deviants. Sagarin's term of becoming "disvalued" persons is appropriate in this context. Deviancy is thus defined as behavior that is personally discreditable departure from a group's normative expectations and one that provokes the hostile reactions just described.

What emerges from the theoretical debates is a newer view of deviancy based upon "labeling." This labeling, in effect, recognizes that deviancy is a social product, an artifact created by virtue of rather formal decisions to so identify it.

Delinquency is a more specific example of deviancy from statutes and regulations imposed by legal authority and has particular application to child offenders or violators of laws or legal orders. Indeed, delinquency is whatever the law declares it to be and is handled in juvenile court systems, usually for persons under eighteen years of age. Otherwise, delinquency is redefined as criminal behavior and is adjudicated in adult courts.

Dependency, the need for care, comfort, and control, is the normal state of affairs for children. Autonomy or self-reliance is denied or delayed because of biological immaturity and social inexperience or knowledge.

It is to be understood, of course, that dependency is not removed upon the achievement of adulthood. The so-called independent adult is also dependent upon others for survival and significance.

Finally, we come to deprivation which involves sociocultural failures to provide essential relationships to guide and guard children as they move through life. Significant others, particularly mothers, fathers, siblings, friends, and peers, are often lacking or separated from growing children who suffer accordingly. Further victimization occurs in the relative deprivations of lower-class life chances.

The basic question that is posed asks to what extent childhood is the prime source or origin of deviancy, delinquency, dependency, and deprivation.

Research strategies have been developed for deviancy behavior in terms of kinds of persons involved, their developmental backgrounds, the situations in which they find themselves, and their deviant careers. Childhood was "acted upon" in this context but could not be considered the prime source or origin of deviancy. We held, instead, that childhood was "left behind" in adolescent and adult behaviors because socialization continues when increasing autonomy and opportunities occur at these later age-grades. Delinquency is much more associated with adolescence, being neither children nor adult, with dependency removed from families to other authority figures. Innovation, ritualism, retreatism, and rebellion characterized adolescent behavior more than the conformity and controls of childhood.

When it came to deprivation, it would appear that childhood was "continued" almost indefinitely. This interpretation is suggested because of the longlasting effects of shattered or broken relationships with significant others, such as parents, as well as the placement of persons at the lower socioeconomic levels of society. Poverty levels continue to mark the lives of some twelve or more percent of the American population and require reassessment monitoring in the years ahead.

15

Handicapped children

The expectations, hopes, wishes, and, we might add, prayers, of parents are for the arrival of healthy children, free from any defects that would threaten their lives or deter them from enjoying a full and happy lifetime. Further, their development—physically, mentally, emotionally, and socially—is expected to run a fairly smooth course, provided appropriate precaution and effort are expended by their caretakers. In the main, these expectations and developments result in "normal" children.

However, this roseate picture seriously overlooks "the special children," those who have handicaps sufficient to warrant attention, adjustments, or modifications in their socialization experiences. It is reliably estimated that some two or three infants per 100,000 births begin their lives with one or more handicaps with which they and those they encounter must cope.[1] To proceed on the assumption that most chil-

[1]James M. Wolf and Robert M. Anderson, eds., *The Multiply Handicapped Child* (Springfield, Illinois: Charles C. Thomas, Publisher, 1969), p. 41.

dren are reasonably healthy and likely not to encounter physical, mental, emotional, or social difficulties is to deny the realities and singular problems confronting handicapped children. There is no tacit conspiracy to neglect handicapped individuals; instead, far too often, the tendency is to plead lack of background or skills in dealing with special children and consequently to delegate responsibilities to professionals, semiprofessionals, or paraprofessionals trained to deal with their cases.

What we are saying by devoting a chapter to an overview of handicapped children is that such children need the support and understanding of all persons, professionals and nonprofessionals alike, if they are to experience a modicum of normative living. Those handicapped persons with whom the authors have dealt frequently express the wish for acceptance on the part of the "nonhandicapped" or the "normals." Robert Kleck, a Dartmouth psychologist, has studied encounters between the handicapped and the nonhandicapped, and his findings affirm there is a wide gap between the verbalizations of the nonhandicapped and their internalized attitudes toward the handicapped.[2]

The nonhandicapped will report, for instance, that they "enjoyed" meeting the handicapped person. But physiological readings suggest that high anxiety or discomfort is experienced in the presence of the handicapped and that eye contact, gestures, and body movements are those tied to avoidance and rejection.

The work of Kleck is further supported by the study of John Tringo of the University of Kentucky who asked his study samples to rank the felt social distance between themselves and persons with twenty-one different disabilities.[3] The rank order, with the most tolerable handicaps first and the least tolerable disabilities last, was established as follows:

1.	Ulcer	12.	Paraplegic
2.	Arthritis	13.	Epilepsy
3.	Asthma	14.	Dwarf
4.	Diabetes	15.	Cerebral Palsy
5.	Heart Disease	16.	Hunchback
6.	Amputee	17.	Tuberculosis
7.	Blindness	18.	Ex-convict
8.	Deafness	19.	Mentally Retarded
9.	Stroke	20.	Alcoholic
10.	Cancer	21.	Mental Illness
11.	Old Age		

[2]"Reactions to the Handicapped—Sweaty Palms and Saccharine Words," *Psychology Today*, 9, No. 6 (November 1975), 122.
[3]Ibid, p. 124.

Obviously, both the subjects and the objects were adults and, as in the cases of "old age" or being an "ex-convict," the list is not exclusively devoted to the handicaps of children. What the rank ordering does suggest, however, is that the hidden or subtle problems of handicaps are more tolerable to non-handicapped persons than the more grossly visible or obvious handicaps. If the dimension of childhood was added to these handicaps, the sympathies and antipathies can be, at least, hypothesized to balance out in the direction of even more rejection because of the prolonged periods of time with which children would have to deal with their disabilities.

What Is a Handicap?

It would seem to be a simple question to ask what a handicap is and to have a simple answer provided. Such is not the case, however. Examination of the literature indicates that what is unequivocally a handicap to some is not viewed as a handicap by others. Further, it is necessary to consider the degrees of severity of a given handicap because some children have borderline symptoms while others have moderate to severe cases of the same disease or physical handicap.

There are, of course, other variables to consider. One of these is the location of the condition on an acute to chronic continuum. If a disability, impairment, or handicap is life-threatening or so dominant that all other life-functions or actions are subordinated to it, then it falls toward the acuity pole. If, however, the problem is recurrent or fairly constant but can be tolerated, modified, or somewhat controlled so that individuals can perform numerous tasks despite its presence, then the handicap is a chronic condition. Perhaps the degree to which a handicap can be managed or bypassed effectively constitutes another variable. Cost factors are also involved. Some handicaps require expensive equipment, prolonged or periodic treatment, possible travel or residency in a particular location, or the specialized services of professional or paraprofessional personnel. Others require the attention of parents, siblings, or other relatives willing to give freely of their time to help handicapped children. Still another vital variable is the degree to which handicapped children themselves can manage normal functions or be helped to help themselves. Finally, reversability or elimination of the handicap is a consideration. Surgery, medication, or other therapeutic measures might achieve such results. In other cases, they would have little or no effect and so are not even considered.

The question remains: what is a handicap? For our purposes and in the context of a sociological approach to childhood, *a handicap is any condition from whatever source—genetic, physical, mental, emotional, or social—that requires attention, adjustments, or special efforts without which the socialization processes of children would be impaired, thwarted, or denied.*

Single or Multiple Handicaps

A handicap, by itself, is troublesome, hazardous, and discomforting. It causes pain and hardship throughout the years of childhood. But when two or more handicaps are suffered by a single child, these problems are compounded. Helen Keller is perhaps one of the best known cases of a child with the dual handicaps of blindness and deafness. She was successfully educated through the remarkable talents of her friend and teacher, Ann Sullivan Macy. It was Helen Keller who once described those who are both deaf and blind as "a comparatively few people surrounded by a multitude of cruel problems."[4]

James M. Wolf and Robert M. Anderson have compiled an excellent source of information on multiply handicapped children in their symposium entitled *The Multiply Handicapped Child*.[5] In their survey, Wolf and Anderson indicate that no major studies have been made on a nationwide scale to ascertain the incidence and prevalence of multiply handicapped children. At the same time, findings of state or local level studies vary widely ranging from about 10 percent to 90 percent depending upon which combination of handicaps is being considered for which population of handicapped children.[6]

Estimations, however, have been made by federal government agencies that some *eight million* handicapped children could be identified in the United States in 1976.[7] That which is often held to be a single handicap, such as "a learning disability," is more likely to be a combination of difficulties through which a particular child must work. Some forty thousand multiply handicapped children have been identified by the federal government's Bureau of Education for the Handicapped in 1976.[8] Table 15–1 provides the overall incidence of handicapped children in 1976. It should be noted that their frequency estimations are based upon the inclusion of "children" from birth to age nineteen,

[4]Helen Keller in a letter to Peter J. Salmon, April 3, 1959 in *World Council for Welfare of the Blind*, Report of Committee on services for the deaf-blind to the world assembly, Rome, Italy, July, 1959 (The Industrial Home for the Blind, 1959), p. 152.
[5]Wolf and Anderson, eds., *Multiply Handicappped Child*.
[6]Ibid, p. 9.
[7]See *Unfinished Revolution: Education for the Handicapped* (Washington, D.C.: U.S. Department of Health, Education and Welfare, Office of Education, Bureau of Education for the Handicapped, 1976), p. 2.
[8]Ibid.

TABLE 15-1   Estimated Number of Handicapped Children Served and Unserved by Type
of Handicap, United States, 1976

	1975–1976 *Served*	*1975–1976* *Unserved*	*Total*	*Percent* *Served*	*Percent* *Unserved*
Total Age 0–19	4,310,000	3,577,000	7,887,000	55%	45%
Total Age 6–19	3,860,000	2,840,000	6,700,000	58%	42%
Total Age 0–5	450,000	737,000	1,187,000	38%	62%
Speech Impaired	2,020,000	273,000	2,293,000	88%	12%
Mentally Retarded	1,350,000	157,000	1,507,000	90%	10%
Learning Disability	260,000	1,706,000	1,966,000	13%	87%
Emotionally Disturbed	255,000	1,055,000	1,310,000	19%	81%
Crippled and Other Health Impairments	255,000	73,000	328,000	78%	22%
Deaf	45,000	4,000	49,000	92%	8%
Hard of Hearing	66,000	262,000	328,000	20%	80%
Visually Handicapped	43,000	23,000	66,000	65%	35%
Deaf-Blind and Other Multiply Handicapped	16,000	24,000	40,000	40%	60%

Source: *Unfinished Revolution: Education for the Handicapped, 1976,* U.S. Department of Health, Education and Welfare, Office of Education, Bureau of Education for the Handicapped, p. 2.

whereas we have defined children as individuals from birth to age twelve.

Noteworthy in the data summarized in Table 15–1 is the uneven distribution of services provided certain categories of handicapped children. Some 92 percent of the deaf children have apparently been served with some 8 percent unserved. Among the "hard of hearing," however, only 20 percent are served while 80 percent are unserved. Among visually handicapped children, some 65 percent are served and 35 percent are unserved, whereas among the deaf-blind or other multiply handicapped children, only 40 percent are helped, leaving 60 percent unserved.

There are, of course, explanations for such results. Some diagnoses of handicaps are easier to make than others. Some specific handicaps have attracted more attention, support, and advocate agencies than other handicaps. Further, there are handicapped children who are hard to reach by reason of residency in remote or isolated sections of the country, lack of funding or facilities in certain locales, and problems in servicing handicapped children at all socioeconomic levels.

Costs of Rehabilitation, Care, or Support of Handicapped Children

The magnitude of the presence of handicapped children can begin to be assessed in terms of the financial investments needed to bring these special children into the mainstream of society. The U.S. Government has appropriated some 387 million dollars for the 1977–78 school year for the education of handicapped children, and the costs are expected to rise to about three billion dollars per year by 1982.[9] Each handicapped child is estimated to cost about twice as much to educate as a normal child, but the promise has long been made that every child is entitled to a free and adequate public school education regardless of special needs or adjustments. These millions of dollars, of course, cannot begin to reflect the other financial investments in terms of hospitals, medical and rehabilitation facilities and staff, or the personal commitments of friends and families in support of handicapped children. Further, and probably more significantly, the dollar investments in handicapped children cannot reflect or measure the emotional investments, individual and family dedication, and high valuations placed upon these special children.

There have been those who ask if all these investments, financial and emotional, are worthwhile. Such questioning does not necessarily reflect a callousness or disregard for human suffering or need but may well be motivated by a desire to know if all the effort has some effect. Those who are close to handicapped children through kinship, servicing them, associating with them, or compassionately considering them in the context of their own values reply in the affirmative. To maximize whatever potentials handicapped children possess is deemed highly worthwhile. Bringing children into their society so they may contribute their talents, their special understanding of coping with problems, or their special courage and zest for living has brought a return that greatly exceeds the costs or investments made in their behalf.

Families With Handicapped Children

Probably the first persons to be concerned and affected by the presence of a handicapped child are his or her family. In some instances, there has been some forewarning or evidence that a child will be born with handicaps. Such indications include the intake of certain drugs, excessive exposure to radiation, a history of possible genetic defects, or difficulties with the carrying period or birth process itself. In

[9]News item reported on December 2, 1975 concerning President Gerald Ford's signing of a bill for the education of handicapped children in the United States.

many other instances, diagnosis or a given child's handicap or combination of handicaps requires careful and prolonged efforts because the evidence of physical defects or of behavioral aberrations cannot be clearly ascertained until the child has developed further. Finally, there are those handicaps that come about as the result of an accident, virus, or disease.

The responses of mothers and fathers to handicapped children can and do run the gamut from negative feelings of remorse, rejection, and self-recrimination to positive feelings of acceptance, understanding, and a determination to make their handicapped child have as happy, safe, and constructive a life as possible under the limits imposed by the circumstances. Some vow never to have children again while others are willing to have other children because they know their handicapped child is the result of a unique set of circumstances which will probably never occur again in their family. Some know how to close ranks and come together to confront their mutual problems of rearing a handicapped child whereas others will turn away from each other or let one carry more than his or her share of the responsibilities of constant and vigilant care. These patternings have been documented by studies that deal with this aspect of the presence of handicapped children.[10] There would seem to be no single, overriding parental reaction to having a handicapped child because each handicap or combination of handicaps brings with it special problems not found in other situations.

Imagine, for example, not being able to call out to a child to warn him or her of danger if he or she is deaf. How does one who is sighted explain to a blind child what a certain scene looks like? What is an appropriate way to handle an autistic child who is unaware of his or her surroundings or is engaged in repetitive random movements that totally absorb his or her attention? How does one communicate with one's own child when the usual avenues of communication are cut off? What can be successfully taught and absorbed by mentally retarded children?

Such questions besiege the parents of handicapped children and do not even begin to touch the surface of the profound adjustments and efforts they make for many, many years. There are costly diagnostic and therapeutic efforts to be made. There is need to participate in the special regimens required by handicapped children in feeding, exercising, entertaining, teaching, clothing, traveling, medicating, guarding, cleaning, or sleeping. At what point does a parent find time for self,

---

[10]See for example, Ray H. Barsch, *The Parent of the Handicapped Child* (Springfield, Illinois: Charles C. Thomas, Publisher, 1968); Susan Gregory, *The Deaf Child and His Family* (New York: John Wiley & Sons, 1976). See also, *The Handicapped Child, Research Review*, Vol. I (London, England: Longman Group, Ltd., 1970 and Vol. II, 1972).

spouse, other children, relatives, friends, and work associates? Small wonder that some men and women find the problems insurmountable and manifest all sorts of anxieties and despairs as a result. Yet the picture is not altogether bleak. With a fortitude born of inner strength and with considerable courage and the help that is available, many parents do manage to deal effectively with their handicapped children. They do not falter or refuse to face the realities of the limitations imposed by a handicapped child because they are resourceful and respond to the knowledge and skills that become known to them.

In addition to the husband-wife relationship, there are other sets of relationships that are tested by the presence of a handicapped child. For example, handicapped children often have nonhandicapped siblings, and aside from the normal difficulties of sibling rivalries, there are problems to be resolved concerning the amount of attention that should be given to a handicapped child beyond that given to his or her brothers or sisters. Decisions must be made concerning the participation of nonhandicapped siblings in the care of their handicapped brother or sister. Some nonhandicapped siblings have uncomplainingly accepted their handicapped brother or sister and become closer to them than many brothers and sisters become. Others have felt that they are neglected or, worse yet, stigmatized for life because of their handicapped brother or sister. It is fairly common to find in families with a handicapped child that nonhandicapped children in the family are quite adaptable to the situation while they, too, are children. It is when they are adolescents or young adults and are concerned with the images they project in the minds of potential friends or marital partners that they may be less well prepared to deal with the negative judgments or rejections that may come their way. The assumption that something is "wrong" with them is more a reflection of the misconceptions of some minds than it is of the fact that they have a handicapped brother or sister.

Lastly, in terms of the families of handicapped children, there are other ramifications among related kin. Grandparents, uncles, aunts, and cousins are also involved, and their reactions to identification with a handicapped child open up a rather neglected research opportunity. Knowing that the responses of the nuclear family encompass a whole spectrum of possibilities when a handicapped child is present, we would hypothesize that the same range of reactions occurs when the universe is enlarged to extended families, with greater numbers reacting in each part of the continuum.

We should, of course, be concerned not only with the various dyadic relationships brought under strain by the presence of a handicapped or multiply handicapped child in a family, i. e., husband-wife, brother-sister, grandchild-grandparents, or niece or nephew with aunts or uncles, but also with those matters of concern in the socialization of such a special child. Normal or nonhandicapped children have ample problems with sexuality, religious training, education, recreation, and choice of occupations. Adding in a baffling array of handicaps presents an awesome, complex dimension that further compounds the already difficult preparation of children for entry into the larger society.

Handicapped Children and the Larger Community

Families with a handicapped child are quite aware that one of their tasks is to explain constantly to comparative strangers just what their special child can and cannot be expected to do. They may have to provide wheelchairs, braces, or crutches. Stairs, curbs, doorways, or rest rooms become inaccessible barriers to movement of the handicapped. Attendance at public events or gatherings call for logistic strategies because most of these affairs do not provide for the participation of the handicapped. Through long-range planning and thoughtful community leaders, there has been some breakthrough; provisions have been made, such as gardens for the blind, removal of physical barriers, special seating arrangements, and the development of sheltered workshops so that handicapped persons may perform useful social tasks and earn a modest income of some sort.

The larger community plays its part through public and private support to aid handicapped children and those seeking to serve them. Through federal, state, and local taxes, the public has indicated a willingness to spread the costs so that all handicapped children may work toward whatever normal goals are possible. In private, nonprofit organizations, tremendous sums are invested in the rehabilitation of handicapped persons, and both professionals and volunteers coordinate their efforts to achieve some positive results for the handicapped. Literally thousands of organizations have proliferated over the years to serve as advocates or champions of the handicapped; each tends to concentrate upon one particular category of handicaps and works to restore handicapped individuals to as much participation in society as possible. Indeed, the involvement of the larger community in easing the burdens imposed on handicapped children and their families amounts to a social movement with its usual broad-based and diffuse impacts on the whole society.

Few would claim that all is now well and that handicapped persons have received their public due. What has been accomplished is a monumental turnabout in public attitudes and support-systems over the past years, but the work is far from complete.

Albert Wessen, a distinguished medical sociologist, has studied hospitals and their settings for many years. It is Wessen's contention that the public, long acquainted with what he calls the "hospital care model," needs to better understand a contrasting model that deals with handicapped individuals, namely, a "rehabilitation model."[11] Figure 15-1 capsulates the chief differences between them.

These two models, while contrasting rather sharply, are not necessarily to be interpreted as totally incompatible with each other. Many hospitals have rehabilitation departments or agencies incorporated into their systems, and many rehabilitation centers have affiliated themselves closely with hospital care units. But, as Wessen's distinctions clearly affirm, the hospital care model and the rehabilitation model operate under quite different philosophies and procedures. It is also clear that the rehabilitation model is much closer to the needs of handicapped children than is the hospital care model. This is not to find fault with medical professionals but rather to point out that sustained, ancillary services are definitely needed once medical professionals have done their best in diagnoses and therapies. The hospital care model is backed by a long and honorable history. The rehabilitation model is less well understood by nonhandicapped persons who are not likely to encounter personal need for their services or for services to be rendered to someone related to them by consanguinity or affinity.

Handicapped Children and the Schools

There is one locus in society that does alert the general public to the long-term needs and care for handicapped children, and that is the

[11]Albert F. Wessen, "The Apparatus of Rehabilitation: An Organizational Analysis," in *Sociology and Rehabilitation,* ed. Marvin B. Sussman (Washington, D.C.: American Sociological Association, 1965), pp. 170–74.

HOSPITAL CARE MODEL	REHABILITATION MODEL
Priorities: Acute conditions of life and death	Priorities: Chronic conditions affecting normal functions
Objectives: Treatment and release to independence	Objectives: Relearning basic daily activities
Patients: To be acted upon; passive recipients	Patients: To be motivated to participate actively
Organization: A clinical chain of command; specialized therapeutic measures	Organization: An interdisciplinary, team approach
Length of Care: Short-term	Length of Care: Long-term

FIGURE 15-1 *Hospital Care Model Contrasted with Rehabilitation Model*

Source: Albert F. Wessen, "The Apparatus of Rehabilitation: An Organizational Analysis," in *Sociology & Rehabilitation.*

schools. There was a time in the history of America when the education of the young was not held to be a collective responsibility. Rather, the view prevailed that only the elite, the specially privileged classes, were to be educated with the costs paid by their respective families. With compulsory, free, tax-supported education for all children, the collective responsibilities were acknowledged and institutionalized. Whether this collective responsibility was to be extended to handicapped children as well as to nonhandicapped children has not been as clear except as more recent events occurred.

Approximately every 40 or 50 years in American history, some major progress was made in the education of handicapped children. Between 1776 and 1817, public education for handicapped children was basically neglected. Beginning in 1817, asylums and residential facilities for handicapped children were established. About 1869, day school classes were developed for handicapped youngsters. Between 1869 and 1913, a dual system of residential and day school classes for the handicapped expanded. Around 1900, state programs for handicapped children supported by state subsidies and supplemental local school programs were initiated. Finally, beginning around 1950, public school programs for handicapped children came to be recognized; a principle known popularly as "mainstreaming" began to take hold.[12] Instead of shunting handicapped children aside to be given some token form of public education, the movement was on to place handicapped children with nonhandicapped children in the course of their public school education experiences. Both handicapped and nonhandicapped children could conceivably learn from each other's presence in the same classrooms or facilities. The isolation of handicapped children is no longer as tolerated as it once was, and with landmark federal legislation and precedent-setting court decisions, more movement has been evident during the recent past than during the past two centuries.[13]

By 1977, 48 states out of 50, Ohio and Mississippi being the exceptions, had passed laws that make education for handicapped children mandatory; in fact, some 20 states not only mandate education for handicapped children but extend that mandate to include preschool ages.[14] In 1972, U.S. District Judge Joseph Waddy, in a case before the Federal Court in the District of Columbia, *Mill* v. *Board of Education*, ruled that all children have a right to "suitable publicly supported education, regardless of the degree of the child's mental, physical, or

---

[12]*Unfinished Revolution: Education for the Handicapped, 1976* (Washington, D.C.: U.S. Department of Health, Education and Welfare, Office of Education, Bureau of Education for the Handicapped), p. 8.
[13]Ibid.
[14]Ibid, pp. 3–4.

emotional disability or impairment."[15] Further, if funds to support needed and desirable educational experiences are limited, these must be distributed in as equitable a manner as possible so that "no child is entirely excluded from publicly supported education . . ."[16] Over 40 cases seeking some easing of the requirements have followed Judge Waddy's rulings but in all cases completed, the court decisions have favored the rights of the handicapped children involved.[17] In a very real sense, "the machinery" is in place to provide a good public education for all children, handicapped and nonhandicapped, under the least restrictions possible in the United States. The smooth functioning of that machinery, however, has yet to begin. Promises have been made to handicapped children. Whether or not these promises will be fulfilled lies in the future.

SUMMARY

Handicapped children, the special children, constitute a relatively neglected group of youngsters whose very real presence provide a serious and important challenge to their parents, relatives, friends, and the larger community in which they live. They are "special" because their single or multiple handicaps do not deter or discourage them from wresting all that is possible from life. To be sure, they are handicapped or impaired in ways that would break the spirit of many nonhandicapped, normal adults. However, with the acceptance and courage that lies deep in their being, these children can be helped to accomplish the necessary tasks of socialization.

Some two or three infants per 100,000 births begin life with one or more handicaps. Handicaps, of course, can have genetic, physical, emotional, or social origins and differ widely in degrees of severity. Large proportions of handicapped children suffer from more than one handicap such as blindness, deafness, and mental retardation. The normal child can be quickly categorized as handicapped should a tragic accident require amputation of a limb or a disease affect the neuromuscular system. The most recent data available indicates that some eight million children in the United States can be classified as "handicapped" because without attention, adjustments, or special efforts, their socialization processes would be impaired, thwarted, or denied.

[15]Ibid, p. 4.
[16]Ibid, p. 4.
[17]Ibid, p. 4.

Dating back to historical periods when handicapped children were rather summarily neglected and thrust aside, tremendous progress has been made to incorporate them into society by maximizing their potential abilities within families, schools, therapeutic communities, and occupational opportunities. The progress has been more successful with some handicapped children than with others. Some 87 percent with learning disabilities, 80 percent who were hard of hearing, and 81 percent who were emotionally disturbed were "unserved" as late as 1977 in the United States. Ten percent of the mentally retarded, 12 percent of the speech impaired, and 8 percent of the deaf were "unserved" in early 1977. The costs of rehabilitation of these special children are in the hundreds of millions of dollars, but there is a commitment to servicing their needs throughout the nation.

Aside from a handicapped boy or girl, the major burdens fall upon parents and the immediate families who have to adjust their lives accordingly. The strains this adjustment imposes upon nuclear and extended families are great and varied, but to their credit, many families do endure and even grow closer because of the presence of the handicapped. Awareness, understanding, and positive aid has been forthcoming from the larger community. Rehabilitation models are gaining more public support than the more traditional hospital care models.

The one locus in society that does involve long-term care and support is the public school system. Learning is the work of children, hence the stress upon this aspect of the lives of handicapped children who seek accommodation in the educational sphere. Major movement, in forty to fifty year intervals, has characterized the growing acceptance of handicapped children and their incorporation into the "mainstream" of public education over the past two hundred years in America. Much of the "social machinery" seems to be in place to serve the special educational needs of handicapped children. Whether or not the machinery will function effectively remains for the future to unfold.

16

Gifted children

At the opposite end of the spectrum from handicapped children, the special children with whom we dealt in the previous chapter, are the gifted children, the exceptional children. In some ways, they may be said to be "mirror images" of the handicapped because these rare children have been given the advantages of excellent health, unusual vigor, keen intellect, tremendous curiosity, swift comprehension, and specialized talents that are lacking in other children. In other ways, however, these gifted children share much in common with all children and so need not necessarily be isolated for special treatment or consideration. Indeed, which strategy in their socialization is best to pursue constitutes one of the basic puzzles with which interested persons have been grappling for many years. We found, it will be recalled, that this same exclusion or inclusion dilemma has occupied the attention of advocates of the disadvantaged, the dependent, the deviant, and the disprivileged children as well.

There may well be other appropriate terminology or nomenclature to identify what we have called gifted children. They are also known in the literature as bright, fast learners, geniuses, prodigies, talented, creative, or those with high potential. In certain contexts, these may well apply to gifted children. In almost all circumstances that we can project, their relative rarity and their unusual aptitudes in comparison with other children well deserve the "exceptional" label. Robert DeHaan and Robert Havighurst have estimated that, perhaps, some two hundred out of every thousand children born in a typical American city in a given year might contain the gifted children of whom we write. Of these, the extremely gifted or "first order" would be those children in the upper one-tenth of 1 per cent. Those children remaining in the upper 10 per cent in a given ability are considered by DeHaan and Havighurst to be of the "second order" or "the solid, superior" children.[1]

The key quality that sets the gifted children apart, of course, is their demonstrated ability to absorb and utilize whatever is set before them in their sociocultural environment. Whereas all children have the task of learning how to live in their respective societies and cultures by acquiring what others before them have acquired, gifted children are precocious in their aptitudes and display a command of complexities that would be a credit to mature, experienced adults. Chronologically, they are young in years, but in terms of socialization, they are well advanced in their absorption of the many complexities that make up the human heritage. Further, they seem to be able to go far beyond the mere absorption or internalization of information. They are creative, innovative, and eager to experiment in new directions. Such children represent pools of talent from which future leadership is anticipated.

Defining "Gifted Children"

There has been both an extensive and intensive debate among scholars as to what precisely constitutes "giftedness," from whence it comes, how to deal with it, and what purposes are achieved by its encouragement. A single definition that satisfies all possible criticisms of what being "gifted" constitutes probably does not exist. All we can do in this overview of exceptional children is to proffer a working definition tailored to our own concerns. In addition, we recognize that such a definition needs the finer honing that can come from many minds and more insights and knowledge than we now command.

The working definition of "gifted children" that we utilize in this chapter designates gifted children as *those children who have the potential or demonstrated capacities to master knowledge, skills, and ideas in a clearly superior fashion and/or are highly innovative, origi-*

---

[1]Robert F. DeHaan and Robert J. Havighurst, *Educating Gifted Children*, rev. and enlarged ed. (Chicago: The University of Chicago Press, 1957, 1961, 1965), pp. 15–16.

nal, or creative in their actions, thoughts, accomplishments, or relation-
ships with materials or people.

In such a definition, we are obviously trying "to touch all bases"
but may or may not have scored "a home run." Note, for example, that
potential is not the same as actual accomplishment. Gifted children
may give promise of great deeds but, for one reason or another may not
fulfill that promise. They may or may not have scored at the highest
levels of intelligence tests. They may show talent in a single specialization or in a number of fields. They may be brilliant in abstractions and
rather inept in dealing with other individuals or groups. None of this
implies that it is not possible to be outstanding in numerous ways;
neither does our definition exclude singlemindedness, excellence, and
high concentration within a single line of endeavor.

James L. Carroll and Lester R. Laming have examined the available literature on gifted children over a period of some sixty years.[2]
Table 16–1 summarizes the characteristics researchers ascribe to gifted
children.

While there may well be exceptions to the research findings concerning the characteristics of gifted children, the general consensus
contradicts the view that gifted children are aloof, disinterested in
other children, and are, in turn, rejected by their peers. On the contrary, the research evidence cited by Carroll and Laming supports the
contention that gifted children are well-rounded individuals, accepted
willingly by their peers, and are frequently recognized for their leadership qualities.

Examples of Precocious Children

Some of the remarkable feats of precocious children are worth
noting because they foreshadow accomplishments yet to be achieved
and shared with the world. In and of itself early mastery of various skills
or knowledge does not prove that precocity is the hallmark of every
gifted child. However, their early facility dramatically illustrates how
some gifted children manifest their intellectual and expressive powers
at very tender ages. Wolfgang Mozart, for instance, was making chords
on the harpsichord and clavichord at age three. At four, Mozart was
learning minuets from his father and by five was composing them. By
age six, he was composing concertos and was on tour before the courts
of Europe. His first opera, *La Finta Semplice*, was completed before he
was twelve.

[2]James L. Carroll and Lester R. Laming, Table 2, in "Giftedness and Creativity:
Recent Attempts at Definition, A Literature Review," *The Gifted Child Quarterly*,
XVIII, No. 2 (Summer 1974), 92.

TABLE 16–1 **Characteristics Ascribed to Gifted Children**

1. The gifted are stronger and healthier than average children. They learn to walk, talk, and have fewer physical and sensory defects than their average peers in school. They are ahead of their peers in school.
2. They are curious, have long memories, and a keen sense of time (keep track of date).
3. They have many different interests and hobbies.
4. The gifted exhibit leadership.
5. They have desirable personalities and possess favorable social characteristics.
6. The gifted have many special talents and abilities. They possess a superior intellectual potential and functional ability and/or one or more unique creative abilities in such areas as mathematics, science, mechanics, creative writing, art, music, and social leadership.
7. They produce work that has freshness, vitality, and uniqueness. They create new ideas, substances, processes, and mechanical devices.
8. The gifted child has unusual abilities in structuring, organizing, integrating, and evaluating ideas (critical thinking).

Source: Adopted from James L. Carroll and Lester R. Laming, Table 2, in "Giftedness and Creativity: Recent Attempts at Definition, A Literature Review," *The Gifted Child Quarterly*, Vol. XVIII, No. 2, (Summer, 1974), p. 92.

Voltaire was able to read the Bible at age three, and Samuel Johnson was reading at age two. Robert Louis Stevenson was climbing stairs at nine months of age and walked unaided by eleven months. Further, Stevenson knew people's names by thirteen months of age. Charles Proteus Steinmetz knew Latin at five years of age and at seven years of age was studying Greek, Hebrew, French, algebra, and geometry. When asked if he was in any pain after a servant accidently spilled hot coffee on him, Thomas Macaulay is reported to have replied, "Thank you, madam, the agony is abated." Macaulay was four years old at the time![3]

Identification of Gifted Children

There is no problem in early identification of the giftedness of precocious children. Their facile attainment of skills, knowledge, and insights while still in their infancy or early childhood indicates the strong possibility of extraordinary accomplishments at maturity. For gifted children, generally those in the "second order" of DeHaan and Havighurst, however, there may well be some delay before their powers can be detected and encouraged.

There was a time when it was held that gifted children would manifest their brilliance and versatility regardless of circumstances.

[3]R. S. and C. M. Illingworth, *Lessons From Childhood* (Edinburgh and London: E. & S. Livingstone, Ltd., 1966), p. 183.

This view may still be held by some. However, for the most part, observers are now more convinced that early identification of gifted children is both necessary and desirable.

This more contemporary view is sustained by reports from the gifted individuals themselves, parents, educators, and others that extenuating circumstances can and do stifle, redirect, or altogether discourage talented youngsters who would otherwise have led happier, fulfilled lives. Poverty probably leads the list of conditions that decrease the chances of demonstrating giftedness. Other conditions such as residency in isolated, remote locales; poor or failing health; special handicaps; or uncaring, ignorant, or callous parents and teachers could also prevent the identification and development of the great abilities of gifted children.

The early identification of gifted children makes good sense in the light of those who could have been encouraged to develop their respective talents but who were, instead, required to conform to the routine, uninspired intellectual processing to which children have been introduced in lock-step fashion. Many years are lost forever when children's caretakers fail to locate and nurture the human resources they once had as their responsibilities. When the Soviet Union launched their pioneering space probes with Sputnik I in 1957, the American nation was jolted into renewed action to recapture scientific leadership backed by solid intellectual training and skills. For some twenty-odd years, that external challenge has been answered by some prodigious accomplishments such as landings and explorations of the lunar surface. Less dramatic, but perhaps far more significant, has been the institutionalization of procedures to assure that gifted individuals are, henceforth, not overlooked or neglected but, instead, given every opportunity to be located and aided. The most precious assets are human lives, and these certainly include gifted children and the wise development of their powers in service to themselves and the less-gifted.

The identifying procedures and tools consist essentially of early screening or nomination by parents and schools followed by both extensive and intensive testing to determine the precise type of talent or potential with which they are dealing.

The early nomination or identification of gifted children by parents and teachers is acceptable as part of the initial screening process, but these judgments are suspect mainly in terms of their subjective nature. Parents, for example, may well be eager to identify their children as "gifted" because there is some vicarious satisfaction, some reflected glory, in having produced and nurtured such children. On the other hand, there may be those who hesitate to suggest that their offspring have superior talents when compared with other children and so are less eager to identify their children as "gifted." Their hesitancy may spring from modesty, fear of rejection by parents or friends who have less-talented "normal" children, and uncertainties as to what having "gifted" children means in the sense of special requirements, costs, or possible adjustments with which they feel they could not cope.

Teachers may also begin the processes of identification of gifted children, but they, too, have been known to judge erroneously the real talents or qualities of their students. This is not to say that they should not be alerted to the exceptionally bright students they encounter, but teachers may select the highly cooperative, obedient, adaptable, privileged, and pleasing youngsters over those who may be negative, recalcitrant, less-prepared, less-motivated underachievers. Their training may or may not include recognition of possible "giftedness" among their pupils, or they may have formed some definite opinions about gifted children that preclude dealing with them in a constructive fashion.

Intelligence tests, of course, are more objective means of identifying gifted children. But much depends upon which types are used, under what circumstances they are administered and interpreted, and how they are utilized. *Group* intelligence tests are valuable aids in the continuing screening process, but these, too, may fail to do the job of adequate identification. Examination under time pressures, vocabulary or reading problems, or emotional upsets and lack of motivation can work against locating certain gifted children. *Individual* intelligence testing by professional specialists is probably a better procedure because extraneous and obscuring variables may be controlled, understood, and given less weight in making a determination about a given child. The costs, availability, and practicality of individual psychological testing or profiling, however, allow an uneven coverage of young students, and many may not be located by either these methods or the general intelligence procedures. *Both* general and individual intelligence testing should be helpful, of course, because much giftedness is rooted in intellectual superiorities, and the examinations are geared along these lines.

Batteries of *achievement* tests have been used in the identification processes in addition to the above procedures. Their limitations are about the same as general intelligence testing. However, they can help assess *some* specially gifted children and cannot be totally rejected because of some of their defects.

The chances for early identification of gifted children are probably highest in the upper socioeconomic classes. By virtue of their privileged class status, many upper socioeconomically advantaged children are exposed to normal *enrichment* experiences well before less privileged youngsters. Such children are often encouraged to read widely, taken on trips to a variety of fascinating places, introduced to many talented or able persons, urged to develop effective study habits, provided with opportunities to experiment with many interests, and aided in following the models set before them by their parents, teachers, or associates who have stimulating ideas. When these are made a part of upper-class children's lives it is no small wonder that objective and subjective measurements would identify the potential results among the particularly gifted.

None of the above should be taken, however, as saying that giftedness lies mainly in the upper-class levels. No single class stratum could be said to be the exclusive source of gifted children. Social mobility studies have established that many in the upper social classes did not necessarily originate there. Many came from more humble or modest socioeconomic levels and brought their extraordinary abilities with them. Social mobility studies have also investigated whether the pace of upward mobility has slowed or been arrested in American society, thus guaranteeing that fewer children would be identified with upper-class living styles than in the past.

What is needed are provisions for as much *enrichment* as possible for all children through public education or broad community support. Such programs do exist but may fall far short of reaching potentially gifted children, identifying them, and sustaining their abilities for their own sake and the sake of others.

There are, undoubtedly, other means of identifying gifted children. Sociometric tests, for instance, have been used to locate child-reported and child-respected leadership. Unusual aptitudes can be reported by specialists in such fields as music, art, mathematics, and the sciences. Work-samples that suggest some previously hidden talents are also useful in the identification process. Finally, underachievers and rebellious youngsters may be telegraphing their distress with run-of-the-mill, boring treatment and, if carefully investigated, may provide a rich resource in gifted children. Systematic and constant awareness that the gifted should be located and encouraged is a responsibility that should be shouldered by those whose actions and decisions affect children's lives.

Families of the Gifted

Families, of course, are the wellsprings from which gifted children originate. Parents in general and mothers in particular have had effective input in the development of gifted children.

Norma Groth, for example, has concentrated her attention on the mothers of gifted children.[4] Some six hundred members of the Gifted

[4]Norma J. Groth, "Mothers of Gifted," *The Gifted Child Quarterly*, XIX, No. 3 (Fall 1975), 217–22.

Children's Association of Greater Los Angeles were mailed question-naires to test a number of null hypotheses for statistically significant differences, if any existed. While not necessarily generalizable or appli-cable to all mothers of gifted children, Groth's sample population based upon a 60 percent return of the questionnaires does suggest that these women, at least, were themselves highly accomplished individuals.

Whereas .1 percent of women in the general population in the United States had secured their doctorates, 1.6 percent had earned master's degrees, and 7.2 percent had secured their baccalaureates, Groth's sample women provided a profile of 2 percent with doctorates, 7 percent with masters' degrees, and 50 percent with baccalaureates.[5] These mothers tended to have smaller families (one or two children) rather than larger families (five or six children), perceived themselves as "younger" than their chronological ages, tended not to be fulltime housewives, had good mental health, and experienced fewer divorces than the general population.[6] In the main, it is not too difficult to understand why these types of mothers could, and did, produce and develop gifted children. They were obviously alert and attuned to intel-lectual superiority or excellence and could move their children toward such goals or objectives.

Juliana Gensley is a recognized specialist in the study and appreci-ation of gifted children and regularly provides editorial leadership in disseminating information and perspectives concerning gifted chil-dren. In a recent discussion of the concerns of parents of gifted chil-dren, Gensley noted the common questions that parents of gifted children frequently raise.[7] They were as follows:

Am I doing the right thing for my child?
Is the teacher doing the right thing for my child?
What school should my child attend to help develop (his/her) potential?
What program is best for my child?
Why does my child seem to be under a strain?
Why does my child seem to be irresponsible?
Why doesn't anybody do anything about my child?
Why is my child bored?
Why is my child involved in so many things that (he/she) doesn't have time for essentials?
Why does my child have a one-track mind and ignores anything that isn't in line with (his/her) specialty?

[5]Ibid, p. 219.
[6]Ibid, p. 218.
[7]Juliana Gensley, "Concerns of Parents," *The Gifted Child Quarterly*, XIX, No. 2 (Summer 1975), 96–97.

In answering such questions, Gensley noted that ". . . nobody can give them a recipe," suggesting, instead, that parents of gifted children will have to tailor-make and individualize procedures for their young-sters. She does, however, recognize that *both* parents constitute "two variables" in whatever decisions or actions are ultimately made. Both mothers and fathers of gifted children have responsibilities for such children and normally should not expect one or the other to carry out the tasks necessary to utilize the "gifts" of their children in constructive and helpful ways.

We can go back to some remarkable fathers of gifted children whose rather unorthodox views on formal education drove them to educate their children at home, as early as possible, and with an inten-sity that is almost unbelievable.[8] The father of Blaise Pascal, for exam-ple, laid out a carefully conceived educational program that he personally supervised fulltime. He not only taught history, geography, and philosophy during meals but also invented games to illustrate their basic principles and precepts. Reasoning was applied to the study of languages and the classics, and in the sciences, particular attention was paid to the experimental method of observing, classifying, generalizing, and testing evidence.

Karl Witte's father, a clergyman, resigned his post to devote his full attention to the education of his son. As an infant-in-arms, Karl was taught the parts of his body and the names of objects all about him. He was surrounded with kindness but was particularly motivated toward diligence, discipline, and harmony. German, French, Italian, English, Latin, and Greek were learned in that order, starting at age six. At about seven and a half, Karl was tested by various reputable scholars, winning him immediate public acclaim. Admitted to the University of Leipzig at age nine, he was given his Ph.D. at age thirteen. Karl's home educa-tion was further justified by his earning of a Doctor of Laws degree at the age of sixteen and his appointment to the staff of the University of Berlin as a professor.

John Stuart Mill's father was more severe in his relentless pursuit of excellence in his child. John, nevertheless, did master Greek, starting at age three, and Latin, starting at age eight. Mill's father then added algebra, geometry, astronomy, physics, philosophy and logic, differen-tial calculus, and political economy, all before his son was thirteen. At fourteen, John was sent to France to learn something of taking his place among his peers, but his intensified earlier training, which had involved a nine-hour daily study period, caused him to feel lost without his world of books and the conscious pursuit of substantive data. John Stuart Mill took his prodigious talents developed by rigorous childhood training

[8]Adopted from Illingworth, *Lessons from Childhood*, pp.48–51, 55–64, 65–68.

under the strict supervision of his father and used them in later life to promote the popular vote, women's rights, universal education, proportional representation, and free discussion.

The dedication of fathers or mothers to the intellectual development of their children is not guaranteed, however. Completely contrary behavioral models for gifted children exist as well. Numerous gifted children have emerged from unhappy, depressing, and uncaring homes.[9] The explanation for their achievements rests upon other sources that encouraged and motivated them to achieve the eminence they did.

Schools and the Gifted

Ultimately, however, parents and families must turn to the school for some formal, specialized training that draws upon resources not readily available to most parents or families. Together, through consultations, cooperation, and mutual agreement, parents and schools attempt to provide the necessary regimen that will enlarge upon the talents and potentials of their gifted children.

A number of options are open to parents, school authorities, and the gifted children themselves. These include the strategies of *acceleration, enrichment, ability-grouping,* and *special classes, schools, or curricula.*

ACCELERATION. Instead of the usual times for entry into the various grade levels, starting with the kindergarten-primary grades, about five years of age for kindergarten and six years of age for the first grade, an early admission policy can begin the formal educational experiences of the exceptionally fast learners. Other procedures include skipping grades and increasing study loads so that gifted children can master materials in a single academic year that would otherwise take two or three years to accomplish. Further along, at both the high school and college levels, individuals who may be chronologically younger than the usual school populations but who can prove their academic abilities, can be given the opportunity to attend advanced trainings that might otherwise be denied them.

The arguments favoring acceleration usually rest upon the thesis that the restriction of each student to the normal rates of promotion to various grades wastes the time of the particularly gifted boy or girl. They become bored, restless, inattentive, and unmotivated because they are forced into marking time while their fellow students go through the usual routines. To endlessly repeat that which they already

[9]Ibid, pp. 1–47.

know is unchallenging and counterproductive as far as the gifted are concerned.

Arguments against acceleration usually focus upon the potential harm done to gifted learners when they find themselves socially, experientially, emotionally, and physically out of synchronization with those with whom they may associate in the school. Further, it is argued, the same situation occurs upon graduation from school programs into the larger community. Why insist upon making gifted children "social misfits" most of their lives?

Both sides of the argument concerning acceleration are cogent and, in certain instances, valid. However, appropriate acceleration or judicious use of acceleration seems to have more to commend it than the refusal to use it in various cases.[10] Terman's classic longitudinal studies of gifted children also confirmed that the social maladaptions that were supposed to ensue from acceleration simply did not occur or were greatly exaggerated.[11]

ENRICHMENT. If acceleration is denied as an option, then enrichment of the curricula might be employed as an alternative. Enrichment simply means that children are provided experiences and information well above that which is normatively given at various grade levels. It may come through imaginative, challenging projects, trips, resource persons or equipment, study of foreign languages, and assignments that require more extensive and intensive reading and reasoning than is usual for a given grade level. In many ways, answers to questions are not readily available, but gifted children are encouraged to interrelate ideas or to deduce possible perspectives from their collected data. As much as possible, the gifted are not isolated from the less-gifted or normal students but may, on occasion, be under the direction of a special teacher qualified to work with highly talented youngsters in some particular subject. Regularly assigned teachers at various grade levels are also specially trained and alerted to deal effectively with gifted children through individual or group assignments, suggestions, or opportunities.

The strengths of enrichment programs lie in their easier administration, their provisions for the continued mixing of talents in class

---

[10]See for example, M. C. Reynolds, "A Framework for Considering Some Issues in Special Education," *Exceptional Children,* 29 (March 1962), 367–370; D. A. Worcester, *The Education of Children of Above-Average Mentality* (Lincoln, Nebraska: University of Nebraska Press), 1956.

[11]Louis M. Terman, ed., *Genetic Studies of Genius, 1925–1959,* Vols. I–V (Stanford, California: Stanford University Press); See also, Louis M. Terman and Melita Oden, "The Stanford Studies of the Gifted," ed. P. Witty, *The Gifted Child* (Boston: D. C. Heath, 1951).

situations, their treatment of teachers as capable educators, and, of course, their understanding that gifted children must be recognized and accorded the opportunities that their aptitudes require for stimulation and further growth.

The weaknesses of enrichment programs, however, remain in the high reliance upon possibly already burdened teachers who may or may not have the necessary skills, personalities, and zest to deal with their extraordinarily talented children. Further, the piecemeal approach calls for the strategic use of time and resources, and gifted children may be left "more on their own," rather than given an appropriate amount of consideration.

ABILITY-GROUPING. A third alternative is to place together children who tend to learn at about the same pace. Such ability-groupings are sometimes called educational "tracks." They allow homogeneous groups of children to compete and cooperate with their peers and prevent them from being held back by slower learners or discouraged by unfavorable performances in comparison with more advanced students. Such tracks avoid the invidious distinctions that come from overly conspicuous acceleration or from enrichment procedures. The tracks may run parallel, cross over at times, or move off in somewhat different directions. Careful placement is necessary to make the system work, and smaller gradations between tracks can help remove some of the labeling effect that may occur. More staff may be required, but ability-grouping does serve the needs of large school systems and larger populations of gifted children.

SPECIAL SCHOOLS OR CLASSES. In special schools or classes, the gifted children can receive the full attention they deserve. Acceleration, enrichment, or tracking become unnecessary. Instead, a forthright, unequivocal recognition that the schools are dealing with gifted children is made operative. The Major Work Classes for gifted children have been a part of the Cleveland, Ohio, Public School System since 1921. Enrichment does occur at the elementary levels, but acceleration does not. Gifted children are placed with gifted children, but in overall school activities, they participate with the entire student body and staff.[12]

Special schools, of course, are quite costly to operate in the same communities as public schools. Rare in contrast with acceleration, enrichment, or even special classes, they can be sustained by affiliation

[12]See Merle R. Sumption, *Three Hundred Gifted Children* (Yonkers-on-Hudson, New York: World Publishing Company, 1941); William B. Barbe, "Evaluation of Special Classes for Gifted Children," *Exceptional Children*, 22 (November 1955), 60–62.

with a university or college that can afford the capital investments in grounds, buildings, staff, and equipment that could best serve gifted children. Private schools with students drawn usually from the higher socioeconomic classes can also aid the gifted, but these can effectively exclude other gifted children from middle- and lower-class levels unless scholarships and deliberate planning are part of the offerings. Much depends upon how willing certain constituencies are to create and support special schools for the gifted.

At the college level, there has been considerable support for "Honors Colleges" that identify gifted students, provide recognition and stimulation for them, and encourage them to use their talents in service to others. If high standards and ethics are set, these special schools can continue to become valuable assets in educational systems.

SUMMARY

Conservation of natural resources, preservation of ecological balances and the intelligent use of fuel and energy sources have been the major concerns of growing numbers in the American population. Failures and shortsightedness in these matters are particularly glaring as the general public becomes involved and finds that business as usual can no longer be sustained.

A parallel case can be made for gifted children. Their presence constitutes a precious human resource that requires attention and intelligent planning. To waste or overlook some of the best minds and finest talents that our people have produced is a serious matter. Indeed, there is rich potential in all children, but this is particularly so with gifted and creative youngsters. The attitude that their abilities will manifest themselves to everyone's advantage without any efforts on the part of families, schools, or the larger community is patently untrue. Instead, valiant efforts are needed if gifted children are to become innovative, creative, effective contributors to their host societies. Otherwise, they have been known to underachieve through lack of motivation and opportunity or to turn their talents toward antisocial actions that bring only pain and suffering to their victims.

Gifted children represent the upper percentiles, usually the upper ten percent, when measured by intelligence tests, achievement tests, and psychological profiles. They have the potential or demonstrated capacities to master knowledge, skills, and ideas in a clearly superior fashion and/or are highly original or creative in their actions, accomplishments, or relationships. Contrary to popular opinion, their giftedness does not set them aside as highly deviant and undesirable individuals. Rather, they are very healthy, physically and mentally; are keenly aware and curious; have multiple interests; exhibit leadership; are chosen by other children as desirable companions and friends; often have special talents in particular fields or subjects; possess a verve and vitality with substances, ideas, processes, and mechanical devices; and possess the unusual abilities of critical thinking.

Their identification as gifted children is contingent upon alert and concerned parents, schools, and the larger community in which they live. Early nomination and screening can come from parents and schools and requires further intensive methods to ascertain the nature of their giftedness or talents. Children from the upper socioeconomic levels are more likely to have the advantages of enrichment experiences well before children in other class levels. On the other hand, as systematic efforts to identify gifted children are developed, more children from middle and lower socioeconomic levels can be located and encouraged.

Parents can begin the fundamental steps in developing, identifying, and encouraging gifted children. Some remarkable mothers and fathers have done so with some very precocious children. In the main, however, schools have the greatest responsibility to train gifted children formally because of their larger community base. Their procedures typically involve the strategies of acceleration, enrichment, ability-grouping, and special classes or schools. Few would hold that these strategems are perfected and highly efficient. However, they do represent some of the best methods and efforts available to provide gifted children with optimal conditions to utilize their great abilities for the good of all concerned.[13]

[13]There are always additional sources to consult and interested scholars could examine: James J. Gallagher, *Teaching the Gifted Child* (Boston: Allyn and Bacon, Inc., 1964); Miriam L. Goldberg, *Research on the Talented* (New York: Bureau of Publications, Teachers College, Columbia University, 1965); William K. Durr, *The Gifted Student* (New York: Oxford University Press, 1964); E. Paul Torrance, *Gifted Children in the Classroom* (New York: The Macmillan Company, 1965); John C. Gowan and E. Paul Torrance, eds., *Educating the Ablest* (Itasca, Illinois: F. E. Peacock Publishers, Inc., 1971); Samuel A. Kirk, *Educating Exceptional Children,* 2nd. ed. (New York: Houghton Mifflin Company, 1972); Donald C. Cushenbery and Helen Howell, *Reading and the Gifted Child, A Guide for Teachers* (Springfield, Illinois: Charles C. Thomas, Publisher, 1974); Lauree A. Pearlman, "A Comparison of Selected Characteristics of Gifted Children Enrolled in Major Work and Regular Curriculums" (Doctoral Dissertation, Kent State University Library, 1971); Richard Keith Seymour, *Comparison Study of Various Methods of Identification of Creativity in Divergent Socioeconomic Strata of Society* (Doctoral Dissertation, Kent State University Library, 1975); T. Ernest Newland, *The Gifted in Socioeducational Perspective* (Englewood Cliffs, N. J.: Prentice-Hall, Inc., 1976).

SIX

Concluding observations

17

*Exiting childhood:
adolescence*

Sooner or later, we must exit childhood and leave it far behind. We have more or less confined childhood to the first twelve years of life, but we know full well that this is merely a convenient way to operationalize our understanding and study of childhood. Most of us still feel and vividly remember our days as children. As one athlete expressed it, "When I play at my game, I feel like a child, but I understand as an adult." The little girl or little boy we once were speaks to us now and then and reminds us of our vulnerability, our earliest ambitions, and our dreams of "growing up." This "growing up" is the *process* of socialization beyond childhood and is the root meaning of the Latin term, *adolescens,* the word from which adolescence is derived.

DEFINING ADOLESCENCE

Adolescence as Status

While we have just stressed adolescence as a process—the dynamic acquisition of the ways of one's society immediately beyond childhood or, in brief, the *continuation* of socialization begun in childhood—there is something to be said for the idea of adolescence as being *another status* in the life cycle. One hint of this treatment of adolescence is the observation that the word adolescence did not appear in our language until about the fifteenth century.[1] For some fourteen hundred years, individuals were either children or adults and not "adolescents" or "teenagers," as some have popularized the term. The sharp distinctions between being either in childhood or in adulthood continue to this day among the remnants of preliterate societies scattered about the world and in some instances can be seen in traditions that keep individuals for many years under the tutelage, guardianship, or domination of much older persons. It is this prolonged subordination to the wishes of others that continues to irk college students who, despite their years past childhood, are often treated as "children" rather than as the young adults they really are.

The older, long-established dichotomy between childhood and adulthood, as two well-defined, clearly distinguishable positions in society with attendant privileges or disprivileges has given way to a trichotomy: childhood, adolescence, and adulthood. Adolescence, from this perspective then, is a period of life, a stage in a lifetime, a status in society in which one is *neither* a child *nor* an adult but "in between" being a child and an adult. It is a *transitional* phase when one is expected to put aside childish things and to turn more toward adults ways.

Adolescence as Marginality

There would be no major quarrel with being neither a child nor an adult if adolescence was clearly set aside from childhood and adulthood. Such, however, is not the case. Rather, there are blurred distinctions, overlaps, and fuzzy borderlines that obscure and confuse these statuses. Persons in the borderline cases are understandably confused, unsure, and without guidelines that might provide some direction for them. Marginality may indeed be the better way to comprehend adolescence. Seeking entry into adulthood, individuals encounter rejec-

[1]Rolf E. Muus, *Theories of Adolescence,* 2nd ed., (New York: Random House, 1968), p. 10.

tion. Regression into childhood is held to be reprehensible or unacceptable. What, then, are adolescents expected to do? They may, of course, accept their marginality, or they may build their own status as nonchildren and nonadults. This is similar to Hollingshead's definition that, sociologically, adolescence is the period in the life of a person when the society in which he or she functions ceases to regard him or her as a child but does not accord him or her full adult status, roles, and functions.[2]

Adolescence as Discontinuity

The conceptualization of adolescence as discontinuity has been derived largely from the field of cultural anthropology and notably from the works of Margaret Mead and Ruth Benedict.[3] Mead's *Coming of Age in Samoa* and Benedict's analysis of adolescence provide the perspective of American adolescence, at least, as an example of discontinuity.

Benedict discusses adolescence as either a continuous, gradual acquisition of adulthood or a discontinuous, disruptive *unlearning* of acquired ways. In three specific aspects—responsibility or nonresponsibility, dominance or submission, and the learning of appropriate sexual behaviors—Benedict explains why American adolescents experience the disruptions in cultural conditioning that remove them from their childhood but keep them from adulthood.

Samoan girls were given responsibility to care for and control their younger brothers and sisters. The Samoan boys, while also quite small, brought in fish from the reefs and learned how to control canoes under rough conditions. These are all responsible tasks that continued into adult life. In the Samoan lifestyle that Mead investigated, dominance-submission patterns were acquired without being perceived as rebellious or stressful. A Samoan girl could dominate her younger charges while she, in turn, learned submission to her older sisters. Boys might not submit to the wishes of their parents and would consequently move to the homes of uncles, for example, without fear of undue comment, social stigma, or emotional upset on anyone's part. In expressing sexuality, girls and boys could observe, experience, and experiment with a

---

[2]August B. Hollingshead, *Elmtown's Youth and Elmtown Revisited* (New York: John Wiley & Sons, Inc., 1975), p. 5.

[3]See Margaret Mead, *Coming of Age in Samoa* (New York: New American Library, 1950); Ruth Benedict, "Continuities and Discontinuities in Cultural Conditioning" eds. W. Martin and C. Stendler, *Readings in Child Development* (New York: Harcourt, Brace, 1954), pp. 142–148; discussion in Muus, *Theories of Adolescence,* pp. 69–74.

wide variety of sexual-release patterns such as masturbation or coital play without moral disapproval.[4]

The rather sharp contrast with the training of American adolescents is clear. Gradual responsibilities are withheld or delayed far beyond childhood. While adults may talk constantly about youngsters taking on responsibilities, adult responsibilities are forbidden to them in actual practice. Submission, too, is held to be a desirable quality for teenagers. Domination or self-assertiveness is considered rebellious behavior and is countered with stronger controls or restrictions. Despite a growing understanding of maturing sexuality in adolescence, sexual expression on the part of adolescents has been viewed as delinquent behavior, immoral, and negative to their emotional-social life. Sexual repression, denial, and diversionary tactics are part of the strategies used to retain the image of sexlessness or sexual disinterest characteristic of former childhood. Such procedures do not foster the gradual acquisition of adult ways as with Samoan youth. Rather, they insist that childhood be prolonged; that learning be kept in abrupt, discrete, differentiated steps; and that adolescence be kept as a period of delayed gratification or minimal satisfaction in terms of adult values. It is the adult world that is in control, and adolescents must wait outside with hats in hand, relatively untutored and ill-prepared in adult behavior when admission to the adult world is ultimately granted.

Adolescence as a Sociocultural Artifact

In addition to status, marginality, and discontinuity, adolescence may also be viewed as a social product. This perspective holds that adolescence is something that is created or brought into being by virtue of social definitions. Musgrove, for example, wrote about "making adolescents"[5] and observed that "the adolescent as a distinct species is the creation of modern social attitudes and institutions."[6]

This type of thinking is also in line with our discussion of the nature and substance of childhood. Childhood, we have contended, is shaped by social forces, variables, or factors that operate with differential effects for children and society. We did not seek to underestimate or exclude other disciplinary contentions or specialized contributions concerning childhood. We merely affirmed that sociological perspectives be incorporated into the mix of elements that produce the childhood data with which we work.

[4]Mead, *Coming of Age*, p. 31.
[5]F. Musgrove, *Youth and the Social Order* (Bloomington, Indiana: Indiana University Press, 1965), p. 13.
[6]Ibid, p.13.

Kiell, who represents a scholarly approach that opposes the view of adolescence as a social product, maintains that adolescence is a universal experience that will occur in any and all societies.[7] Kiell draws heavily upon literary evidence that adolescence is a distinguishable feature of any individual's life cycle despite the wide variations in society or cultural differences. He wrote, "It is my thesis that the great internal turmoil and external disorder of adolescence are universal and only moderately affected by cultural determinants."[8] Documents collected from every Western European nation, Russia, Poland, Lithuania, Hungary, Moravia, England, Scotland, Wales, Ireland, Canada, United States, Brazil, Argentina, Venezuela, Persia, Turkey, Syria, China, Manchuria, Korea, Japan, India, Siam, Australia, Macao, Philippine Islands, and from Mexican, Canadian, and American Indians testify to Kiell's thesis of the universality of adolescence.[9]

Adolescence as a Biological-Physiological Phase, Socially Defined

Expressed in slightly different terms, adolescence could be said to be rooted in the biological-physiological changes that occur universally to boys and girls but which are defined differently in various societies; Samoan society, for example, provides a smoother transition out of childhood into adulthood while American society tends to make it a period in life discontinuous with childhood and distinguishable from adulthood. Winter offers a useful summary of the changes that occur during adolescence for girls and boys.[10] (See Figure 17–1)

These physically obvious changes to the individual girls and boys, to their families and intimate friends, and to others with whom they associate can be variously defined. To some they are a signal of impending adulthood with its awesome responsibilities. To some, they are a distressful farewell to childhood. To others, they are a welcome sign of new freedoms and experiences. To still others, they are merely a biological phase in life that shows development, but not in the abilities to act as all other adults. It is this latter definition that sets the stage for adolescence as it appears generally throughout American society. The familiar line that is repeated endlessly to American adolescents is, "You may be growing up, but you have a long way to go and much to learn before you will ever be an adult." It is this advancement of the body

[7]Norman Kiell, *The Universal Experience of Adolescence* (Boston: Beacon Press, 1967, Copyright 1964, by International Universities Press, Inc.), Preface, p. 9.
[8]Ibid. p. 9.
[9]Ibid, p. 9.
[10]Gerald D. Winter and Eugene M. Nuss, *The Young Adult, Identity and Awareness* (Glenview, Illinois: Scott, Foresman and Company, 1969), p. 88.

FIGURE 17-1   *Changes During Adolescence by Sex*

Girls	Boys
Growth of pubic hair	Growth of pubic hair
Growth of hair under arms	Growth of hair under arms
Light growth of hair on face	Heavy growth of hair on face
Light growth of hair on body	Heavy growth of hair on body
Slight growth of larynx	Considerable growth of larynx
Moderate lowering of voice	Considerable lowering of voice
Eruption of second molars	Eruption of second molars
Slight thickening of muscles	Considerable thickening of muscles
Widening of hips	Widening of shoulders
Increase in perspiration	Increase in perspiration
Development of breasts	Slight temporary development of breasts around nipples
No change in hairline	Receding hairline at temples
Menstrual cycle	Involuntary ejaculations
No change in neck size	Enlargement of neck
Growth of ovaries and uterus	Growth of penis and testicles

Source: Gerald D. Winter and Eugene N. Nuss, eds., *The Young Adult, Identity and Awareness.*

set against the jarring deemphasis of body changes that generates the discontent and malaise that can keep adolescents in direct conflict with their elders. Physiologically ready to father or mother a child, adolescents discover the delays in gratification required to be psychologically, emotionally, economically, and sociologically prepared for adulthood.

The conflict model dates back many years but was probably given its greatest support in the works of G. Stanley Hall who characterized adolescence as *Sturm und Drang,* storm and stress, a time when the naïveté of childhood is displaced by great swings in moods and ideas.[11] Whereas Hall's treatment stressed the biogenetic psychological processes, our own predilections call for greater attention to the sociocultural definitions of adolescence.

Thus, there is something to be said in support of the variant definitions of adolescence as process, status, marginality, discontinuity, sociocultural artifact, and biological-physiological phase, socially defined. These perspectives, however, by no means exhaust the full array of explanatory theories of adolescence that have been advanced from ancient times to the present. Rolf Muuss has brought together a most

[11]G. Stanley Hall, *Adolescence* In 2 Vols., (New York: Appleton-Century-Crofts), 1916.

helpful series of theories of adolescence.[12] A shorter, but insightful source may also be found in Dorothy Eichorn's statement on adolescence in the *International Encyclopedia of the Social Sciences.*[13]

ADOLESCENCE AND THE CONTINUING SOCIALIZATION PROCESS

Socialization, of course, does not end with childhood. It continues in adolescence and takes on the qualities given to it by the overall social system or the subsystems that particular adolescents encounter.

In former times and particularly in preliterate societies, "rites of passage" clearly marked the transition from childhood to adulthood. Adolescence, as we previously noted, was not recognized as a distinct phase of an individual's life for some fourteen centuries. An individual was either a child or an adult. A child was "admitted" to adulthood by reason of some ritual or procedure that conspicuously marked off the ending of childhood and the beginning of adulthood.

We may see a remnant or survival of such a rite of passage in the Jewish custom of Bar and Bas Mitzvah ceremonials for boys and girls, respectively, at age thirteen. An extended period of training is undertaken by preadolescent boys and girls in anticipation of ceremonies before the entire congregation at a time close to their thirteenth birthday. Their twelfth year is usually a year of increased activity and final preparations for the ritual which demonstrates to all persons assembled their facility with Hebrew, the language of prayer, and their dedication as inheritors of Jewish traditions. Through the rituals, the girls and boys become "daughters and sons of the Commandments" and are recognized, thence forward, as religious "adults." In secular affairs, however, they are treated as adolescents, and their lives are not markedly different from other adolescents.

In preliterate societies or in the tradition-oriented societies that still survive, the menarche is quite commonly the occasion for fairly elaborate ceremonials to welcome girls into womanhood. For boys, there may be circumcision ceremonials or other rituals to mark their transformation from boyhood to manhood. In American society, at least, such sexually explicit events are more matters of privacy and are given no particular prominence. Instead, birthdays are celebrated or

[12]Muuss, *Theories of Adolescence.*
[13]Dorothy Eichorn, "Adolescence," in *International Encyclopedia of the Social Sciences* David L. Sills, ed., Vol. I, (New York: The Macmillan Company and The Free Press, 1968), pp. 84–96.

graduation ceremonials occur as children move from elementary grades to middle schools or from junior high schools to senior high schools. Although the passing from one grade level to another does not carry with it the emotional-social impacts of religious or sexually-cued rituals of the past, youngsters can use such means to tell how far along they are in comparison with other youngsters. Such observances are helpful because they serve as landmarks or reference points in what seem like unstructured, unguided, uncertain pathways to adolescents.

Van Gennep, almost a century ago, detailed the significance of rites of passage.[14] We draw upon his recognition of three phases or functions performed in these rites of passage as children move out of their childhood into adolescence and finally into adulthood. These are: (1) Separation, (2) Transition, (3) Incorporation.

Separation

In whatever form it takes, there appears to be a need to differentiate between childhood and the period in life we now call adolescence. To be sure, the need will reoccur in the drawing of boundary lines between adolescence and adulthood or, in adulthood, in further socialization for adult vocations or roles. For present purposes, however, we can profitably observe the separation between childhood and adolescence as it seems to occur for most youngsters in American society.

It should be recalled that in an earlier chapter we sought to understand what prominence or importance should be assigned to families in shaping the lives of children in contemporary American society. We noted that there was competition among several institutions to make appropriate inputs such as in religious training, in educational processing, in mass media, in politicalization, in economic considerations, or in leisure activities. Nevertheless, families remained the central locus in most childhood experiences. It follows, then, that one of the major hallmarks of leaving childhood is to separate or remove oneself from familial influences as much as possible.

This separation from families usually takes the form of investing more and more of one's time with peers or being more concerned with peer affairs. Ties with one's home are not severed, but they are no longer as paramount as they once were. In a sense, adolescents break with their familiar home surroundings and take their chances in the company of same-sex, same-age, or mixed-sex, similar-age groups. It is an exciting world for many as they try their adolescent "wings." But it is also one in which their families can no longer protect them as they

[14]A. Van Gennep, *Les Rites De Passage* (Paris: Nourry, 1909).

once did as children. The important step to take, however, is to establish that separation has begun from childhood and that adolescents must find their way among their friends, their casual acquaintances, and their own generational comrades. There will be penalties and suffering for mistakes, but there will also be new learning in autonomy and even some sweet victories.

Transition

Once the separation has begun from childhood, there is minimal room for retreat. Adolescents move forward into the marginality of being neither child nor adult. At times, childish and, at other times, adultlike in orientation, their actions often speak louder than their words. Somewhat akin to the movement of homing pigeons that fly in growing circles to find some major direction, they mill about, group together, and begin to follow some direction that beckons them into the unknown. It is a time-consuming process to find one's way, particularly when there are few structures or guidelines to aid them.

The very lack of guidelines or structure provides a void that can and must be filled by adolescents. Cut off from both childhood and adulthood, adolescents are relatively free to innovate or create life styles of their own. This they have been doing in American society for some time. It effectively provides the structure for which adolescents long. They can speak their own argot, develop their tastes and talents, and, figuratively, provide a world in which children or adults cannot truly enter.[15] This, to adolescents, is "where the action is," and as they are immersed in activities that are the sole concern of other adolescents, they are for all intents and purposes in transition between a childhood that is swiftly fading into memory and an adulthood they can only faintly see in the distant future. Peer pressures mount at this time, and nonconformity entails an isolation that is threatening or decidedly uncompromising for a tremendous number of adolescents. A few can throw off the tyranny of their peers by moving closer to adult values and adult guides.

Incorporation

The last of Van Gennep's phases of the rites of passage concerns the movement away from the pristine state of adolescence to the ultimate goal of incorporation into adulthood. The earlier nonserious, less responsible, often idealistic responses of adolescents give way to serious,

[15]A useful source is Hans Sebald, *Adolescence, A Social Psychological Analysis,* 2nd ed. (Englewood Cliffs, New Jersey: Prentice-Hall, Inc., 1977), pp. 227–37

responsible, realistic acts of commitment and concern. Dating, casual affairs, or group affairs are displaced by serious attachment to one man or woman. Job skills become focused on working careers and full economic independence. Fun and games no longer satisfy the longing to be a part of the human group. Instead, long-range objectives are laid down, and youngsters seriously prepare themselves for full adulthood. These are sobering decisions to make, but they constitute the means by which adolescents can enter maturity assured that they will be acceptable and capable when they arrive. Marriage and parenthood, sometimes and sometimes not delayed, provide young adults with a view of life that their parents before them experienced. Where before they were the children being socialized by parents, they now stand as parents shaping, where they can, the new lives in their safekeeping. In this status and role reversal, novice adults begin to understand their own strengths and limitations. No longer adolescents-in-training, they are adults newly initiated and still learning.

Incorporation into adulthood, of course, consumes a tremendous amount of time and energy. Incorporation means schooling in whatever their specific lines of endeavor may be, and young adults find a great difference between "learning by-the-book" and "learning on-the-job." There was a time when apprenticeship under the guidance of a master-specialist was the chief way to enter professions or skilled trades. Some of this tradition still remains but is handled by a larger number of individuals and in a complex, bureaucratic manner. Incorporation, nevertheless, does involve a protracted apprenticeship or promotional ladder that becomes more difficult to climb as one approaches the highest or most responsible positions. In short, incorporation into adulthood is a prolonged, often anxiety-ridden period in which young men and women, newly arrived and "freshly minted," discover there are still rungs to climb "up the ladder" of adulthood. "Freshmen" in adulthood, they will seek whatever levels in adulthood beckon them on. It does not seem to matter in what field of endeavor one is working, seniority or public acknowledgment that one is fully adult takes many years to establish.

ADOLESCENT SUBCULTURES

In our descriptions and analyses of exiting childhood and entering adolescence, as well as in leaving adolescence, we need to be as clear as possible that our generalized portrayal of adolescence does not overlook or omit numerous subdivisions or, if you will, subcultures among adolescents. By this, we mean that certain variables, often sociogenic, either by themselves or in concert, tend to manifest their influences in shaping rather distinctive adolescent life styles. They are not necessarily exclusive to adolescence but are often the identical variables with which we dealt in childhood. They consist of such matters as social class differences; racial, religious, regional, or ethnic factors; educational, economic, familial orientations; and identification with legal or illegal activities. Sexuality or sexual identification also may be sufficient to set some adolescents apart from other adolescents, depending upon the paths open to them and which paths were taken.

We do not propose to provide the chapter-length attention to these differences as we did in childhood. Applied to adolescence, they would require a book-length treatment that is far beyond the scope of our concerns with childhood.[16] What is possible is to highlight one or two selected features of adolescent subcultures as illustrative of our analysis of adolescence.

Persistent Social Class Differences

One striking difference among adolescents appears to be a result of social class differentials. The work of August Hollingshead, for instance, is pertinent in this regard.[17] In the early 1940s, Hollingshead intensively examined adolescence in a Midwestern community with the fictionalized name of "Elmtown." Hollingshead returned to Elmtown in the early 1970s and reexamined what changes, if any, existed after the passage of some thirty years. It is an excellent documentary on the persistence of social class differences despite the extensive changes brought about by three major wars, sustained prosperity, and increasing industrialization.[18] Some adolescents of the 1940s had moved out of the community, and their adult lives are essentially unknown to Elmtowners or to Hollingshead. Such outward-bound youth

[16]Some useful book-length treatments include: Denise B. Kandel and Gerald S. Lesser, *Youth in Two Worlds, United States and Denmark* (San Francisco: Jossey-Bass, Inc., Publishers, 1972); Harry Silverstein, *The Sociology of Youth, Evolution and Revolution* (New York: The Macmillan Company, 1973); John C. Cileman, *Relationships in Adolescence* (London: Routledge & Kegan Paul, 1974); Robert E. Grinder, ed., *Studies in Adolescence, A Book of Readings in Adolescent Development*, 3rd ed. (New York: Macmillan Publishing Company, Inc. 1975). See also, Robert C. Sorensen, *Adolescent Sexuality in Contemporary America, Personal Values and Sexual Behavior, Ages 13-19* (New York: World Publishing, 1973), and recent issues of *Adolescence*, a quarterly published by Libra Publishers, Inc. and *Youth and Society*, a quarterly published by Sage Publications. See also, *Daedalus*, Journal of the American Academy of Arts and Sciences, 100 No. 4 (Fall 1971), Issue on *Twelve to Sixteen: Early Adolescence*.
[17]Hollingshead, *Elmtown's Youth*.
[18]Ibid, p. 385.

were particularly noticeable among those youngsters who were "out-of-school" in the 1940s. But, in the main, the five status classes remained intact and viable and continued to affect and delineate the different lifestyles of Elmtown's youth.

Persistence of Racial Separations

It would be in keeping with the widely proclaimed idealism held out to American youth that racial differences are inconsequential for equal opportunities and personal growth. However, the bulk of the evidence reported through the mass media, documented by untold scores of specialized studies, and obvious to the most casual observer is the persistence of racial divisiveness in contemporary American society. For adolescents in particular, "black experiences" seem to be in striking contrast with "white experiences." American Indians have a growing sense of urgency that they, too, have been shunted from the mainstream or asked to abandon their past traditions. One might seek out Mexican-Americans, Chinese or Japanese-Americans, or others with so-called "visible racial features" with similar results. As we noted in childhood, racism affects or mars the earliest, formative years. In adolescence, racism continues relatively unabated despite valiant efforts on the part of some schools and some political breakthroughs. Adolescents are less complacent, however, than children, and they frequently constitute the "flashpoint" or "critical mass" that aggressively proclaims their identity and search for freedom and self-expression at long last.

An Easing of Religious or Ethnic Differences Among Adolescents

We must also recognize the concern of dedicated adolescents over their respective religious or ethnic heritages. Plurality in these matters is a part of the contemporary American scene. However, we also sense that there is more easing of tensions and differences religiously and ethnically among American adolescents than in the recent past. Perhaps this is a function of the passage of years in which religious and ethnic differences have been given less prominence and similarities, more attention. For adolescents, at least, the bitterness experienced by their parents or elders seems to have eased and given way to a newer era of tolerance, appreciation, and understanding. This type of relaxation of tensions has not yet occurred for racially different peoples because the "physical differences" are acted upon in housing, employment, education, welfare, criminal behavior, legalities, and political tests of strength. Although labeling and reification go hand in hand in racism or other preconceived notions, they occur far less frequently now in matters relating to religion or national origins. In this sense, we see assimilation or, more cautiously, accommodation at work in America.

Liberalism in the Education of Adolescents

While far from satisfied with the formal educational training of adolescents, we do commend the educators and communities who seek to provide multiple paths for adolescents to explore. Relevant curricula, varied offerings, and person-centered counseling offer much more help for adolescents than in past years in American schools. Havighurst's "action-education" seems to be recognized so that classroom confinements are minimized and adolescents can become far more aware of the adult life they are about to enter than ever before.[19]

We see this "learning-by-doing" syndrome in such areas as community services, practical training in the field, and volunteer work in a variety of agencies outside the limits of traditional class routines. One high school with which we are affiliated, for example, runs a restaurant for the general public. The entire operation run by student-trainees and their advisors compares quite favorably with some commercial enterprises catering to a discriminating set of customers.

Further, there is a growing respect for adolescents who earnestly want to know how they might best deal with sensitive social problems such as human sexuality or integrity among public officials. Adolescents cannot be denied access to adulthood forever, and mutual appreciation between the generations begins with opening the lines of communication with them.

SUMMARY

Beyond childhood, there lies an interim status of adolescence before adulthood is achieved in American society. It is a status that is relatively new in human history and almost unknown in those societies in which one is either a child or an adult. There are other valid ways to comprehend adolescence such as by stressing its marginality between childhood and adulthood, its discontinuity with training begun in childhood, its boundary determination by reason of insisting upon a delayed entrance into adulthood, or socially-defining the acceleration of biological-physiological changes that may or may not lead to "storm

---

[19]See Robert J. Havighurst, Richard A. Graham, and Donald Eberly, "American Youth in the Mid-Seventies" (*The Bulletin of the National Association of Secondary School Principals*, LVI, 1972), pp. 1–13.

and stress" among teenagers or outright conflict with authority figures such as parents or teachers.

Socialization continues in adolescence and will continue in adulthood. The rites of passage once used to symbolize the transformation of children into adults are no longer given prominence, but they continue to exist in multiple ways such as movement through the schools and the marking of birthdays. In whatever form, the years past childhood separate individuals from their childish ways, help them establish a transitional identity with their peers, and finally, allow them to become incorporated into adulthood by serious commitments in vocations and family responsibilities.

There has always been some academic debate about the overall nature of a distinct adolescent culture in the midst of American society. In some ways, there is reason to believe that the ways of adolescents are much admired and envied by both children and adults. For children, they may serve as models of what lies ahead. For adults, there may be a certain nostalgia and longing to relive the carefree days of youth. However, there would appear to be stronger support for the contention that adolescence is heterogeneous and is divided into numerous subcultures depending upon how strong certain variables are operative. Differences by social class, race, religion, ethnicity, education, region, family orientations, and identification with legal or illegal activities crisscross adolescence and distinguish numerous subtypes of youngsters. Social class differences and racial distinctions persist in contemporary America, but we sense some easing of religious or ethnic differences among American adolescents. Lastly, we tentatively postulate a growing liberalism in the education of adolescents that is action-oriented, respectful of the thinking and experiences of adolescents, and willing to keep open communication with adolescents about their needs and problems, many of which are not of their own making.

18

Where do we grow from here?

Growth, developing, experienceing changes are all part of life processes that move children past their childhood into adolescence and adulthood. It cannot be otherwise for regression contradicts all that we know about the nature of "growing up." We may *look* back on our lives to assess where we have been, but we cannot *go* back to our childhoods. So it must be with our studies of childhood and with this text. Just as persons remember their earliest years, the foundations of their uniqueness, so we can review our understanding of childhood in this concluding chapter and move on from there.

THEORIES, APPROACHES, AND CONCEPTS IN THE STUDY OF CHILDHOOD

Childhood Is a Multidimensional Status.

During the first twelve years of life, children occupy a position in human society unique to their age-set. No single discipline can illuminate the subject of childhood fully because childhood is a complex, multifaceted status that yields to no singular analysis and synthesis. Rather, each specialization provides valuable insights into childhood. Historical, developmental, psychological, educational, or therapeutic theories, approaches, and concepts need not be overlooked. What we have suggested is that a *sociological* approach to childhood should be included in its study. We sought to indicate what might be gained by examining childhood from a sociological perspective.

Structural-functionalism and Socialization Dominate Sociological Study of Childhood.

Fundamentally, children are brought into contact with preexisting social order and taught to conform, to adapt, to adopt, or to internalize the ways of adults. The process by which they acquire the ways of their society is through conscious and unconscious socialization in their most formative years. Structural-functionalism and socialization, however, are not sufficient explanatory tools. Over the past ten or fifteen years, symbolic-interaction, exchange, conflict, and control theories have tempered sociological studies and are particularly useful in the study of childhood. Children are bonded to their society to the extent that they join with their elders in the acceptance and usage of common signs and symbols. Exchanges go on constantly through rewards and punishments, moves and countermoves, or gains and losses between children and their caretakers. Further, the exchanges involve both violent and nonviolent forms of nonalignment, nonacceptance, or nonagreement with proponents of social systems. In some ways, the conflicts between youngsters and their teachers involve who shall control situations and who shall determine the end results of power-in-action. We can see instances in which elders "win" and other instances in which children have their way.

Social Systems Are Child-Centered, Child-Oriented, or Child-Dominated.

Distinctive social systems to which children are introduced are either child-centered child-oriented, or child-dominated. Child-centered systems are concerned with the total personality, the total being of children, whereas child-oriented systems are concerned with segments or portions of children's lives. Families are prime examples of child-centered systems; schools are key examples of child-oriented systems. Schools may claim to be concerned with the total being of children, but they fall short in their focus upon formal educational processing of large numbers of children. Adult-designed, adult-created, and adult-sponsored "prepackages" of programs said to be "for the good of children" are clearly in the child-oriented syndrome. Finally, there are the child-dominated systems in which children themselves determine how they shall act. Peers or peer-groups are central to child-dominated systems, and much socialization occurs in company with them.

**Childhood Is a Recognized Age-Grade
Differentiated from Other Generations
and Accorded Differential Treatment.**

Universally, societies distinguish between the newest generations and the oldest. Persons are held to be either children or adults in preliterate, hunting-gathering societies. Rituals or ceremonials mark the passage from childhood into adulthood. As societies become literate, more complex, and industrialized-urbanized, high-energy users, with elaborate divisons of labor, finer distinctions are made among age-grades. A greater social distance is maintained between childhood and adulthood, and entry into adulthood is delayed.

Childhood May Be a Dependent or Independent Variable.

As a dependent variable, childhood may be treated as a status being acted upon by a host of factors or variables. As an independent variable, childhood may vary widely and actively affect societies and their respective cultures. The former circumstance suggests that childhood is shaped by what other age-grades bring to bear upon it. The latter circumstance suggests that children themselves can and do become agents of social change.

Parents and parent-surrogates have "a developmental stake" in their efforts to impose their will upon children, but children, in turn, have wills of their own and seek to validate or affirm their own ideas. Prejudgments that children are to be submissive, malleable creatures provide the setting for "the self-fulfilling prophecy" of conformity to normative expectations. Resistance, rebellious behavior, or refusals on the part of children become signals for labeling them as deviant, difficult, or problem children requiring special attention. An extreme labeling occurs if children are viewed as invading, threatening "barbarians" who must be subdued lest they destroy revered traditions.

In the end, the ethos or underlying sentiments or values of societies determine the degree to which childhood may or may not be granted latitude to affect all other age-grades. In American society, at least, the value of individual freedom reduces the severity of restraints or controls on childhood but at the same time raises questions as to how much encouragement and permissiveness should occur.

Much of the Sociology of Childhood Consists
of Examining What Happens to Children
as They Move from Group to Group.

Shifting between primary and secondary groups, children experience sociocultural inputs that set limits upon their pluripotentials. If treated categorically or as tabula rasa, certain expectations or outcomes are predictable. On the other hand, if the thesis of childhood's "privilege of backwardness" has merit, children are less convinced that what is set before them must be adopted wholesale, without criticism or modification.

Social Stratification, In General, and Open-Class
Estate, or Castelike Systems, In Particular
Affect Life-Chances of Children.

Differential opportunity is a fact of life in childhood. Depending upon which social class system is operative, children are granted maximal or minimal chances to self-actualize. When restricted to barest survival levels, children are denied need-fulfillment. Encouraged by meeting higher levels of needs such as security, love, and esteem, children can develop the self-respect and self-understanding necessary to express their unique qualities within their society.

CHANGING SOCIETAL ISSUES AND CHILDHOOD

Sex or Sexuality Pose Sensitive Issues for Childhood.

Gender is "a fact of life," but its social definition determines in large measure just how boys and girls are treated. In American society, unconscious sexism has operated for decades, ascribing females to positions of social inferiority in relation to males. Language and mass media have reflected and reinforced this posture but are being met with considerable opposition in contemporary American society. Accordingly, the socialization of children has been deliberately altered to operationalize a more equalitarian view of gender distinctions. Sex-role taking in terms of social definitions of masculinity and femininity is to be distinguished from the expression of sexuality itself. Modesty taboos and toilet training are early manifestations of dealing with sexuality in childhood. A final consideration, although still unresolved, is the growing recognition of the pleasure principle in sexuality as opposed to past emphasis upon sexuality for reproductive purposes. Teachable goals in childhood sexuality involve concern, affection, gentleness and abiding responsibility toward others.

Sacred and Secular Religious Systems Provide
Emotion-Laden, Morality Decisions in Childhood.

In addition to sex and sexuality, religion occupies a highly sensitive area in the socialization of children. Diversity of religious views, religious conservatism or liberalism, civil religion, separation of church and state—particularly in public schools, models of morality, and comprehension of the significance of life and death are but a few of the issues that touch childhood deeply.

Entrenched Racism in American Society Continues
to Blight Childhood.

Most pernicious of all, racism, which holds that one people or another are superior or inferior by reason of genetics, has made children "the little victims." Studies of both black and white children in America detail the depth and breadth of this categorical denial of full participation in American society. Sociology and other scientific disciplines, however, provide mounting evidence that racial prejudice and discrimination have no basis in fact and cannot continue indefinitely in a society devoted to human dignity. There will undoubtedly be "ordeal in change," but that change must come if American society is to endure.

SOCIAL INSTITUTIONS AND CHILDHOOD

Families Are the Initial Groups for Childhood,
But Traditional Forms and Functions Are Challenged
by Competing Alternatives.

Pro and antifamily forces have emerged in contemporary America to dispute appropriate ways and means of dealing with childhood. Peer groups or coevals seem to be initiating agencies that test earlier socialization begun in families. Pronatalism and antinatalism advocates have brought into question the quantities and qualities of children to be brought into families and society. Families, whether traditional or nontraditional, continue to perform vital functions for childhood despite premature declarations of disorganization or disarray.

Children are Educated or Miseducated
in Contemporary America Depending Upon One's Criteria.

Compulsory, formal education from about five or six years of age to about seventeen or eighteen has become a battleground involving those who believe the public schools are doing an admirable job, given the conditions in which they are forced to operate, and those who contend that children are "miseducated!" Equality or inequality of educational opportunity, segregation and busing, domination of classroom teachers, and classrooms and "containers" of children are among the moot questions being openly debated among professionals and nonprofessionals. The ideology of the public school movement, or the PSM$_i$ in Pratte's terminology, sets the tone or objectives of formal education, whereas the PSM$_{si}$, the social institution of the public school movement, has been repeatedly revised as America moved through preindustrial, industrial and postindustrial stages. Until Americans achieve consensus over their public school movement ideology, there will be continued argument as to how the public school movement as a social institution should operate for the sake of children.

Childhood Is Intimately Associated with Political Power.

Childhood is targeted as the appropriate period in life in which to prepare children for their future participation as adult citizens in support of established political norms. However, with growing awareness of power and autonomy, the rights of children can no longer be set aside or ignored. Childhood advocates have emerged to articulate those objectives that would provide maximal chances for children to grow and express their many potentials. The achievement of such objectives requires the abandonment of a posture of over-protection and control over children in favor of a newer stance dedicated to providing children with positive freedoms and every possible means of developing their many capacities for constructive living.

In Childhood, Play, Games, and Work Are Interconnected.

Play has long been assigned to the world of children, and work to the world of adults. Economic linkages, however, have been established through organized play, such as games; through the marketing of toys; through entertainment via mass media; through promotion of pets; through imitation of adult occupations; and through direct effects because of the presence or absence of working parents. In the future, socialization of children in relationship to the economy may move away from exploitation of consumers and workers toward a concern for goods and services that enhance life for consumers and producers alike.

SOCIAL PSYCHOLOGY OF CHILDHOOD

A Sociology of Childhood Includes a Concern for Each Child.

Sociological study of childhood with its focus on group impacts upon the status of children does not preclude a concern for each unique child. Rather, it calls attention to the social sources of self-concepts, conflicting self-images, and symptoms of psychic stress. Further, it recognizes the damaging self-concepts of minority children, the significance of self-insulation, and the ramifications of "the self-awareness trap."

Central to Each Child's Well-Being Is Health.

Health is a tripartite unity of physical, mental-emotional, and social components; shortcomings in any one or combination of these factors detracts from the life of each child. Child abuse, mental health, and social health are among the key topics of concern. Significant others, particularly symbionts, are vital models in promoting the well-being of each child.

Symbolic Interaction in Childhood, Notably Language Acquisition and Understanding of Semantic Differentials, Brings Each Child Into Human Society.

Acquisition of oral and written symbols provides a major means by which each child is brought into touch with his or her world. Semantic referents can be a source of humor, a barrier to communication, or the appropriate knowledge needed for an effective social life for each individual child.

PROBLEMS IN CHILDHOOD

Less-Than-Perfect Social Systems Produce Less-Than-Perfect Children.

Deviancy, delinquency, dependency, and deprivation in childhood make up a large part of the problems confronting American children. A sociological analysis of childhood indicates why and how they occur and what might be done to modify or eliminate them.

Handicapped Children Provide Lessons In Humane Treatment From Which All May Learn.

Conditions that impair, thwart, or deny socialization processes are receiving increased attention from children's advocates. Few would deny that the costs of rehabilitation, care, or support are rising, but these are surmountable expenditures necessary to a respect for human potentials. In the humane treatment of handicapped children, Americans demonstrate their dedication to the dignity and worth of each life. Efforts seem to be in the direction of bringing handicapped children from the backwaters of society into the mainstream of social living.

Gifted Children Represent Pools of Talent from Which Future Leadership May Come.

Gifted children are those exceptional children who master knowledge, skills, and ideas in a clearly superior fashion and/or are highly innovative, original, or creative in their thoughts, accomplishments, or relationships with materials or people. Socialization is rapid or advanced far beyond the chronological years of such children, and the talents and abilities gained can be directed for the good of the human condition. Identification, encouragement, and enrichment procedures go a long way toward the conservation of these invaluable human resources. Still problematic is the adoption of strategies capable of drawing upon these exceptional children with consideration for all concerned.

CONCLUDING OBSERVATIONS

Children Exit Their Childhood Through Adolescence.

A new status has been emerging in American society. It is the status of adolescence that may or may not be a departure from childhood and may or may not be preparatory for entry into adulthood. Adolescence seems to be a period in life that places individuals somewhere "in between" childhood and adulthood. It is a transitional period in which there is some discontinuity or break from childhood and some experimentation and preparation for adult status. Sometimes characterized as a period of "storm and stress," adolescence is mainly the continuation of socialization begun in childhood, but with characteristics of its own. Biological-physiological "readiness" for adulthood is socially defined as still "not ready" for the mantle of adulthood. In response, a subculture of adolescence has been growing to accommodate the half-children, half-adult participants.

An Ending Is Also a Beginning.

In the summary statements and capsulated explanations in this concluding chapter, we have reviewed some of the highlights of the sociology of childhood. We have also suggested that *growth* consists of moving forward and that childhood and adolescence are not the be-alls and end-alls of life. Rather, there is more to learn, more to gain, and more to accomplish.

Education, Counseling, and Research in Childhood Are Essential.

Many students of childhood ask what they can do in behalf of childhood and children. For our part, we follow what might be called "a medical model" of prevention, therapy, and the advancement of new knowledge.

Education in childhood corresponds to the preventive medical approach that does whatever it can to ward off dangerous or life-threatening possibilities. We are saying that there exists a large body of time-tested information concerning childhood and children that needs to be known and applied by potential or actual parents, by parental surrogates, and by children's caretakers. "Parenting" need not be a hit-or-miss, trial-and-error process in which children become learning objects. Rather, there must be serious pursuit of sound knowledge that provides children and childhood with informed, sensitized adult-guides and adult-models capable of making the most of children's capacities. The data upon which such persons draw come from many fields of knowledge and inquiry, including, as we have stressed, sociology.

Counseling in childhood corresponds to the therapies required for those who have already suffered because of prior lack of knowledge or ineptitude. In our "free" society, neither those who deal with children nor children themselves are mindless puppets who can be manipulated and controlled. Instead, individuals are relatively "free" to do as they please in child rearing or in experiencing childhood as children themselves. The results are "mixed," with some achieving admirable results, others reaching some levels of success, and still others failing miserably and suffering the consequences of foolish or thoughless actions. It is when "things go wrong" in the processes of socialization that calls for help are raised. These "calls for help" need answering by qualified, well-schooled, motivated childhood counselors who can help modify, restore, and make tolerable the lives of those who come to their attention. Counselors, too, are caught up in the same social systems with which we dealt in this text. Their work reflects, and is limited by, the same social fabric that we tried to examine in some detail. The work of counseling in childhood will probably continue for many years to come because, while social change is inescapable, changes usually come slowly and subtly.

Research in childhood is the growing edge of any science or field of knowledge, including sociology. It is the work of sociologists to ask the questions that need answers and then to devise ways and means of seeking out the necessary information or insights. Undoubtedly, in this text and in studying childhood, we have probably raised more questions than we have answered. But this is worthwhile if it becomes the first step in the growth of sociological efforts to comprehend childhood beyond the present state of our knowledge.

Some of the research will be repetitive or involve replication to make certain that what we say we know about childhood or children still applies to ongoing generations of youngsters with changed, contemporary circumstances. Some research will seek out those areas that are "gaps in the knowledge" so that we no longer have to "guesstimate" what they contain. Some research will take cross-sectional samples from specified universes within rather limited time-frames. Other research will be longitudinal and will study panels of respondents over extended periods of time or over lifetimes.

It is worth noting that research may or may not achieve consistent findings. Some students who encounter the inconsistent results of research studies are troubled, confused, and dismayed that data do not seem to fall into some anticipated order. However, we would point out that such contradictory material mirrors our pluralistic society in which children live in a wide variety of circumstances. Perhaps more to the point, the counter data also reflects the differing qualities of research skills brought to bear upon such conditions. Finally, conflicting information suggests that interpretations, applications, and generalizations should be *tentative* until the preponderance of information clearly show what appropriate conclusions or actions should be followed.

Research and theory, of course, go hand-in-glove. When highly motivated students of sociology enter upon their training, they are tempted, at times, to favor either research procedures, design, methodologies, techniques, and statistical measurements or theoretical considerations of integrating bits and pieces of documented data to formulate a comprehensive schema or macrosocial system. In an age of specialization, investment in a single, vital service is understandable and commendable. However, in engaging in divisions of labor, it is easy to lose sight of bigger pictures to such an extent that experts speak only to experts and fail to address the general public of which they are a part. So long as they or others can fit research and theory together, the danger of knowing "a great deal about a little" is averted.

Oscar Ritchie used to introduce himself to his audiences with the following bit of doggerel that made this identical point:

> I once had a friend named Guessor
> Whose knowledge grew lesser and lesser.
> It grew so small,

That he knew nothing at all,
And now he's a college professor[1]

As research grows, so also does theory in the sense that there are more data upon which to base ideas or to suggest that the ideas need further testing or modifications. As theory grows, so also does research in the sense that further documentation is needed or new exploratory directions are found. Research and theory are thus twofold aspects of the same discipline. Texts such as ours attempt to weave them together to provide the whole tapestry for interested students, in our case, of the sociology of childhood.

In a brilliantly executed work, Leslie Stevenson has brought together some seven major theories that attempt to explain the nature of human nature.[2] Stevenson surveys the intellectual landscape in an exposition of the theories advanced by Plato, Christianity, Marx, Freud, Sartre, Skinner, and Lorenz. These theories are, respectively, the rule of the wise, God's salvation, Communist revolution, psychoanalysis, atheistic existentialism, conditioning of behavior, and innate aggression. Each is critiqued in a most effective way by Stevenson. Such theories have provided the guiding philosophies that motivate human actions involving millions of lives.

We do not claim that we have produced on these pages a definitive statement of all there is to know about the sociology of childhood by pulling together all known research and theory. Instead, we have introduced some selected studies in childhood and have provided perspectives derived from our sociological concerns that can encourage ongoing study and applications of children and childhood.

Our Guiding Philosophy is the Preciousness of Childhood and Life Itself.

It is neither customary nor fashionable in a college text to intrude upon value-orientations or the guiding philosophies of its readers. As much as possible, we have tried to respect that custom or folkway so that each student would be free to arrive at any conclusions he or she feels are legitimate distillations of hundreds of pages of reading and months of soul-searching and group discussions.

The value-free stance, neutrality, and the presentation of as many views as possible was uppermost in our minds as we discussed a wide

---

[1]To the best of our knowledge, this doggerel's authorship is unknown. It is also possible that Oscar Ritchie created the lines in keeping with his own humility and character.

[2]Leslie Stevenson, *Seven Theories of Human Nature* (London: Oxford University Press, 1974).

variety of childhood issues, many of which we dubbed as "sensitive," "unresolved," or controversial. On the other hand, over the years, we have become aware that there has been a growing awareness on the part of some students that "sitting on the fence" and refusing "to stand up and be counted" is not always the posture that best serves their interests. Conclusions, even tentative ones, are asked of them, but not of us as authors or teachers. There have been many times when students have asked in class, "Where do you stand on this issue?" or "What is your judgment on this matter?" A reluctance or refusal to answer, motivated by a desire not to unduly influence the reasoning, thoughtways, and actions of others, has not been received with much appreciation.

Accordingly, we affirm that our guidng philosophy is the *preciousness* of childhood, the high valuation we place upon children who have just entered the first major threshold of life. One of the most vivid recollections of one of the authors is that of receiving a birth notice from a relative while serving as a soldier in the South Pacific. The notice was edged in black and contained not only the good news of the arrival of a little girl, but also a caption, "What better answer to death than to bring forth life." It took a while for the import of the message to sink in, but it was, indeed, a marvelous thing to know that despite the tragedies and losses of lives in combat, there were still those who cherished life and encouraged it. It is in the "choosing of life" that we see promise for brighter futures than most of us have witnessed in our own lifetimes.

We know that there are those who reject such a philosophy, and we will not fault them for it. We are conscious of those who, by other standards, are *antichildren* in what they think and do. We have, at times, discussed three aspects of love as eros, agape, and filial love. The first, *eros,* is the erotic or self-centered love in which a man or woman receives personal gratifications. *Agape* is the sacrificial love that gives to others far more than one receives in return. *Filial* love refers to the love between parents and children or, by extension, to the whole human family. We seek no quarrel with those who are self-centered and have no time or room for children and childhood. Nor do we insist that childhood and children are so important and precious that we call for extreme self-sacrifices and disinterest in maturity and adulthood. Rather, we are motivated by a filial love that is *prochildren* and dedicated to making the initial years of childhood the best possible foundations for children to grow upon.

The twenty-first century is almost here and we look to it and the centuries to come as a future in which children and childhood will be recognized as treasures beyond measure, worth cherishing and appreciating. Like the Roman matron who brought her child in front of her guests, we say, "Here are my jewels."

GLOSSARY

This glossary of terms, alphabetized for easier access, refers to key concepts utilized throughout the text. They are not intended to be memorized as immutable definitions but are offered simply as useful explanations. It is suggested that students will have much to gain if they can express in their own words what these terms really mean to them in a wide variety of contexts.

Abused Children Children who are physically, mentally, emotionally, and socially damaged through excessive punishments and controls for alleged misdeeds.

Adolescence Social status between childhood and adulthood comprised of youngsters from approximately thirteen to eighteen years of age.

Agape Sacrificial love; giving of oneself to others for their gain and the individual's possible loss.

Age-Grade Social recognition that persons of approximately the same age are to be treated differentially from all other persons of other ages.

Andragogy Education of adults.

Antinatalism A gathering of social forces against the birth of children for such reasons as overpopulation, unwanted children, defective or handicapped children, freedom from unwanted pregnancy, or inability to support and appropriately rear children.

Approaches The varied ways and means to comprehend childhood; each perspective, procedure, or philosophy adding its particular skills and insights but undoubtedly not providing a totally comprehensive picture of childhood.

Artifact A socially derived product; a creation of tangible or intangible items designed to serve human needs.

Attitude The tendency to act toward an object (human or non-human, material or nonmaterial) or class of objects in a particular way.

Autonomy Control over one's own behavior within the limits imposed by acquired social and cultural systems.

Barbarian Thesis The idea that children are "barbarians" or "uncivilized savages" who do not know the ways of humans and so may wittingly or unwittingly undermine or destroy social and cultural systems carefully built up by past generations.

Carrot-and-Stick Principle Rewards and punishments.

Castelike An approximation of rigid social class distinctions so that persons are confined by reason of birth to certain life-opportunities regardless of what they may achieve in their lifetimes.

Categories Groupings of persons thought to belong together because of some common feature or features.

Categorical Thinking   Treating persons in some arbitrary fashion because it is believed they are identified as part of a socially ascribed category.

Child-Centered System   Adult-designed system in which children are the centers of attention and concern, their whole personalities are involved, and continuing supervision and control by adults occurs in the best interests of children.

Child-Dominated System   Child-designed and controlled system from which adults are excluded and in which children themselves determine group structures and activities.

Child-Oriented System   Adult-created, adult-sponsored, and adult-controlled programs or offerings alleged to serve the needs of children.

Childhood   Multidimensional status assigned to children during the first twelve years of their lives.

Coevals   Persons of the same or equivalent age-grade.

Cohorts   The thousands of persons born about the same year as a given individual.

Conflict Theory   Nonagreement, nonacceptance, and nonalignment with other persons or systems; may occur in violent, highly aggressive, hostile behavior or may be nonviolent and nonconforming through rejection, deviance, or nonadaptations of ways promoted by others.

Continuity   A smooth, gradual, following-through of training and experiences from prior years so that accumulative knowledge can be utilized under present circumstances.

Control Theory   Applied to childhood, a theory that questions the assumptions that children must be docile, compliant, cooperative individuals who accept a priori conditions; it suggests, instead, that children may also determine the extent to which they conform to social pressures or develop new behaviors.

Contraculture   (Also known as Counter-culture) Life styles that disagree with established, normative ways and so provide alternatives for persons to adopt.

Culture   The totality of shared, learned behavior and the products of that behavior, including values, attitudes, norms, overt behavior, and material objects with which participants in a society live.

De Facto Segregation   Separation of persons of different backgrounds who choose to live apart from each other and so maintain their own territoriality; a condition in which distinct boundary lines are maintained between persons of different backgrounds, heritages, or experiences.

Delinquency   Acts on the part of children and adolescents judged to be in defiance of laws and established authority.

Dependency   The need to rely upon others in order to survive or live within a social system.

Deprivation   Failures, losses, and suffering due to inability to gain acess to opportunities, advantages, or resources open to most participants in a society.

De Jure Segregation   Separation of persons of different backgrounds by reason of law.

Developmental Approach   A perspective of childhood as a time of growth and learning in graduated stages or levels so that further growth and learning can occur at more advanced, mature, or complex levels.

Deviancy Differing from certain social expectations in favor of other norms or procedures.

Dichotomy Having at least two parts or subdivisions; an either-or proposition.

Differential Opportunity A condition in which some participants in society have more or less opportunity to take advantage of available resources, power, and prestige.

Differential Treatment Handling persons in contrasting ways by reason of who they are or what their potentials may be.

Ego An individual, himself or herself; also, a Freudian construct said to be the moderating factor or element in an individual's makeup between the demanding Id and the highly socialized Superego.

Eros Erotic, body-oriented, sensual love.

Estate System Social class system in which there is some upward mobility by reason of pleasing those in higher social levels of society than one's own level.

Ethos The composite system of values that dominate the orientations, concerns, and behavior of a human society.

Eugenics A program of procedures to produce the healthiest, most genetically sound infants and children possible.

Euthenics Design to provide the best possible social experiences for children and childhood.

Exchange Theory The conceptualization of reciprocity, interchanges, checks and balances, rewards and punishments, gains and losses, moves and countermoves among participants in social settings.

Filial Love Concern, support, and affection expressed among family members, with particular emphasis upon the parents and children, and, by extension, to the whole human "family" or to all human beings.

Folkways The expected or customary ways of behavior that regulate or characterize the people of a society.

Freedom, Negative Absence of prohibitions on desired behavior; no restraints or impeding of what a child or a person seeks to do.

Freedom, Positive The provision of constructive help and encouragement so that capacities and talents may be realized or activated.

Function The consequences or actions that emerge from a structure or social system.

Function, Latent The unintended, unexpected, unanticipated consequences of social forms or structures.

Function, Manifest The intended, expected, or announced objectives or consequences of bringing persons together.

Games Organized, formalized play through the acceptance of rules.

Gender Category or labeling usually applied to distinguishing between the male and female sexes.

Gerontology The study of aging as it affects individuals and their societies or specialized groups.

Gestalt Philosophy Concern for understanding the whole patterning, picture, or phenomenon rather than particular portions of the patterning, picture, or phenomenon.

Gifted Children   Exceptional, talented, precocious children who rapidly learn, create, express, and innovate in the context of their society and culture.

Group   Two or more persons interacting and mutually affecting each other according to a set of interconnected statuses.

Handicapped Children   Those "special children" whose socialization processes are impaired, thwarted, or denied unless attention, adjustments, or special efforts are devised to overcome conditions derived from genetic, physical, mental, emotional or social sources.

Health   The state of complete physical, mental, and social well-being, not merely the absence of disease or infirmity.

Hierarchy of Needs   The conceptualization of the ability to self-actualize or self-express, providing basic needs are first met.

Horizontal Mobility   Movement and placement within a single social stratum in human society.

I, Mead's   That portion of the self that remains unpredictably aloof, removed, or insulated from the attitudes of others.

Id, Freud's   The unconscious, animalistic, primitive, basic component of self, usually identified as sexual and aggressive.

Infant   Child, one year of age or younger.

Infant Mortality Rate   Number of infants who die per one thousand living children under one year of age.

In-Group   Those individuals with whom a person associates within a limited circle of interacting persons.

In Loco Parentis   In place of the parents.

Institutions, Social   Those systems that embody and promote fundamental values within a society, such as family, religion, education, economy, and polity.

Invidious Comparisons   Arbitrary contrasting of one or more persons to other persons who obviously have different qualities.

Language   Arbitrary vocal, written, or visual symbols or signs by which persons communicate.

Life-Chances   The probabilities that children or persons may be able to fulfill their needs, express their capacities or qualities, and contribute in some way to all other persons and their social ways.

Life-Space   The degree of leeway or latitude open to all persons to achieve life-chances.

Looking-Glass Self   The mirroring, reflecting, or understanding of oneself through the perceived reactions of others.

Macro-Social Theory   Those theories that seek to take the broadest, most comprehensive view of social conditions in order to understand and predict its nature and behavior.

Mainstreaming   A term used mainly by educators to describe the inclusion of all children or students in current educational practices; can be broadened to refer to the assurance that all children are brought into contact with ongoing society.

Marginality   Participating in two or more groups or life styles but never fully identifying oneself with a single group or life style.

Masculinity-Femininity Social definitions of appropriate behavior for males or females with possible shades of differences, sharing of behavior, or provisions for clearly designated and differential roles.

Mass Media Those means or devices by which the general public or specific parts of the public are reached; usually includes newspapers, radio, television, magazines, motion pictures, records, tapes, and books.

Mestizos Spanish term used to refer to those persons of mixed racial origins.

Micro-Social Theory Those theories that deal with highly specific aspects of social patterning.

Miscegenation Genetic pooling between persons of different races.

Miseducation The charge that education does not accomplish what it alleges to accomplish and, instead, misleads and misdirects children.

Models Persons to be emulated or social patterns worth following.

Norms Social expectations concerning behavior; often are folkways, mores, or rules and regulations such as laws.

Nouveau Riche The newly rich; those who have recently acquired wealth.

Nuclear Family Usually postulated as consisting of a husband, a wife, and their biological or adopted offspring.

Open-Class System The social class sytem that maximizes opportunities to improve one's status on the basis of sheer merit.

Out-Group That group to which one does not belong; strangers and unknown others.

Pedagogy The education of children.

Peers Those equal in age, status, power, or other qualities such as sex or social background.

Personality The totality of an individual's traits or qualities.

Play Mental and physical activity for expressive purposes, for sheer enjoyment, amusement, or abandonment to feeling-states.

Pluralism The conception of a society with numerous life styles or ways to behave or think.

Pluripotentials The many possibilities within children to use their talents, aptitudes, and interests in human society.

Precocious Children Those children who exhibit learning abilities far in advance of their ages.

Prejudice An attitude of prejudgment, favorable or unfavorable, often without valid or complete information.

Primary Groups Those groups in which fundamental personality qualities are acquired; often characterized as small, intimate, face-to-face, and of long duration.

Privilege of Backwardness A condition that allows persons such as children, who lack commitment and involvement, to learn from the mistakes of others and to seek new, more effective alternatives.

Pronatalism Those social forces that favor the birth of children because of confidence that youngsters have the potentials both to bring about social improvements and to self-actualize.

PSM   Public School Movement; if written with a subscript of "i," it refers to formal schooling as an ideology; if written with a subscript of "si," it refers to formal schooling as a social institution.

Race   Category in which people are ascribed a particular status because they are alleged to have a common set of distinguishing physical qualities or traits.

Racism   The contention that one race or another, one people or another, is either superior or inferior by reason of genetics to any other race or people.

Reference Group   Those groups from which individuals take their cues to behavior.

Reification   Making real one's abstract ideas or fantasies.

Relative Deprivation   The condition that results when comparisons are made between what one has and what others have.

Religion   Beliefs, emotions, and conduct appropriate to sacred or secular systems of thought or social organization.

Replication Studies   Those studies that repeat or duplicate other research in an effort to recheck or verify findings.

Repro-Sex   Sexual activity for purposes of human reproduction.

Reverse Racism   The application of racism to those who practiced racism against one's own group or category.

Rites of Passage   Those cermonials or rituals that publicly acknowledge major events in the individual life cycle and so mark the shedding of one status for another.

Role   Behavior or actions that individuals use in their interpretations of how to conduct themselves in a given status.

Sample   A portion of a universe under study, which may or may not be representative of the whole universe under investigation.

Secondary Group   Group in which only a portion of a person's personality is known or is involved; usually large, impersonal, of short duration, and operative for specific purposes.

Self-Actualization   To express oneself or one's potentials as fully as possible.

Self-Concept   The ideas and attitudes an individual holds concerning his or her own being; may or may not differ from the judgments of others concerning that individual.

Self-Fulfilling Prophecy   An idea or judgment becomes a reality in an unconscious way because it has been articulated repeatedly, is eventually accepted, and affirmed, despite the fact it has no basis in truth or fact.

Semantic Differentials   Differing or contrasting references or meanings attached to the same terms or words.

Sexism   The prejudgment that one sex or another is either superior or inferior to another sex as a basis for differential treatment.

Sex-of-Assignment   Placement of an individual into one sexual category or another whether that sexual ascription is appropriate or not.

Significant Others   Those persons who negatively or positively affect an individual's life, personality, or orientations.

Social Psychology   Specialization that studies the impacts of groups upon individual behavior.

Socialization The process by which an individual acquires human nature, develops a personality, and participates with similarly processed persons in a society.

Society An organized group of people distinguished by a common culture that is distinctive from other ways of life.

Status A position within a social system to which roles or a set of behavioral expectations are attached.

Status, Achieved A position earned in a society by the efforts of an individual and the acceptance of others.

Status, Ascribed A position assigned to an individual in a society on different bases; often on bases that are undeniable such as race, sex, or age.

Status Quo Conditions as they currently exist.

Stratification, Social Differing levels or ranks in society based on such criteria as prestige, power, education, occupation, wealth, family name, length of residence, and allegations of personality qualities.

Structural-Functionalism Theory that deals with social forms, patterns, or systems and the resulting actions or services performed by or though these organized patterns.

Subculture A portion of a total culture that seems to operate somewhat apart from a whole way of life within a total society.

Superego Freudian construct of that portion of a person's being that has been most influenced by social training or experiences to consider the needs of others.

Symbionts Those persons with whom one can form mutually helpful relations.

Symbolic-Interaction Theory that human beings are bonded to each other through meanings attached to symbols.

Tabula Rasa A conceptualization of children as tablets not yet written upon or used, unspoiled, new, and receptive.

Temporocentrism The idea that one's own times represent the pinnacle of human history and that all other times are inconsequential.

Theory The bringing together of assumptions and tested hypotheses to explain complex phenomena.

Unisex Ideology that asserts that sexual differences should be blurred or overlooked so that gender no longer is used to the advantage or disadvantage of males or females.

Universe The total population under investigation or being researched.

Variable, Dependent That factor or those factors being studied and so held constant in research efforts.

Variable, Independent Those factors that are allowed to vary, or change as they will, that may affect the phenomenon under study.

Vertical Mobility Rising or falling within a social stratification system.

Work Productive labor, usually for economic reasons.

Youth Orientation The idea that being young is better than being old.

ZPG Zero Population Growth, movement that seeks a balance between losses and gains in population.

AUTHOR INDEX

Adamek, Raymond J., 114
Adams, James T., 41
Adams, Paul, 136
Allen, R., 209
Amory, Cleveland, 41
Anderson, C. A., 142
Anderson, Robert M., 243, 246
Anderson, Walt, 146
Argyle, Michael, 73
Arterton, F. Christopher, 37
Atchley, Robert C., 7, 112

Bain, Joyce Koym, 118
Bain, Read, 168–69
Banks, Olive, 140–41
Barbe, William B., 267
Barsch, Ray H., 249
Baughman, E. Earl, 87, 91
Beck, Rochelle, 153–54
Becker, Howard S., 230, 238
Begles, Jeanne, 93
Bellah, Robert N., 72
Benedict, Ruth, 275
Bengston, Vern L., 24
Berardo, Felix M., 16
Bernard, Jessie, 95, 117
Berry, Brewton, 99
Bettelheim, Bruno, 202
Bettmann, Otto L., 6
Bierstedt, Robert, 5
Billingsley, Andrew, 95, 101–3
Birenbaum, Arnold, 228
Blau, Peter, 16
Boles, Donald E., 79
Boll, Eleanor, 120
Bonjean, Charles M., 92
Borgatta, Edgar F., 89
Bossard, James H. S., 120, 168
Bowlby, John, 232
Boyd, Rosamonde, 112
Brasch, R., 22
Breasted, James H., 5
Brogan, Donna, 58
Brookover, Wilbur, 140
Brown, Dee, 87
Brown, Joe David, 146
Burr, Wesley, R., 118
Busby, Linda Jean, 58
Buxton, Thomas H., 138
Byer, Curtis O., 67

Campbell, Ernest Q., 133
Campbell, Thomas C., 77
Cannon, Kenneth L., 118
Cantaldo, Everett F., 94
Carmichael, Stokeley, 89
Caroll, James W., 112
Carroll, James L., 258–59
Carter, T. P., 189

Cavan, Ruth S., 41
Chand, Ian P., 111
Cherniak, Donna, 114
Chesney-Lind, Meda, 58
Chesterton, G. K., 69
Christensen, Harold, 117
Cileman, John C., 283
Clark, Kenneth, 9
Clarke, Helen I., 231
Clinard, Marshall B., 190, 228
Cohen, Albert K., 230, 234–36
Coleman, James, 133–34
Coles, Robert, 111
Comte, Auguste, 72
Constantine, Joan and Larry, 117
Constanzo, Joseph F., 83
Cooley, Charles H., 119, 182
Corbett, Kathryn, 112
Corsi, James R., 90
Crain, Robert L., 93
Cranston, Maurice, 157–58
Crider, Donald M., 111
Cuber, John F., 116
Cushenberg, Donald C., 269
Cutler, Donald R., 72

Dahlstrom, W. Grant, 91
D'Alessio, Edward R., 81
Davis, Fred, 230
Davis, Kingsley, 109, 115
DeHaan, Robert F., 257, 259
DeSola Pool, Ithiel, 221
Dinitz, Simon, 48, 190
Dispenza, Joseph E., 57
Donovan, Michael, 78
Douglas, Jack D., 228
Dreikors, Rudolf, 11
Dreyer, Albert and Cecily, 120
Duberman, Lucille, 57
Duke, James T., 16
Durkheim, Emile, 72
Durr, William K., 269
Duster, Troy, 89

Eaton, Joseph W., 113
Eberly, Donald, 285
Ehrhardt, Anke A., 59
Eichorn, Dorothy, 279
Engle, David E., 69
Erickson, Edsel L., 140
Erikson, Erik H., 160–61
Erman, Adolf, 5

Farber, Seymour M., 57
Feingold, Allan, 114
Feldman, Harold, 117–18
Fichter, Joseph H., 77
Field, Frank, 240
Finnegan, Dana G., 118

306

SUBJECT INDEX

Black power, 89
Bruised self, 187–88
Bureaucracy, 140
Busing, 135–37

Career model, 236
Carrot-stick principle, 11
Categorical thinking, 90
Categories, 28, 90
Change, family, 117
Child abuse, 8–9
Child-centered systems, 17
Child-dominated systems, 17–18
Childhood:
    age-grading, 289; definition, 3–4;
    dependent-independent variable,
    23–30; economy, 160–75; equality, 10;
    exiting, 273–86; privilege of
    backwardness, 30; social stratification,
    32–50; sociocultural settings, 32–50;
    source of delinquency, dependency,
    deprivation, deviation, 234–40;
    symbolic-interaction, 208–23
Child labor, 6
Child-oriented systems, 17
Child rearing strategies, middle-class,
    46–48
Children:
    busing, 135–37; comparison, invidious,
    10; dependency, 13; discipline, 5–7;
    exploitation, 6; family, 17, 107–29;
    general, 4; gifted, 256–69; handicapped,
    243–55; health, 193–207; inner-outer
    environments, 11; little victims, 103;
    minority, 133; morality, 75–78; pets,
    167–69; precocious, 10; racism, 86–104;
    religion, 69–85; rights, 152–58;
    self-attitudes, 92–93; self-concepts,
    179–92; sexuality, 53–68; social agents,
    24; value, 6
Christianity, 74, 82
Civil religion, 72–73
Classroom teacher, 137–39
Coevals, 109–11
Community and the handicapped,
    251–53
Conflict:
    parent-youth, 109–10; school, 139–41;
    selves, 186–88; theory, 16, 110
Containment, 139–41
Control, 16–17, 40, 139–41, 147, 152
Costs, rehabilitation, 248
Criticisms, contemporary education,
    132–42
Culture-carrier, family, 122

Day-care centers, 109
Death, 22, 82–83
Delinquency, 231
Dependency, 231–33
Deprivation, 233–39
Desegregation, 135–37
Deviancy, 228–31
Differential opportunities, 33
Disabilities, 244

Discipline, family, 124
Discontinuity, adolescent, 275–76
Discrimination, racial, 97–100
Divorced parents, 186–87
Doll-play, 163
Doll-preference, 93
Double-entendre, 215

Economy, childhood, 160–75
Education:
    children, 130–44, 291–92, 295; religion,
    79–81; segregation, 135–37
Elementary schools, 131–32
Enrichment:
    family life, 127; school, 266–67
Equality, educational opportunity,
    132–34
Ethos, 26–27
Eugenics-euthenics, 195
Exchange, 16, 111, 139

Factors, politicalization, 151–52
Factory model, schools, 133
Family, 17, 44, 47, 94–97, 107–29,
    133–34, 248–51, 291
Fecundity, 113
Femininity, 61, 63
Fertility, 113–14
Freedom, 27, 37, 125–26, 147
Functions:
    black families, 102–3; families, 122–28;
    religion, 71; schools, 142–43

Games, 160–61, 292
Generations, 21–22, 110
Gerontology, 112
Gifted children, 256–69, 294
Groups:
    initiating, 107–11; primary, 28, 119–22;
    secondary, 28, 119–20; sociology of
    childhood, 290

Handicapped children, 243–55
Health, 193–207, 293
Heredity-Environment, 194–95
Hippies, 146, 238
Humor, 215–21
Husbands-Wives, 119

Identification, gifted children, 260–62
Imagination, 182
Incorporation phase, adolescence, 281–82
Individuality, 11
Infant Mortality Rates, 38, 60
Infants, 8, 37, 111, 121, 180–82, 196
Initiating-initial groups, 107–11
In loco parentis, 156
Institutions, social, 291–92
Interdependency, 233
Interpretation, family, 123–24
Interracial marriages, 99

Judaism, 74, 82, 279
Juvenile Court, 231
Juvenile Delinquency, 39, 58–59

Kerner Report, 88

Supreme Court, decisions (continued)
v. Board of Education, 80; Walz v. Tax
Commissioners, 80–81
Symbolic interaction, 16, 208–23
Symbionts, 206–7
Symbols:
abstract, 213–14; oral, 209–11; written, 211–13
Systems:
castelike, 36; child-centered, 17, 288–89; child-dominated, 17, 288–89; child-oriented, 17–18, 288–89; estate, 35; social class, 32–50; open-class, 33–35

Tabula Rasa, 29–30
Teachers, 151, 261
Television, 108–9, 167
Temporocentrism, 5
Theory:
conflict, 16, 110; control, 16–17, 40; exchange, 16, 111; Freudian, 184; hierarchy of needs, 38–39; Mead's, 183–84; Myrdal's, 98; Nozick's, 134; Rawl's, 134; research, 296–97; structural-functionalism, 15; symbolic interaction, 16
Toilet training, 65–66, 181–82
Toys:
commercial, 164–65; dangerous, 164;

general, 161, 163–69; living, 167–69; popular, 165
Transition, phase of adolescence, 281
Types, teacher, 138–39

Unisex, 61, 63
United Nations, Declaration of Human Rights, 154–55
Upper-class children, 41–45

Values, 26–27
Violence, 90, 166–67

Wanted children, 118
War, 152, 213
War on poverty, 40, 53
Watergate, impact, 37, 237
Weaning, 9
White House Conference on Children, 153–54
White racism, 87–88, 92
Work, 61, 160–63, 172–74, 292
Work ethic, 47
Working, fathers-mothers, 172–74

Youth-orientation, 6

Zero Population Growth, 115–16